JOSÉ ORTEGA Y GASSET

Recent Titles in
Contributions in Philosophy

Nature, Human Nature, and Society: Marx, Darwin, Biology, and the Human Sciences
Paul Heyer

The Meaning of Suffering: An Interpretation of Human Existence From the Viewpoint
of Time
Adrian C. Moulyn

Ethics of Withdrawal of Life-Support Systems: Case Studies on Decision Making in
Intensive Care
Douglas N. Walton

Insight-Imagination: The Emancipation of Thought and the Modern World
Douglas Sloan

Making Believe: Philosophical Reflections on Fiction
C. G. Prado

Arguer's Position: A Pragmatic Study of *Ad Hominem* Attack, Criticism, Refutation,
and Fallacy
Douglas N. Walton

Physician-Patient Decision-Making: A Study in Medical Ethics
Douglas N. Walton

Rethinking How We Age: A New View of the Aging Mind
C. G. Prado

Rationality in Thought and Action
Martin Tamny and K. D. Irani, editors

The Logic of Liberty
G. B. Madison

Coercion and Autonomy: Philosophical Foundations, Issues, and Practices
Alan S. Rosenbaum

Einstein and the Humanities
Dennis P. Ryan, editor

From Science to Subjectivity: An Interpretation of Descartes' *Meditations*
Walter Soffer

JOSÉ ORTEGA Y GASSET

Proceedings of the
Espectador universal
International Interdisciplinary Conference

Edited by
NORA DE MARVAL-McNAIR

Prepared under the auspices of Hofstra University

Contributions in Philosophy, Number 34

Greenwood Press
New York • Westport, Connecticut • London

Library of Congress Cataloging-in-Publication Data

Espectador universal International Interdisciplinary
  Conference (1983 : Hofstra University)
  José Ortega y Gasset : proceedings of the Espectador
universal International Interdisciplinary Conference.

  (Contributions in philosophy, ISSN 0084-926X ; no. 34)
  Conference held at Hofstra University in November
1983.
  Includes index.
  1. Ortega y Gasset, José, 1883-1955.
I. Marval-McNair, Nora de.   II. Hofstra University.
III. Title.   IV. Series.
B4568.O74J663   1987   196'.1   87-330
ISBN 0-313-25896-1 (lib. bdg. : alk. paper)

British Library Cataloguing in Publication Data is available.

Library of Congress Catalog Card Number: 87-330
ISBN: 0-313-25896-1
ISSN: 0084-926X

First published in 1987

Greenwood Press, Inc.
88 Post Road West, Westport, Connecticut 06881

Printed in the United States of America

The paper used in this book complies with the
Permanent Paper Standard issued by the National
Information Standards Organization (Z39.48-1984).

10 9 8 7 6 5 4 3 2 1

Contents

1.
Preface. José Ortega y Gasset:
Espectador universal
NORA DE MARVAL-MCNAIR

In 1916, when José Ortega y Gasset (1883-1955) decided to embark on writing El Espectador, a series of articles that would eventually evolve into eight published volumes of essays, he received letters of praise and encouragement from his numerous readers. One of them, however, although extremely supportive of his effort, ended on a note of dismay. The correspondent had remarked, "I regret that you will devote yourself exclusively to being a spectator."

In his reply in "Verdad y perspectiva" ("Truth and Perspective"),(1) Ortega stated that at that point in his life he had found the need to devote a part of himself to pure contemplation. In support of this decision, he invoked the examples of Plato and Goethe. In The Republic, Plato had defined philosophers as theorists, or philoteamones, that is, those who enjoy watching. Goethe held that the only way he could understand the world was through his own eyes. Following in this tradition, Ortega decided to write for a public made up of amigos de mirar, of readers both interested in life as it flowed before their eyes, and concerned about truth as they perceived it from their own personal perspectives.

But since for Ortega living preceded theorizing, essence followed existence. His oft-quoted statement, "I am myself and my circumstance, and if I do not save the latter, I cannot save myself,"(2) which had appeared in 1914 in his Meditaciones del Quijote (Meditations on Quixote), summarizes his belief that man has the obligation not only to look at his surroundings, at his past and present circumstances, but to interact with them. The Spanish philosopher Julián Marías explains that according to Ortega man's concrete destiny — when he is faithful to his situation — is "to give sense to that which has none, to extract the logos from the inert, brutish, and il-logical, to convert that which is simply 'there around me' (circumstance) into a real world, into personal human life."(3)

With Meditaciones del Quijote Ortega began, in the words of Marías, "a series of salvations" by unveiling the meaning of man as hero or Quixote who "fights with his environment and tries to achieve the humanization of his surroundings in order to make a world out of them, while material things press heavily upon him with their meaninglessness and absurdity, trying to suffocate the flame of his projects and aspirations."(4) Authentic human condition is therefore, for Ortega, the unattainable and ever-renewed struggle of living, of trying to be a human being.(5)

José Ortega y Gasset was a professor of metaphysics at the University of Madrid from 1910 to 1929, and a prolific writer on all aspects of Western culture. His books and essays on philosophy, literary criticism, pedagogy, painting and sculpture, politics, history, sociology, music, and even hunting and golf, are contained in the twelve massive volumes of his Obras

completas, and in posthumous publications that continue to appear periodi-
cally.   In describing Ortega's plurality and universality, Ernst Robert
Curtius had remarked that Ortega was perhaps the only man in Europe who
could speak on Marcel Proust or Max Scheler, on Kant or Debussy, with the
same intensity and serenity of judgement, and with equal brilliance of exposition.

Regarded as the intellectual leader of a whole generation, it has been
said that through Ortega y Gasset Spaniards became better acquainted with
the rest of Europe, and Europe with Spain.   Furthermore, because of the
variety of his intellectual interests and his profoundly human focus on contemporary problems, he has been called the prototype of the twentieth-century humanist, and compared to Erasmus.

Not only was Ortega hailed for his philosophical system, but even his
detractors (he had quite a few) are unanimous in applauding his style. His
prose, as elegant, subtle, precise and inspiring as his thought, makes him
one of the leading writers of modern Spain.

Espectador universal, the international interdisciplinary conference
held at Hofstra University in November 1983 to mark the one-hundredth anniversary of José Ortega y Gasset's birth, endeavored to open new perspectives
on his thought and work, and to deepen our appreciation for his unique outlook as universal observer. The following contributions should prove that
our objectives were fulfilled.

NOTES

1.   José Ortega y Gasset, Obras completas, 6th ed. (Madrid: Revista
de Occidente, 1963), vol II, pp. 15-21.

2.   Ortega y Gasset, Meditaciones del Quijote e Ideas sobre la novela,
9th ed. (Madrid: Revista de Occidente, 1975), p. 30.

3.   Ortega y Gasset, Meditations on Quixote, with an introduction and
notes by Julián Marías, trans. Evelyn Rugg and Diego Marín. (New York: W.
W. Norton, 1961), p. 172, n. 7.

4.   Ibid., p. 10.

5.   Ibid., p. 173, n. 7.

JOSÉ ORTEGA Y GASSET

2.
Introduction. Ortega y Gasset:
A Tribute
IGNACIO L. GÖTZ

It is both an honor and a privilege for me to be able to participate in the celebrations marking the passage of one hundred years since the birth of Don José Ortega y Gasset. I am grateful to the editors of these proceedings for having accepted this modest tribute to a man whose work represents a significant contribution to the understanding of the human condition.

Hermann Hesse, Ortega's contemporary, considered him "one of the few men who have a real knowledge of the nature of mankind;"(1) and Camus, in an oft-quoted phrase, called him "perhaps the greatest European writer after Nietzsche."(2) "And yet," Camus added, "it would be hard to be more Spanish." Indeed, in his early Meditaciones del Quijote (1914), Ortega had maintained that all his thinking, directly or indirectly, referred ultimately to Spanish circumstances.(3) The effect that his years of study in Germany had had on him, he observed, was the decision to accept, wholly and without reserve, his Spanish destiny.(4) Nevertheless, his thinking never became narrow or provincial; rather, it was thoroughly steeped in the European intellectual tradition.

Ortega was born and raised in Madrid. He was schooled by the Jesuits, and did his graduate work at the universities of Madrid, Leipzig, Berlin, and Marburg. He taught metaphysics at the University of Madrid until 1929, when he resigned, along with most professors, in opposition to the government of Primo de Rivera. Characteristically, however, after his resignation, Ortega rented a hall, the Sala Rex, in order to continue his lectures to the general public. The interest generated was enormous; due to the large crowds, he moved to the more spacious Teatro Infanta Beatriz. The theater overflowed with listeners, and the newspapers published detailed accounts of the lectures. The initial situation was described by a reporter in El Sol, May 21, 1929, as follows:

> The theater was full. The public was numerous and diverse. Neither a single group, nor a single color, nor a single sex, nor a single class of society. It is an intellectual selection, but one made up spontaneously, freely . . . An excellent symptom. A favorable sign of the times. Now in Madrid people fill a theater, day after day, only to learn philosophy.(5)

A philosophy course in a theater! There is some incongruity here, some paradox -- like St. Paul preaching to the Athenian assembly, or pianist Ian Shapinsky concertizing in a service station. Yet, of the many episodes from Ortega's life one could choose to narrate, I wish to single this one out because it highlights the sporting character of life and of thinking that Ortega stressed in so many of his writings.

I shall not dwell on this element here, however, even though the lectures in the theater provide a most suitable context for a discussion of play. Rather, I wish to spend some time on three aspects of Ortega's thought that I believe to be highly significant, and which are also illustrated by this episode. They are circumstance, care, and institutional atheism. I wish, in short, to effect the "salvation" of this event -- that is, to bring it to the fullness of meaning of which it is possible.(6) Even though the constraints of our time and our circumstances may render this salvation partial -- one step out of purgatory, perhaps, or one step into the lower heavens -- that may be sufficient tribute to the man who actually lived the circumstances under consideration.

On the face of it, and given the political climate, the decision to offer a cycle of lectures open to the public must have struck Ortega's friends as foolhardy. On top of it, to make it a course in philosophy, must have seemed to many an invitation to disaster. Who would pack a hall to hear a lecture on philosophy? And who would pay 30 pesetas (half for students) for abstraction? And Ortega was determined to make this a rigorous intellectual enterprise -- a philosophical examination of philosophical thinking itself, something in the nature of the task attempted years later (and with less clarity) by Heidegger in What is Called Thinking? (1954) and in Discourse on Thinking (1959).

The success of the lectures proved that, appearances notwithstanding, Ortega had diagnosed the nature of the circumstances with sensitivity and accuracy. And that had been possible because he was a man who cared about his situation. For, as he had already written, "We use our capacities to the utmost when we are fully aware of our circumstances."(7)

Circumstances -- this is the word that has come to characterize Ortega's understanding of the immediate world. He writes:

> Circum-stantia! The wordless things that stand closely
> around us! Close, very close to us, they raise their
> silent visage with a gesture of humility and hope, need-
> ing our acceptance of their gift, yet ashamed of its
> seeming lowliness. And we walk in their midst with nary
> a glance toward them, our eyes fixed upon some future
> enterprise, projecting the conquest of far off, imagi-
> nary citadels.(8)

We are what we are in our circumstances, and Ortega understood this very well. Given the temper of the times, and the volatile nature of the situation, it would have been possible, and even advisable, for him to withdraw from public utterance and to dream of a utopian future when the political and social circumstances would be different. That would have meant a surrender to illusion. It would have been possible for him, on the other hand, to heed the political demands of the hour and embark on a voyage of action. That would have meant surrender to the fashionable. He did neither, for to choose between polarities is to betray the circumstances, which are always complex, multifarious, polymorphous. Instead, he embraced the circumstance as a whole, in its history and its presentness, in both its practical and its theoretical aspects. He moved from the classroom to the theater, but in doing so he did not lose himself. Rather, he sought to maintain the concrete synthesis of the "I" and its circumstances through which alone the human element can be saved.(9) What he did, he had described prophetically in an earlier essay:

> There are moments when Nature performs a quick turn, and
> yesterday's circumstances are replaced by others of such
> opposite character that persons endowed with an insuffi-
> cient sense of balance feel catapulted toward a moral
> vacuum. The world has changed and they know not how.

It is different from yesterday's, but its features are
not yet familiar. They only sense in the present the
absence of the usual looks. One does not believe today
what one did yesterday; therefore, they suppose one does
not believe in anything. The new faith acts subcon-
sciously in them, but they lack the spiritual strength
needed to define it.
     On the other hand, it is a pleasure to see how, when
Nature turns, those used to keeping it company, like ex-
pert racing sailors, keep close to the sudden turn, get
over the difficult point, and never lose contact, adher-
ing intimately to the new circumstance. They are infinitely malleable souls, capable of the finest adjustments to the cosmic turns.(10)

     True to his prophesy, in his own hour of crisis, Ortega showed himself
the master navigator, the consummate helmsman — in short, the accomplished
sportsman.
     I said earlier that Ortega cared about his situation. That word, care,
requires some elucidation. Care comes from cura, Ortega writes:

In old Spanish cuidar meant to be concerned, curare.
This original meaning of cura or care survives in many
of our current words, such as curator, procurator, cure,
and in the very word curate, which was applied to the
priest because he took care of the soul. . . . Conversely, incuria means carelessness, lack of concern; and
security — securitas — is the absence of concern and
preoccupation.(11)

     Ortega ties the meaning of care to that developed by Heidegger. For
Heidegger, to care is essentially to live authentically in this world.(12)
Care does not mean anxiety, worry, or concern for the practical consequences
of our actions. Rather, care expresses the essential relationship between
us and our circumstances; it characterizes the nature of our being insofar
as we exist concretely in a world made up of those wordless things that
surround us, as well as of humans who address us. Care marks the fact that
when human living is authentic, the "I" is concerned about its own being in
the midst of its circumstances. In short, to be authentically human in this
world is to be careful about ourselves in our circumstances.
     When care is understood thus it is not difficult to see how careful
Ortega was about his situation. Here he was, a professor of philosophy,
accustomed to the intense intellectual climate of the classroom and to a
self-imposed urge to write — suddenly catapulted into a hostile milieu,
without a job, and in the center of a political amphitheater.
     Had he not cared for the fundamental activity that tied him to his
circumstances — for that amor intellectualis, as he called it, echoing
Spinoza — we would not be celebrating the centenary of his birth. Similarly, as Kierkegaard has reminded us, had Abraham's arm not been raised to
sacrifice his son Isaac, his life would be nothing to us. But they cared,
each for his own circumstance, each through his own action, and in their
circumstances they have been preserved for us.
     "Within each thing," Ortega wrote, "there is a hint of its possible
fullness. An open and noble spirit will desire to perfect it, to help it
reach its fullness. This is love — love for the perfection of the loved
one."(13) In the situation I have been trying to "save," Ortega glimpsed a
hint of fullness, and he committed himself to its fulfillment. I am referring to the fact that he was able to seize the opportunity and move from an
institutional teaching situation to an anti-institutional one; from teaching
in the university to lecturing in the theater under no aegis but his own.

4   Ignacio L. Götz

In other words, Ortega glimpsed the human element latent in the institutional situation; he plucked from its shell the kernel of meaning, and he was able to transfer it, intact, even enhanced, to a set of circumstances sui generis within which it could prosper and find fulfillment.

Here we have a perfect example of what Ortega called "a curious institutional atheism"(14) -- that is, the use of structures and institutions without believing in them. The paradigm is the atheist who swears "by God;" or Galileo's legendary "Eppure si muove!" Only those who have grasped the human meanings enshrined in institutions can move freely in and out of institutional settings, and even dispense with institutions altogether, if the circumstances and the treasure they enshrine demand it.

There is a lesson here, and it is an important one, for our age is crumbling, partly due to an inveterate adherence to moribund institutions. Listen to the contemporary defenders of the public schools, of the electoral college, or of institutional capitalism, who claim those institutions are "essential" to the survival of the democratic compact. Their fanatical faith in institutions blinds them to the urgency of the situation and the need for change. They stick to their course even when the winds have changed, leaving them becalmed and stagnant in the middle of nowhere. Even those who speak the language of reform and advocate moderate changes, are still fixated in institutional belief. Such belief differs toto coelo from the institutional atheism of Ortega.

The crucial difference between reformers and institutional atheists is the attitude they bear toward institutional structures. Reformers, while working within institutions, still maintain their faith in the need, value, and importance of specific structures. For institutional atheists, on the other hand, such a faith is not justifiable. Belief can be given only to the permanent, and the only abiding value is that of the human. Therefore they may create structures, if these serve their purposes, but they do not believe in them, because their only belief centers around humans and their ever changing circumstances. Such a belief, and the lives grounded in it, are indeed paradoxical, for they require the use of means without attachment to them. Only skillful, experienced players can afford to confront these elusive, powerful, bicornuous questions.

Ortega went eventually into exile, where he continued to teach and to write. He did not go back to Madrid until the late 1940s, after sojourns in France, Argentina, and Lisbon. Upon his return, he picked up where he had left off: he founded an institution sui generis, the Institute for the Humanities, whose purport was the study, precisely, of "the most diverse dimensions which make up the gigantic project that is the 'human life.'"(15) Eventually, the ultimate human circumstance overtook him. He died in 1955.

Few of us will be around for the celebration of the centenary of his death. That is as it should be. But perhaps his death is an event that should not be commemorated. For he was a man enamored of living, for whom life raised constantly inexorable problems, who devoted himself to the salvation of his circumstances, whose living was itself a meditatio vitae, a meditation on life.

NOTES

1.   Hermann Hesse, My Belief (New York: Noonday Press, 1975), p. 371.

2.   Albert Camus, "The Wager of Our Generation," in Resistance, Rebellion, and Death (New York: Modern Library, 1963), p. 186.

3.   José Ortega y Gasset, "Meditaciones del Quijote," in Obras completas (Madrid: Revista de Occidente, 1966), vol. I, p. 311.

4.   Ortega y Gasset, Obras VIII, p. 55.

5.   Luis de Zulueta, "Lecciones de Ortega y Gasset," El Sol, May 21, 1929, cited by Robert McClintock, Man and His Circumstances: Ortega as Educator (New York: Teachers College Press, 1971), p. 215.

6.   Ortega y Gasset, Obras I, p. 311.

7.   Ibid., p. 319. Unless otherwise indicated, all translations from the Spanish are mine.

8.   Ibid.

9.   Cf. Ibid., p. 322.

10.   Ortega y Gasset, "Reforma de la inteligencia" (1926), Obras IV, p. 494.

11.   Ortega y Gasset, "Sobre el estudiar y el estudiante" (1933), Obras IV, p. 550.

12.   Martin Heidegger, Being and Time (New York: Harper & Row, 1962), p. 237.

13.   Ortega y Gasset, Obras I, p. 311.

14.   "¿Instituciones?" Obras IV, p. 363.

15.   Ortega y Gasset, "Prospecto del Instituto de Humanidades," Obras VII, p. 17

Part I

Philosophy, History, Literature

3.
From Ortega y Gasset to
R. S. Hartman:
Thoughts on Value Theory
GARY J. ACQUAVIVA

José Ortega y Gasset has been associated with several movements within philosophy: existentialism, life philosophy, and phenomenology, to name a few. Many have written of his influence by Nietzsche, Husserl, Dilthey, Scheler and others, influences Ortega would never have denied, particularly since one of the central themes of his metaphysics is "I am I and my circumstance." He has not, however, received the credit due him in value theory, in axiology. This is not unexpected considering the traditions within academic philosophy. Only recently, in 1977, Walter Kaufmann revised his popular reader on existentialism to include a selection from Ortega with an extensive introduction in which he states that Ortega "has been widely underestimated as a philosopher."(1) Though Julián Marías wrote that Ortega attempted to "rid himself from the beginning of an existentialism,"(2) Kaufmann's inclusion represents a significant — if late — recognition of Ortega's stature.

Albert Camus referred to Ortega as "one of the greatest philosophers of the 20th century."(3) Ortega not only acclaimed the value of life within his philosophy, but he also lived his philosophy. While he did not construct a formal theory of axiology, his work did influence and inspire the development of such a theory by R. S. Hartman. The novel approach to the concept of human reality shared by both Hartman and Ortega is the value dynamics existing between human consciousness and the phenomena it either experiences by choice or avoids by choice.

We shall begin our journey through the landscape of Ortega's philosophy intending to uncover the metaphysical frame encompassing Espectador Universal de Vital Valors. "Imagination is more important than intellect," Einstein once wrote. So, let us use our imagination and paint the metaphysical landscape that Ortega y Gasset left us. Imagine us shipwrecked, drifting through the vast expanses of the universe, drifting at Ortega's "crossroad," and each of us has the choice to direct our attention wherever circumstances gives us access. Choosing to experience aletheia, truth, is a matter of an individual's will. It is the choice to uncover the interpretations that make up our separate perspectives. It is also the choice of opening oneself to interpenetrate with each other's perspective in order to understand the inter-individual structure of the human self. Interdependence and coexistence are fundamental to Ortega's philosophy. He wrote, "Between the world and the self there is no priority; neither comes first, but both come at the same time."(4)

Our metaphysical landscape would be incomplete without vital reason, which brings value and meaning to Ortega's metaphysics. Vital reason together with aletheia, one's circumstance, one's crossroad, living together, coexistence, inter-individuality and attention interwoven into a dynamic unity, make up Ortega's axiology, or what Marías and Mora have referred to as his metaphysics of human life. Our landscape would be incomplete if any one were absent. We now begin with Ortega's first book Meditations on Quixote, written in 1914.

The philosophical significance of the Meditations is aptly expressed in Julián Marías illuminating introduction, which stresses that the fulcrum upon which Ortega's metaphysics rests is found within his statement "I am I and my circumstance." Since each individual is born into a world not of his choosing, neither nation, parents, race, nor sex are a matter of choice. From the day of birth, circumstance surrounds each of us and affects our development. Essentially we exist shipwrecked at a crossroad.

The concept of encrucijada (crossroad) is central to Ortega's theory of perspectivism; for it is at one's crossroad where one's circumstance is experienced.   Perhaps the novelist Herman Hesse captured the meaning of Ortega's crossroad best when he wrote, in 1919, that each person "represents the unique, the very special and always significant and remarkable point at which the world's phenomena intersect, only once in this way and never again."(5) Or as Ortega wrote in his essay "Truth and Perspective:" "Each nation and each individual perceives reality in a different way, like a tentacle reaching towards those inaccessible fragments of the universe."(6)

While Ortega acclaims the uniqueness of each human perspective, he reminds us that many have a "humble desire to be like everybody else" by "letting customs, prejudices, habits, topics be installed within them."(7) Consequently, many individuals choose to ignore and avoid the uniqueness of their encrucijada and, consequently, ignore the uniqueness of their perspective.   Individuals who make this choice ignore the crossroad that is uniquely theirs and live as participants in a carnival disguised as someone they are not. "The world is a constant carnival," Ortega wrote in Concord and Liberty, "Masks surround us."(8) Psychologists may attempt to explain why some individuals conceal their identity behind a mask; for Ortega, when living a mask, they remain shipwrecked within their inner self. Never having learned to appreciate the uniqueness of their crossroad, their existence, they have also failed in learning to appreciate others' perspectives. The masked perspective of this type of individual shuts out the world preventing him from experiencing his circumstance.

In the recent Pulitzer Prize-winning book The Denial of Death, cultural anthropologist Ernest Becker develops a similar point, explaining that the neurotic "fences himself off and becomes his own world (narcissism)."(9) As a result, "the neurotic exhausts himself not only in self-preoccupations like hypochondriacal fears and all sorts of fantasies, but also in others . . . he takes out his subjective problems on them."(10) To the degree that the individual refuses to open and share his perspective with others and, thus, refuses to experience lived reality, neurotic symptoms emerge. As Ortega expressed it, "a perspective is perfected by the multiplication of its viewpoints and the precision with which we react to each one of its planes."(11) What we discover in the masked individual is the opposite. For the masked individual, a perspective becomes more imperfect the less he multiplies his viewpoints. The dehumanization of one's perspective is accompanied by negative forms of neurosis; both are symptoms of a dehumanized perspective -- an axiological distortion of values. Rather than directing one's life energy toward a positive valuation of the uniqueness, the neurotic's energy and attention are directed at reinforcing the belief in the mask he lives.

The inter-individual, on the other hand, may avoid neurosis and choose to discover the uniqueness of his existence. The self, Ortega has told us, is "far from being closed; it is par excellence the open being."(12) But, this openness exists as a potential whose actualization depends upon the individual's choice to experience or not to experience aletheia. Aletheia is the intricate ingredient of the lived experience of life, requiring the interpenetration of one's own with the perspective of others. Interpenetration may accurately be referred to as an act of loving, for this is

essentially what is needed for the enrichment of one's perspective. Ortega
writes, "In loving, as differentiated from desiring, we are trying to live
from within the other and unlive ourselves for the sake of the other."(13)
The perspective of the individual is expanded through such acts of love so
that there is a change within the individual from the isolation of his perspective to the perspective of the inter-individual. In his book El hombre
y la gente (Man and People), Ortega explains that it is through the experience of convivencia that the uniqueness of the inter-individual develops.(14) In value terms the act of loving is a mutual and intrinsic sharing of two encrucijadas, which occurs simultaneously with the experience of
aletheia: a sharing of the experience of truth. The openness of our human
perspectives is also as fundamental as is making the choice to enrich our
perspectives, and aletheia is the doorway allowing us. Ortega qualifies
being open as an active state and not a passive state; this active openness
is necessary to convivencia, which we will refer to as "open reciprocity."(15) Furthermore, let us clarify that open reciprocity is a precondition for living within the other, for loving; and, consequently, experiencing love is a precondition for the expansion of one's perspective.

It is through open reciprocity that unique experiences occur and here
where the inter-individual develops and grows. Both humanistic and growth
psychology inadvertently followed Ortega's lead; however, his philosophy is
not as similar to self-actualization psychologies, such as Abraham Maslows',
as it is to Victor Frankl's logotherapy.(16) Ortega explicitly refers to
"trans-mine," "transcendent,"(17) and "transmigration."(18) There is a
significant difference between the two theories. On the one hand, the emphasis is placed upon the actualization of an individual self that remains
self-centered by focusing upon pursuits of personal goals. From selective
exclusions of other perspectives, a variety of types of egotism evolve. On
the other hand, if the emphasis is placed upon actualizing one's potential
by sharing perspectives with others, psychological health results. Those
inter-individuals who transcend narrow self-interest with acts of love discover and enrich the meaning and value of life. Once placed within the
metaphysics of Ortega's value theory, the dynamic of aletheia, of uncovering
the truth, is translated into a living activity of discovering a structure
of value previously undisclosed.

What we have observed are two distinct paths separated by fundamentally
different value perspectives. On the other hand, the inter-individual en-
richens and expands his encrucijada and becomes his mask, fearing to open
himself to others. Consequently failing to enrich or expand his perspective, he stifles his growth as a human being, or what is the same thing, the
growth of his relations with others. A vivid contrast: the positive valuation of the dynamics of humans living together versus the valuation of a
static mask -- the dehumanization of man. In The Dehumanization of Art,
Ortega wrote a brief essay entitled "A Few Drops of Phenomenology."(19) In
it he describes the scene of a great man dying, with four witnesses present.

In order to dramatize Ortega's example, we will expand the number of
persons present in the example, and we will consider the specific scene of
the death of a recent, most popular president of the United States, the
assassination of President John F. Kennedy, on November 22, 1963. For
Ortega, the perspectives of all individuals are authentic. The sum total of
all perspectives represents various aspects of the event. Those exhibiting
greater sensitivity are, to a greater degree, experiencing the real event,
while those desensitized or insensitive are not involved in the real event.
Respectively, these extremes represent Ortega's notions of "lived reality"
and "observed reality."

Consider the following individuals and their respective points-of-view:
The president's wife, Jacqueline Kennedy, the Secret Service agents, the
chauffeur, the citizen who filmed the assassination with his home camera,
the assassin and, perhaps, your own point-of-view when you first learned of
the assassination. The authenticity of all perspectives does not mean that

all involve the same reality. Opposite points-of-view are represented by
the assassin and the president's wife. The assassin calculatedly and un-
feelingly aimed his rifle and shot the president. He was not involved in
the "real event." He performed his job perfunctorily while living within
what Ortega describes as "observed reality." At the other extreme, we discover the president's wife involved in experiencing the most intimate form
of anguish, despair, and helplessness, as she held her dying husband's body.
Her experience of his tragic death represented the closest form of empathy,
illustrating Ortega's "lived reality."

Between these two extremes, between unfeeling, calculating insensiti-
vity and spontaneous, empathic sensitivity, exist various mixtures of perspectives. Neither the chauffeur nor the Secret Service could allow themselves to become emotionally involved. The unknown citizen filming the
event did not drop his camera, did not stop filming, for he may have sensed
that he was filming history. The assassination may have affected him in
such away that he felt a mixture of disturbed emotions and a sense of responsibility to history. Eventually the historians identified the film with
his name, and it is now referred to as the Zapruder film. Ortega does not
exclude perspectives, but outlines in "A Few Drops of Phenomenology" a meth-
odology to classify and measure the various value dimensions.

It is from this essay that R. S. Hartman quotes Ortega and explains
axiologically in The Structure of Value,(20) one of the few books that ac-
claim Ortega as an axiologist. Hartman wrote, "These 'drops' of phenomenology can be formalized . . . . The axiological variations of the situation
are expressible in a symbolism which faithfully represents the 'measure'
given us by Ortega y Gasset. The value symbolism is isomorphous with the
value reality."(21)

A few years after the Meditations, in The Modern Theme, Ortega wrote,
"Every object enjoys, on identical grounds, a kind of dual existence. On
the one hand it is a structure of real qualities, which we can perceive; on
the other it is a structure of real qualities, which are only apparent to
our assessive capacity."(22) Ortega also knew that the task of mathematically structuring a hierarchy of values had to be undertaken, for he wrote,
"Mathematics is an a priori science of absolute truths. Well then, axiology, or value theory, is likewise a system of evident and unchangeable
truths of a type similar to mathematics."(23) Ortega's notion of measuring
value perspectives can be traced back to his Meditations(24), and his theory
of values can be found throughout his works. Ortega also explained, "It is
essential, for instance, for every value to be positive or negative: there
is no middle term . . . when we have a clear intuition of any two, we observe that one exceeds the other and is set above it, each remaining in a
different rank."(25)

The ranking of a hierarchy of values is what Ortega focuses attention
on; but, unlike other objectivists, Ortega's hierarchy places human life as
the highest value of this world. And, similarly, Hartman's Value Questionnaire which is based upon his formal theory of values, places a baby as the
highest value and mathematically defines human life as the greatest number
-- a nondenumerable infinity, a continuum.

While Ortega divides values into three categories, persons, things and
situations, Hartman's axiology mathematically distinguishes three value
dimensions as intrinsic values, extrinsic values, and systemic values.
While Ortega divides "reality" into lived and observed, Hartman axiologically distinguishes the individual's value perspective of his self from the
individual's value perspective of his world. Whereas in Ortega's earliest
writings on values he distinguishes negative values from positive while
denying the possibility of neutral values, Hartman also separates negative
from positive values, with no neutral values. The positive valuation of an
intrinsic value or a human being valuing the positive value properties of
the uniqueness of another human being ranks as Hartman's highest value.

The most relevant application of axiology is the analysis of the value structure of personality. Such an analysis is no small undertaking for it purports to describe the values of the individual while diagnosing and predicting his behavior. Few psychologists since Verner, Lindsey, and Allport in their Study of Values in 1951, have realized the significance of values in understanding human behavior. Several, however, have found the Hartman Value Questionnaire useful in psychological counseling. Dr. Leon Pomeroy, psychologist at the Biofeedback and Stress Control Unit of the Veterans Administration Clinic, has completed a study comparing the Hartman Value Questionnaire with the most widely accepted personality test in the United States, the Minnesota Multiphasic Personality Inventory. I have since designed a value questionnaire to be more aligned to Ortega's germinal point: "Life is preoccupation and not only in moments which are difficult, but all the time; in essence it is no more than this, to be preoccupied."(26) And, this questionnaire has recently been used to assess the value characteristics unique to criminals on probation.

Preoccupation or attention is determined by the value structure of the personality. The fundamental claim of value theory is that human behavior is determined primarily by the values of the individual and that these values can be scientifically studied. Psychology and axiology may not yet, and may never, be able to determine the entire structure, personality, and motivations of an individual. However, it is clear that if the unique perspective of another individual is to be investigated and understood, an understanding of his or her values is needed.

Basing their early research upon Ortega and Hartman, these two giants of axiology value, theorists have begun applying their skills in Sweden, Mexico, Canada, and the United States. I have been living at the crossroad of this rapidly expanding computerized science of human behavior. Will such computerization dehumanize man's understanding of man? No, it is not the machine that dehumanizes man; it is man alone, man falsely confusing observed with lived reality, or confusing dynamic coexistence with static objectification.

Both Ortega y Gasset and R. S. Hartman give directions whereby man might humanize his world and prevent its further dehumanization. Computerized technology will only accelerate their dreams of further discovering once inaccessible human perspectives. Then, the study of man will return again to accentuate the unique rather than common types. Our axiological vocabulary to describe man will have as many terms as there are colors, shades, and hues in an artist's eye, and Ortega's values will become a lived reality.

NOTES

1. Walter Kaufmann, Existentialism from Dostoyevsky to Sartre (New York: The World Publishing Company, 1956), pp. 152-58.

2. José Ortega y Gasset, Meditations on Quijote, with an introduction and notes by Julián Marías, trans. Evelyn Rugg and Diego Marín (New York: W. W. Norton, 1961) p. 25.

3. Ibid., Preface, p. 1.

4. Ortega y Gasset, What is Philosophy?, trans. Mildred Adams (New York: W. W. Norton, 1960), p. 219.

5. Hermann Hesse, Demian, trans. Michael Roloff and Michael LeGeek (New York: Bantam Books, 1965), p. 4.

6. Ortega y Gasset, Obras completas (Madrid: España, 1955), vol. I, p. 129. Translation is mine.

7.   Ortega y Gasset, Philosophy, p. 251.

8.   Ortega y Gasset, Concord and Liberty, trans. Helene Weyl (New York: W. W. Norton, 1946), p. 59.

9.   Ernest Becker, The Denial of Death (New York: Free Press, 1973), p. 183.

10.   Ibid., p. 184.

11.   Ortega y Gasset, Meditations on Quixote (New York: W. W. Norton, 1961), p. 12.

12.   Ortega y Gasset, Philosophy, p. 201.

13.   Ibid., p. 239.

14.   Ortega y Gasset, El hombre y la gente, (Man and People) (Madrid: Revista de Occidente, 1970), pp. 151–52. Translation is mine.

15.   Ibid,. p. 150.

16.   Victor Frankl, Man's Search for Meaning (Boston: Beacon Press, 1962), p. 112.

17.   Ortega y Gasset, Hombre, p. 134.

18.   Ortega y Gasset, Philosophy, pp. 238–39.

19.   Ortega y Gasset, The Dehumanization of Art, trans. Helene Weyl (Princeton, N. J.: Princeton University Press, 1968), pp. 14–15.

20.   R. S. Hartman, The Structure of Value (Carbondale, Ill.: Southern Illinois University Press, 1967), p. 259.

21.   Ibid., p. 260.

22.   Ortega y Gasset, Obras, III, p. 180. Translation is mine.

23.   Risieri Frondizi, What is Value? (La Salle, Ill.: Opencourt Publishing Company, 1971), p. 48.

24.   Ortega y Gasset, Obras, I, p. 12. Translation is mine.

25.   Ortega y Gasset, The Modern Theme, trans. James Cleugh (New York: Harper and Row, 1961), pp. 62–63.

26.   Ortega y Gasset, Philosophy, p. 249.

4.
Between Philosophy and Literature: Ortega's *Meditations on Quixote*
ANTHONY J. CASCARDI

In Ortega's own description, the Meditaciones del Quijote (Meditations on Quixote, 1914) is the work of a philosopher in part disloyal to his calling, "in partibus infidelium," as it is put in the text. Just why Ortega chose to publish these reflections on the Quixote as his first book is open to some debate, not all of it bearing directly on Ortega's philosophical interests, yet this unconventional blend of philosophy and literary criticism may seem less strange to us today than it did to readers in 1914.

Looking back on Ortega's work, we can place the Meditations in the middle of a series of philosophical reflections that take the novel as a genre, and Don Quixote in particular, as their point of departure. When writing the Meditations, Ortega no doubt had Unamuno in mind, even though Ortega's writing is so unlike Unamuno's in style and tone; Unamuno's Vida de Don Quijote y Sancho (Life of Don Quixote and Sancho) had been published in 1905, and Del sentimiento trágico de la vida (The Tragic Sense of Life) of 1912 concludes with a section on "Don Quijote en la tragi-comedia europea contemporánea" ("Don Quixote in the Contemporary European Tragicomedy"). Just after Ortega's Meditations, Georg Lukács published Die Theorie des Romans (The Theory of the Novel), its first appearance being in an academic journal, the Zeitschrift fur Aesthetic und Allgemeine Kunstwissenschaft of 1916.

To be sure, Ortega's Meditations on Quixote is an idiosyncratic work of philosophy, but certainly not more so than either Unamuno's or Lukács' work. The text is deceptively modest and unassuming, nearly elusive of its subject, and scarcely leaves room for allusion to the whole process by which Ortega was measuring his distance from German phenomenology; Philip Silver could rightly speak of Ortega's "invisible philosophy" in this regard.(1) The essays are moved by "philosophical desires" (Ortega's phrase), even if they are not orthodox philosophy; or rather, they are philosophy minus the philosophical apparatus ("science, minus the explicit proof").(2) As literary criticism, they are equally disarming. Whole stretches of Ortega's text are free from reference to Cervantes' work. Just why Ortega chose to approach the Quixote in his first published book, and what his philosophical and literary purposes may have been in so doing, may become apparent if we consider the work in the tradition of philosophical reflection on the novel, in the line of Unamuno and Lukács.

At the end of The Tragic Sense of Life Unamuno says, in words which would mark him as one of the strongest of Harold Bloom's "strong readers" of literature (and, arguably, as a belated Romantic as well), "What do I care what Cervantes did or did not put into Don Quixote or what he actually did put into it? The living part of it for me is whatever I discover in it — whether Cervantes put it there or not — and whatever it is I myself put into or under or over it, and whatever all of us put into it. And I sought to track down our philosophy in it."(3)   Unamuno makes these remarks in the face of claims that there has never been such a thing as Spanish philosophy; in his Life of Don Quixote and Sancho, and in the essays surrounding it -- I am thinking, for instance, of "Ganivet, filósofo" ("Ganivet, Philosopher") and "Sobre la lectura e interpretación de Don Quijote" ("On the Reading and Interpretation of Don Quixote") -- he says that he is not sure whether there ought to be a Spanish philosophy; but how one takes that remark will depend on what one takes philosophy itself to be.

For Unamuno, this was the lingering idealism and budding positivism prevalent in Germany, ultimately part of the Kantian legacy from which Ortega similarly wanted to clear free. Kant customarily provokes Unamuno to sly, even dyspeptic remarks, but in dealing with the Quixote Unamuno was not interested in campaigning against schools or doctrines per se.   Rather, he wanted to find a philosophy capable of binding together the active and con- templative sides of man, and in finding a mode of knowledge responsive to the integrity of human existence. Given such an interest, he could only see contemporary European thought as effete, as incapable of fashioning a re- sponse to the historical forms of human life: "When scientific thought at- tains an independent existence as a desire for knowledge for the sake of knowledge, it takes the name of philosophy," Unamuno says, quoting from Windelband; "and when subsequently integral knowledge divides into branches, philosophy becomes the general knowledge of the world, embracing all other knowledge (The Tragic Sense of Life, p. 343)."   Unamuno wanted instead a nonspecialized, or rather a noncompartmentalized philosophy, so that philos- ophy as a whole might find itself capable of dealing with human life in all its particularity.

For direction, he turned to Cervantes' novel.   There, he saw the out- lines of a "philosophy for the world and not for philosophers alone" (Medi- tations, p. 356), of a "mundane philosophy," one capable of coming to grips with lived experience, with human history, and with the phenomenon of embod- iment. In the Quixote, and above all in Cervantes' hero, Unamuno found evi- dence of this desired philosophy: in Don Quixote's will to be who he is, in his clashes with the world and his defeat at its hands, and in the human conditions of life which are made apparent in his association with Sancho. Don Quixote, who is willing for adventure and risk, is able to live a life open to its own tragic possibilities (Kierkegaard here would have seen him as open to ridicule, hence to the comic possibilities of life); as such, he becomes the hero of Unamuno's work, On the Tragic Sense of Life.

In the Life of Don Quixote and Sancho, Unamuno chastizes the Spanish people for their "spiritual sloth," for "moral cowardice," for their failure to open themselves to turmoil and anguish. Where they have looked to Euro- pean and, in particular, to German ideas, they have betrayed their own iden- tity. It may well be that the Spanish people do not have a "philosophical" destiny, Unamuno says; certainly they do not if one identifies "philosophy" with the abstract and specialized "science" he describes in The Tragic Sense of Life; however, they have a destiny to follow Don Quixote's example, and in so doing Unamuno implies that they will be meeting their spiritual obli- gations to themselves. He asks his countrymen to seek out anguish and un- rest in their thinking in order to open themselves to the philosophical pos- sibilities inherent in themselves, rather than import inauthentic "sciences" from Europe. Were they to achieve this, they would fulfill the mission that Unamuno saw for himself as philosopher in The Tragic Sense of Life. They would, for instance, succeed in reversing the Cartesian cogito, on which Western rational thinking in the modern world is based, revising it to place the fact of human existence over and above the human capacity for intellec- tion or thought. They would learn to set aside ideas of social justice and human order founded on the supposed existence of a detached, transcendent point of view, and learn instead to respond to immediate situations, active- ly to involve themselves in circumstances, as Don Quixote does when he lib- erates the galley slaves or frees the punished servant boy Andrés.   They

would learn, in short, to behave quixotically, which in Unamuno's framework
means to act in ignorance of any breach between action and thought.

Unamuno's diagnosis of the "spiritlessness of the age" has obvious
roots in Kierkegaard, whom he refers to in fraternal terms at various points
in The Tragic Sense of Life, but it passes to Ortega in a rather different
guise. Ortega's antipathy to Unamuno is too well-known to require special
comment here, but he has also expressed an aversion to Kierkegaard; as an
author, Ortega says, Kierkegaard is virtually unreadable. (One can well
imagine the aversion of Ortega, philosopher of clarity and light, to Kierk-
egaards's poetic writing, especially in the pseudonymous works, but one remarks also the limitations of Ortega's poetic sensibility at this point.)

Ortega's appraisal of the "spiritlessness of the age," for which he
will seek his solution through the Quixote is, like Unamuno's, closely bound
up in the modern Spanish political and social crisis, but Ortega's claim
that the Meditations on Quixote have a "patriotic preoccupation" may seem
puzzling at first. Ortega addresses matters Spanish, and is concerned with
national patterns of understanding, but we hear no call to unity, no exhortation for Spaniards to turn inward, as in Unamuno. Still, Ortega can say
that "if we were observed in our most intimate and personal meditations, we
should be found trying out new experiments on a new Spain with the humblest
fibres of our soul" (Meditations, p. 53). In order for this to happen, however, Spaniards must tear down one Spain and build another: "The author who
is writing (these Meditations) and those to whom they are addressed have
their spiritual origin in a denial of a decrepit Spain" (ibid.) Ortega's
idea of a solution to the malaise of the Spanish spirit would require looking to Don Quixote for direction, although Ortega's Quixote is markedly different from Unamuno's.

Ortega identifies division and pessimism as plaguing the present age;
instead, there should be optimism and unity. What is needed to save the
Spanish circumstance — by which Ortega means saving it from divisiveness
and ultimately from destruction — is a new awareness of our relationship to
our circumstances, a relationship founded on "love." "We have reached the
depth of pessimism and do not seem to find anything positive enough in the
universe to save us," he writes (Meditations, p. 47) — and we will be unable to do so until we learn to approach our circumstances with what he
calls "love." "Owing to unknown causes, the inner dwelling of the Spaniards
was captured long ago by hate" (Meditations, p. 32). There is evidence of
such hate for example in the work of Mateo Alemán, and in Quevedo's sardonic
wit. "We Spaniards offer life a heart shielded by the armor of rancor, and
objects, rebounding from it, are cruelly driven away. For centuries we have
been involved in an incessant and progressive collapse of values" (Meditations, p. 34). By finding what Ortega means by "love," to replace the re-
pulsions generated by this hate, Spaniards will further the work of understanding, hence saving themselves and their circumstances.

Ortega finds his model for love and salvation in the Quixote, not only
because Cervantes' benevolent irony is powerful enough to offset the darkness of Quevedo and Mateo Alemán, but because the Quixote is the model of a
work concerned with circumstances. Reality as portrayed in Cervantes' novel, Ortega says, has two sides — a material side, and a poetic side, which
could also be called, respectively, a substantive side and an interpreted
side. More than this, each encountered reality is presented in its different perspectives in the Quixote, and it was Cervantes' genius to have as-
sembled a world which gives internal evidence of its many perspectives
(hence of the radically circumstantial nature of that world). This is why
Ortega privileges Cervantes over Don Quixote in his philosophical model,
whereas Unamuno had so highly prized the hero of Cervantes' book.

In Ortega's high regard for the Quixote we find, as in Unamuno, that a
literary work is presented as the model for philosophical change: in
Unamuno's case, by urging Spaniards to respond to their own spiritual
destiny as Don Quixote did to his, and in Ortega's case by urging Spaniards

to be as Cervantes, to place themselves in an open and caring relationship to their circumstances. Lukács likewise looks to the novel for philosophical reasons in his famous work of 1916, but his purpose is markedly different from that of Ortega and Unamuno. I do not mean simply the obvious fact that the Quixote could not have the same national significance for Lukács that it did for them, but that in Lukács the philosophical dimension of the novel serves a different end. The Theory of the Novel was, on Lukács' own account, an attempt to give an "historico-philosophical" explanation of the modern novel, that is, a placing of the novel as a genre (and of the Quixote as the first exemplar of this genre) in the history of forms. This attempt is evidence of one major portion of Lukács' intellectual inheritance in The Theory of the Novel, namely his reliance on Hegel's Aesthetik. (Another major portion of Lukács' inspiration derives from Kierkegaard.)

In The Theory of the Novel, the novelistic genre is evidence of the same philosophical situation to which Ortega and Unamuno had responded, and which in broad terms proves the lasting impact of German Romanticism on modern thought: a breach of subject and object, a split of thought and being in man. Indeed, it is only in light of this predicament that one can approach Lukács' more famous pronouncement linking the novel to epic literature: "The epic and the novel, these two major forms of great epic literature, differ from one another not by their author's fundamental intentions but by the given historico-philosophical realities with which the authors were confronted. The novel is the epic of an age in which the extensive totality of life is no longer directly given, in which the immanence of meaning in life has become a problem, yet which still thinks in terms of totality."(4) In the epic world as Lukács saw it, the sword is an extension of the arm, its presence is imbued with an active sense; but in the novel, whether in Cervantes, in Tolstoy, or in Proust, we have evidence of a world which is "incomplete" (the Romantic's eternal complaint), a world in which man is deeply estranged from his surroundings and wanders, unsheltered, in search of lost meaning.

If The Theory of the Novel is read today as a statement of the material or simply of literary conditions that preclude the integrity of thought and action, or the recuperation of wholeness and meaning in the world, that is in part because our image of Lukács and of the importance of his work derives largely from the later Marxist writings. But it is also because the Lukács of 1916, fresh from his readings of Hegel and Kierkegaard, did not himself see the full philosophical implications of his insights. Lukács', for instance, skirted the deep questions of the place of philosophy in this fragmented modern world and of the role of philosophy not only in diagnosing its problems but in working towards solutions of them. Lukács' The Theory of the Novel remains striking not only for its Romantic affinities, but also for its anticipation of the modernist concern with fragmentation and englobing order within works of art.

In comparison to The Theory of the Novel, Ortega's Meditations on Quixote are not impressive as an anticipation of the modern; whatever claim Ortega might lay to that accomplishment will have to rest with La deshumanización del arte (The Dehumanization of Art), itself a text of much debated value. Yet, two years earlier than Lukács, Ortega had succeeded in recognizing the place of philosophy in a modern world, and in envisioning such a place as shared by philosophy and the novel. Having identified, as did Unamuno and Lukács, a "spiritlessness" in the age, and having seen the possibilities for remedying that condition, it was up to Ortega to offer an example of the new mode of understanding he was proposing in his own work on Don Quixote. Taking up the form in which Descartes had begun what for us counts as "modern" philosophy, Ortega turned to the meditation, which for him means the contemplation of a world in its circumstantial nature. Ortega sets a scene near the Escorial, at the foot of the mountains outside Madrid. There is a grove of oak and ash trees, green grass and leaves, and patches of purple, yellow, and lavender flowers. This image, with its strong

emphasis on the continuities of color, is that of a world. The concept of a
world as a horizon-bound whole, as a field of circumstantial reality, is
central to Ortega's conception of the novel and the opportunity for meditative thought that the novel will also offer: "The forest opens up its
depths around me. A book is in my hand: Don Quixote, an ideal forest . . .
Don Quixote is the foreshortening book par excellence" (Meditations, p. 70).
The Quixote is an "ideal forest" because it is, by virtue of Cervantes'
intuition of perspective and circumstance, an "ideal world."

What Ortega means more deeply by this is that the novel has the possibility of showing us the sense of things, their meaning, in addition to
their materiality. Thus he can say that the novel is especially apt to the
"meditative cult," in other words, to the attempt to understand things in
their relationship to others, as embedded in a network of significance. The
novel, like the forest, and like a world, is defined in terms of the relationships among its parts and also by our relationship to it; the forest,
for example, is defined by how we stand among its trees. What lay in the
novel for Spaniards to discover was the creation of a world in literature,
and all that that implies; what Ortega urged his countrymen to do in the
Meditations on Quixote was to learn to interpret a world, to see in Cervantes' novel the possibility for replacing themselves in the proper relationship to their own world. In Ortega's vision, this could not be done
by the kind of transcendental reduction of the world that phenomenology had
sought. Instead, it would require the spiritual benevolence which he called
love and care, terms which, respectively, recall Kierkegaard and anticipate
Heidegger, but which Ortega on his own discovered could not be exiled from
philosophical thought.

NOTES

   1. Philip W. Silver, Ortega as Phenomenologist: The Genesis of
"Meditations on Quixote" (New York: Columbia University Press, 1978).

   2. José Ortega y Gasset, Meditations on Quixote, trans. Evelyn Rugg
and Diego Marín (1961; reprint, New York: W. W. Norton, Norton Library,
1963), p. 40.

   3. Miguel de Unamuno, The Tragic Sense of Life in Men and Nations,
trans. Anthony Kerrigan (1972; reprint, Princeton, N.J.: Princeton University Press, Bollingen Series LXXXV, 1977), pp. 335-336.

   4. Georg Lukács, The Theory of the Novel, trans. Anna Bostock (1971;
reprint, Cambridge, Mass.: The MIT Press, 1977), p. 56.

5.

The Influence of José Ortega y Gasset's Thought on Hungarian Spiritual Life (1928-1945)

DEZSØ CSEJTEI

First of all should be discussed those previous spiritual-cultural conditions that determined from the very first the spreading of Ortega's ideas in
Hungary, particularly the state of academic philosophy and the presence of
the literary "essayist generation."

To begin with, Ortega did not (and could not) exert any considerable
influence upon Hungarian official, academic philosophy. There are several
reasons for this: First, Hungarian academic philosophy was from the very
beginning essentially German-oriented. It was rather epigone-like; as a
consequence, it had constant phase-lagging. At the universities the various
branches of traditional, epistemology-centered neo-Kantianism maintained
rather strong positions, whereas there was not so much room for irrational
currents, Hungarian academic philosophy was also Christian; first of all,
Catholic philosophies had very strong positions during this whole period,
from the directly political-ideological "Christian Course" through the cool-
er, tradition-centered neo-Thomism up to the various currents of contemporary neo-Catholicism.

Secondly, Ortega's philosophy did exercise an influence on the members
of the so-called "essayist generation," on writers, first of all, and, to a
lesser extent, on political publicism. (I count Antal Szerb (1902-1945),
Gábor Halász (1902-1945) and László Németh (1901-1975), as the most outstanding representatives of this generation.) The reasons for this could,
perhaps, be summarized by the traditions of Hungarian essay-writing; I could
say that the Hungarian essay exhibits the following characteristics:

a) It is of a literary character (apart from some
exceptions);

b) Therefore, a characteristic of it is its lyrical
tone;

c) Furthermore, beside its lyrical coloring, there is a
deep conceptional content in it, which is due to the
fact that for lack of a highly developed philosophical life the burden of expressing the Hungarian
philosophical spirit had been, for the most part,
imposed on the genre of essay;

d) Lastly, it always had a deep ethical content, which
grew stronger especially in critical periods, and
the events in 1918-1920 (defeat in war, overthrown
revolutions, the unjust Paris Peace Treaty, the end
of Hungary's position as a great power with the

collapse of the Austro–Hungarian monarchy) caused,
to   be sure, the greatest historical crisis of the
Hungarians since the Mohacs battle (1526).

Ortega's appearance in Hungary could be characterized as a fortunate
spiritual meeting of two complementary essay styles; Ortega is an outstanding representative of the philosophical essay, although his style is a bit
milder than that of the so–called didactic essay; lyrical insets and poetic
fantasy are peculiar to it.   The members of the essayist generation, in
turn, cultivated the genre of the literary essay, with a strong philosophical coloring.   German spirituality, inherent in most of Ortega's writings,
contributed on a large scale to the dissemination of his ideas in Hungary;
it facilitated his adaptations.

The consequence of all these above–mentioned circumstances is that the
essayist generation was able to command a greater popularity for Ortega's
ideas, as though his message could only have been received by a limited,
professional circle.

Third, Ortega's thoughts helped the members of the essayist generation
to discover themselves, to make them conscious of their mission — partly
against the so–called "official Hungary" and partly against the generation
just ahead of them.

What were the nation's fundamental problems?   The first factor was ac-
complishing the recovery of a broken country.   Here I would refer to the
above–mentioned components of our national catastophe.   In fact, the situation in Hungary after 1918–1920 reminds one of that in Spain after 1898.
Both countries fell into a state of national catastrophe, which called forth
with unprecedented strength the imperative of national regeneration.

The second problem was gaining the assurance of regeneration as a special program of the intellectuals.   The members of the essayist generation
thought that the country, fainting with inability, should regain her consciousness mostly with the help of the intellectuals; they regarded the intellectual class as the thinking organ, the living conscience of the country.   The missionary zeal of the intelligentsia bears a strong resemblance
to the Orteguian conception of authentic minority.

The third task was reformulating the Europe–Hungary relationship.   (The
fundamental situation resembles that of the Europe–Spain relationship, with
considerable differences, naturally, in the details.)   The point of crucial
importance is to place the Hungarian people within the frame of the new,
contemporary Europe.   This Europe, towards which the essayist generation
tried to find its way, was by no means identical to the Europe of the "merry
old times" but a Europe torn and tormented by the Great War and revolutions.
So Hungarians were looking for their place in a Europe which for her part
was trying to find her place as well.

The fourth problem was the surpassing of the spiritual horizon of the
so–called "official neo–Catholicism."   A remarkable comparison can be drawn
between Hungarian and Spanish spirituality from this respect, too, for the
official neo–baroque Catholicism which became the most important ideological
supporter of the restoration after the revolutions in Hungary, bears a close
resemblance to that official Spanish neo–Catholicism which became the spiritual supporter of Francoism.   The common motive between Ortega and the essayist generation is the following one: the appearance of Orteguian
thoughts in Spain, as the expression of philosophy that is indifferent from
the religious point of view, betrays a close similarity to that spiritual
atmosphere in which the intellectual horizon of the essayist generation took
shape, for their range of thought was directed against neo–Catholicism in
some respects as well.

Antal Szerb dealt with the Spanish thinker in his History of World Literature.   Speaking about Ortega's style, it was Szerb who elucidated one of

the main reasons of his Hungarian popularity: "His essays brilliantly hit
the right middle course between philosophy and lyricism; in them, reason and
emotions are balanced in a Latin harmony."(1)   A certain duality is characteristic of Szerb's views concerning Ortega. He writes: "Ortega's central
message is that of the Nietzschean elite-thought; society should be governed
not by the masses but by the chosen minority."(2)   It is a matter of fact
that the so-called elite-thought is really one of the cornerstones of Ortega's thought (how Szerb interprets it, is another question; I shall come
back to this later); his statement, however, that this thought is of an essentially Nietzschean origin, could be conceived partly as an association
based on distant analogies and partly as an exact expression of the prevailing tone of his age in which Nietzsche really became an important point of
reference. But this could not be considered, by any means, the final conclusion of a detailed analysis.

Naturally, Nietzsche deeply influenced Ortega's thought (this is precisely demonstrated by Sobejano);(3) nevertheless, on the basis of an ex-
haustive analysis it can be pointed out that, though both of them have a
fundamentally aristocratic view of man and society, their concept of the
elite is different in many respects. Furthermore, by reason of Orringer's
research work(4) it can be taken for certain that Verweyen's book(5) had
been one of the main spiritual inspirers of the Orteguian minority-concept.
(Let it be said on Szerb's behalf that in his time he could scarcely have
known anything about these connections.)   One point is, however, of the
greatest importance, and this is the notion of a close Nietzsche-Ortega
parallel which could have -- especially in the 1930s -- serious ideological
consequences. (I hasten to emphasize that Szerb did not belong to this line
of thought; he was a Jew by origin and he died in a labor camp in 1945.)
This problem could, perhaps, be formulated as that of the double shadow; by
this I mean that the gloomy shadow, which fell onto Nietzsche's philosophy
as a result of the Nazi interpretations in the thirties, could easily be
directed towards Ortega's philosophy, bringing about the danger that his
thought can be interpreted as an ideological forerunner of Fascism, which is
obviously nonsense. Szerb's intention was to bring Ortega closer to the
Hungarian public through Nietzsche's figure, who was very popular at that
time in Hungary; but this comparison had its disadvantages as well.

There are slight problems concerning his interpretation of the Orteguian minority-concept, too, for Szerb here speaks about "scientists, physicians and engineers," that is to say, he identifies the elite with trade and
professionals. In this way the central Orteguian tenet, according to which
minority is above all a human quality, which can make its appearance in
every field of social being, fell completely into the background. In turn,
another observation of his is quite right when he writes that "Ortega's
whole conception comes very near to that of the most exquisite representatives of German human studies (Geisteswissenschaften)."(6) Here Szerb takes
notice of a resemblance that Ortega himself became aware of only in the
thirties having made himself familiar with Dilthey's philosophy.

To the best of my knowledge it was Gábor Halász, who, in 1928 in the
columns of Napkelet,(7) first called attention in Hungary to Ortega's philosophy. It can be demonstrated philologically that in his essays written
during that time (e.g., On Recent Novels, The Death of Lyricism) he made
much use of Ortega's writings as well, especially those of Ideas sobre la
novela and La deshumanización del arte.

If now I compare Ortega's theory of the novel with that of Halász's, I
can point out the main difference in the fact that whereas Ortega's analysis
is multi-layered, Halász's line of thought stays on the same ground all the
way. One can clearly feel out the philosophical-anthropological background
behind Ortega's train of thought, whereas Halász's analysis continues on the
aesthetical plane all the while. At the same time the lack of a deeper

philosophical foundation provides greater theoretical free scope for Halász his argumentation is breezier than that of Ortega (though the latter's analysis is more virtuosic), and, furthermore, his scope is greater than that of the Spanish thinker. In the main, Halász accepts Ortega's elucidations concerning the crisis of the novel and, besides this, two further requirements for novel-composition: first, the necessity of creating a closed, hermetic, inner world of the novel; second, that the author should not define his own characters. There are, however, significant discrepancies, too, such as the following ones: the first is that whereas Ortega insists on the ever more perfect representation of the figures, Halász assigns an important place to occurrence. Another difference is this: Ortega states that the impeding of the infiltration of outer (social, political and ideological) influences on the part of the novelist is the basic requirement of aesthetical immanentism of form in general; Halász, on the contrary, calls for the representation of social contents, too, though he himself is against the so-called "sociological novel" of the nineteenth-century.

I think that Halász's partly restrained aesthetical conservativism manifests itself in his way of thinking. And here we can see another thing, which, perhaps, explains the conservativist tone of his aesthetical judgement. At the end of his essay he writes that "after the war the new self-esteem of the intellect became more and more evident in novel writing as well. Thought gradually regains its previously lost prestige, its directing rule over art, literature, life."(8) These are the words of a Central-European intellectual who lived through, almost as a child, the bloodthirsty years of the Great War. Whilst in Western-European philosophical life, as in Ortega's thinking as well, the reevaluation of the positions of traditional rationalism was at issue, in Central-Eastern Europe, where the development of classical bourgeois rationalism was behind time, Halász's conservative-colored neorationalism, his supplication to the authority of thought can be valued as an unambiguously progressive intellectual deed.

In his essay, The Death of Lyricism, it is a typically Orteguian trait that, in his view, the basic characteristic of the nineteenth-century — romantic — verse consists in the hypertrophy of the poetic self, in the exaggerated emphasis of the lyrical subject. Furthermore, Halász agrees with the Spanish thinker that new lyricism will bring about the revival of aristocratic sensibility, the respect for form and moderation. This is another question that the sociology of art, which underlines the whole Orteguian conception, is completely missing in Halász. But here again the cool intellectualism of the Hungarian aesthete gets the upper hand, for he writes that "in its fundamental ambitions the new lyricism in the making will bear a resemblance to its classical predecessors;"(9) that is, besides novelty, Halász cherishes the preservation of classical traditions too.

Let us take a glance, finally, at his essay, entitled José Ortega y Gasset, in which he summarizes in brief the main tenets of Ortega's teaching. The most important idea is concealed in the first lines: "The unity of Europe is due to her thinkers. However divided she was in power, rivalry, hatred, some immaculate souls sent a message to one another and their ideas bound, like a hoop, the ribs that were falling apart."(10)

We are listening to a voice in 1944, the sixth year of the Second World War, and Europe is bleeding with a thousand wounds, she is dying; and in the midst of these circumstances the author — a year before his cruel death in the labor camp — turns to Europe taken as a unit, turns to the eternal, spiritual Europe and, evoking Ortega's spirit, he writes: "The unity of thought is again ahead of political reconciliation. Europe, in Ortega's esteem, is the company of European peoples; she is not a 'thing,' but a brilliantly realized balance."(11) Nevertheless, at this point of his exposition Halász's voice falters, he is unable to bear the vast moral burden his century has imposed on him. In order to gather strength he turns to the nineteenth-century, to that very century, the spiritual atmosphere of which he — just like Ortega — always tried to escape: "Our point of view cannot

be that of a simple reaction in relation to the great century of civilization; having gotten acquainted with its virtues and faults we have to continue right there where it fell short of the work of perfection."(12)

Paradoxes at the crossroads: a twentieth-century Hungarian intellectual who had concentrated in his self both sides of our century -- with his
life, its intellect, victorious over the whole universe, and, with his
death, its crude, unrestrained barbarism -- becomes converted this way into
his antagonist, the nineteenth-century, out of which he had been born.

It is undeniable that Ortega exercised on László Németh the deepest
influence during these years. In connection with their spiritual meeting
two things should be initially mentioned; on the one hand, Ortega's discovery on Németh's part is by no means an isolated phenomenon, but it is only a
combing wave among the flow of European influences pouring in on Németh at
that time; on the other, it is not a theoretical meeting, but the point,
rather, is that Németh is fighting with real, living problems, and all of a
sudden he finds another fellow arm in arm with whom he can conclude a spiritual alliance. What were the main questions?

To begin with, the missionary zeal was incredibly strong in Németh from
the very beginning. It is an almost physiologically determined feeling in
him, for he speaks about "mission written into the viscera."(13) All this
could form open doors admitting Ortega's notions concerning quality.

The radiation of the missionary zeal goes into two directions; one is
Németh's religiosity, or what is, strictly speaking, a profane substitute
for religiosity. Németh does not accept the neo-Catholicism of his age; his
religiosity is that of a struggle against the norm, which supposes the notion of self-redemption and which, in the last analysis, leads into an inner, impelling notion about a God who is dissolved in moral feeling. "It is
a nice thing to profess togetherness with the centuries, but it is still
more important to feel at one with ourselves."(14) Németh's profane religiosity stands near to Ortega's conception of mission, which, for its part,
is, perhaps, of krausist origin.

The other direction is the problem of Hungary, as a mission directed
towards ourselves. Németh is of the opinion that the country, as a consequence of the national catastrophe of 1918-1920, has even ceased to be in
command of herself, sinking into indigenous conditions; that is why the
country is in such bad need of conversion. The work of converting Hungarians, however, should be done by Hungarians themselves. This circle of
problems has remained an inexhaustible fountainhead of Németh's uncompelled
missionary zeal and it is inwardly akin to the Orteguian program aiming at
the regeneration of Spain.

The connection to Europe is inseparable from the problem of Hungary:
Europe as a concept, equivalent to culture, has always been a fixed point of
reference in Németh's scale of values. Yes, but which Europe? Well, this
is precisely the point where Ortega could particularly come to Németh's
help. It could be asserted that Ortega's discovery in Europe procured, in a
certain sense, the discovery of Europe herself for Németh.

It was exactly at this moment when he discovered Ortega. He remembers
the fascination of the find, as follows:

> Chance, which always throws in front of a real writer
> the book he most needs, has made me know Ortega these
> days. I have read all his published works in a little
> over a week. He was the most suitable writer to console
> me from the mire, into which I have sunk. He has led me
> to the coherent view of the twentieth-century as out-
> lined by a philosopher being on the move from the great
> bulk of the nineteenth-century.(15)

His long essay on Ortega, which appeared on the first of July, 1930, reflects truly that dazed state which the fresh reading of the works of the
Spanish magician has caused. Ortega exercised a double influence on him; on
the one hand he was dazzled by the knowledge and style of the Spanish thinker, but this spell, on the other, precipitated the spontaneous reaction of
trying to free himself from his hypnotic power, too. For a moment he felt
that in Ortega he, at last, had found the very key by the help of which he
could open wide the gates of the new Europe through which to explore. Ortega is, for him, "an ear leaning over the heart-throb of the century";(16)
his work "is an inexhaustible charge against the nineteenth-century, still
inherent in us."(17)

Németh's enthusiasm is completely to be understood. It was exactly
three months before, when Babits's famous essay, Silver-age, had appeared;
in comparison to the lively flaming lights of the Grand siècle, our age --
the author states -- is that of a lightened graveyard; furthermore, the only
task of this age consists in keeping a watch over the treasures of the past.
Németh did not want to be a treasurer; he endeavored to discover precisely
the new values and style of the new century.

What are these values? One is a respect to measure, first of all; the
main spheres of collective life -- arts, science, politics -- will, at last,
give up their megalomaniac aspirations, and each will retire within its own
confines, respectively; and the standard of the new age is life. "The child
has become the symbol of his century for life is less restrained in him.
The child has not been subjugated by reason, duty and dignity. His twentieth-century is that of respect to life."(18) He is impressed by that inner, coherent unity into which Ortega is able to fasten together all the
main manifestations of life in our age. He sees in him the counterpoint of
our culture getting drawn into specialization, the first champion of the so-
called new encyclopedism.

Again, new encyclopedism requires an overall new view of system; its
principle of arrangement should be the inner perspectivism of life, of the
essay that of its form and, lastly, its soul should be puerility, sportive-
ness. In his essay, entitled New Encyclopedism, Németh writes that Ortega
"is a new Atlas who does not carry the immense body of science across his
humped back any more, but he is spinning it on the top of an acrobat's rod
and, though he himself has worked tremendously hard, he bids us smiling:
learning is just a sport and not work. What has been gambled away by hard-
working scientists will be regained by the players. He is a lively, bril-
liant man, at the head of whose works, had I to pick out an epigraph, I
should print: Socrates does not sweat."(19)

Special attention should be paid to Tanú, Németh's critical review, as
a most distinguished example of the effect Ortega has exercised on him.
(Tanú could be rendered into English as "Witness;" the term, however, is
used in another sense, the ancient Greek equivalent of which is "martyr";
or, as he writes in the opening announcement, Tanú is "not only a witness to
what is actually going on, but, in addition, is a testifier to what is eternal. It is, more than writing: moral.")(20) In starting his review, pre-
sumably, Ortega's periodical, El Espectador must have been in Németh's mind;
yet, in contrast with the touch of passivity that the title El Espectador
suggests, that of the Tanú means rather an active participation, espousal.

Tanú has proved to be a unique enterprise in twentieth-century Hungarian cultural life; all the numbers were personally written by Németh; in addition he was involved in the printing and publishing. The schedule of Tanú
was grandiose (at that time this author was only 31 years old): to follow
closely contemporary European literature, to keep a watch over the treasures
of the Ancient and Medieval Ages, new encyclopedism (really in the Orteguian
sense), to follow up both intra- and extra-European social life. Central
Europe had a special column; he was looking for a common ground to bring together at last, so to speak, as twin brothers, Central European peoples who,
notwithstanding the identity of fate of the recent past and present, had

been at age-old odds with one another. This way of putting the question was something completely new at that time and the realization of this noble purpose now is more urgent than ever. Finally, the search for the role of Hungarians can also be found in the schedule. In choosing the analogy, he turns to Spain: "Not one of the new Spanish writers has written a book on Don Quixote. They confess through him what the Spanish people are to Europe. We, Hungarians, have no Don Quixote. The 'legitimation' of our life should be picked out of an enormous bulk of works, figures and experiences."(21)

Ortega's name is mentioned in several essays: for instance, he writes a criticism of La rebelión de las masas in the very first number. In contrast with later interpretations, in many respects oversimplified, he correctly states from the beginning that the Orteguian concepts of "mass" and "minority" should not be taken in a sociological or political sense; the point, rather, is that they denote a determined, generic, human quality. "Mass does not mean the proletariat but those living in the line of least resistance, which may happen to be, incidentally, even the aristocracy; the members of the nobility, the elite, on the other hand, are those searching out real tasks, working beyond their call, the creative ones."(22) During that time Németh often mentions the category of the "new nobility" -- precisely in the Orteguian sense. But the most important place of Ortega's spirit is the review, as an enterprise, taken as a whole; so I can assert without any exaggeration that during the years of Tanú two Ortegas existed in Europe: one, the real one, in Spain, and the other in Hungary.

Tanú appeared seventeen times between 1932 and 1936, and though sometimes it could not bring about the expected effect, it always remained true to its spirit. Németh writes in the last number, taking his farewell of the readers: "I was almost a child then -- viz., when the journal started --, I have become almost a greybeard by now. If there are works, which have burnt their authors, then Tanú is surely one of them."(23)

The Hungarian edition of a few works of Ortega commenced in 1938, with the appearance of La rebelión de las masas. After this, the number of shorter articles, critiques of minor importance, increased, but the theoretical level of these writings fell short of those written by Szerb, Halász and Németh. These writers were the real introducers of Ortega's philosophy in Hungary.

NOTES

1. Antal Szerb, A vilagirodalom tortenete (Budapest: Magveto Konyvkiado, 1973), p. 954.

2. Ibid.

3. Gonzalo Sobejano, Nietzsche en España (Madrid: Editorial Gredos, 1967), pp. 527-65.

4. Nelson R. Orringer, Ortega y sus fuentes germánicas (Madrid: Editorial Gredos, 1979), pp. 265-91.

5. Johannes M. Verweyen, Der Edelmensch und seine Werte (Munich: Ernst Reinhardt, 1922).

6. Antal Szerb, A vilagirodalom tortenete, p. 955.

7. Gábor Halász, "José Ortega y Gasset," Napkelet, (1928), p. 696.

8. Gábor Halász, "Az ujabb regenyrol" (1929) in Tiltakozo nemzedek

(Budapest: Magveto Konyvkiado, 1981), p. 982.

9. Gábor Halász, "A lira halala" (1929) in Tiltakozo nemzedek, p. 966.

10. Gábor Halász, "Ortega y Gasset" (1944) in Tiltakozo nemzedek, p. 933.

11. Ibid., p. 937.

12. Ibid., p. 938.

13. László Németh, "Magam helyett" (1943) in Homalybol homalyba. Eletrajzi irasok (Budapest: Magveto es Szepirodalmi Konyvkiado, 1977), p. 83.

14. László Németh, "Ember es szerep" (1933) in Homalybol homalyba, p. 361.

15. Ibid., p. 402.

16. László Németh, "Ortega y Gasset" (1930) in Europai utas (Budapest: Magveto es Szepirodalmi Konyvkiado, 1973), p. 390.

17. Ibid.

18. Ibid., p. 404.

19. László Németh, "Uj enciklopedia" (1931) in Europai utas, p. 520.

20. László Németh, "Tanú-evek" (1938) in Homalybol homalyba, p. 453.

21. Ibid., p. 514.

22. László Németh, Tanú, 1932. Kritikai naplo, p. 55.

23. László Németh, "Tanú-evek" op. cit., p. 526.

HUNGARIAN TRANSLATIONS OF JOSÉ ORTEGA Y GASSET'S WORKS

A tomegek lazadasa (La rebelión de las masas) (Budapest: Egyetemi nyomda, 1938).

A szerelemrol (Estudios sobre el amor) (Budapest: Bibliotheca. 1942).

Don Quijote nyomaban. Atlantisz (Meditaciones del Quijote. Las Atlántidas) (Budapest: Bibliotheca, 1943).

Korunk feladata. Gondolatok a regenyrol. Az "emberi" kiesese a muveszetbol (El tema de nuestro tiempo. Ideas sobre la novela. La deshumanización del arte) (Budapest: ABC Könyvkiadó, 1944).

Gerinctelen Spanyolország. A történelem mint rendszer (España invertebrada. Historia como sistema) (Budapest: Európa Könyvkiadó, 1983).

Goya. (Budapest: Helikon Kiadó, 1983).

Elmélkedés az Escorialról. Idö, távolság és forma Proust müvészetében. Az ember szocializációja (Meditación de El Escorial. Tiempo, distancia y forma en el arte de Proust. Socialización del hombre) (Uj Irás Budapest: 1984-86), pp. 85-98.

6.
The Problematicity of Life: Towards the Orteguian Notion of Universal Spectator

JORGE GARCÍA-GÓMEZ

Here we are concerned with a type of man, indeed with a manner of being human, which preoccupied, even defined, the work of José Ortega y Gasset. We are interested in that form of life which may be characterized as that of the espectador universal, and I wish to come to terms with it as the great Spanish philosopher thought of it and wrestled with it.

As a style of living and constituted standpoint, being a "universal spectator" must be approached as an accomplishment (rather than as a permanent human possibility) and as an issue of the manifold but specific activity of understanding that is coextensive with life. And this is as it should be, for nobody is born as a "spectator," much less as one whose scope is universal. On the contrary, we must learn how to become such (if really our vocation is so defined), and the clues for such a task -- if any -- must be found and be present for us in our experience of the immediately surrounding world as the only reality spontaneously at our disposal. In fact, our very way of access to the everyday world must be purified in style and become proportionate to the world of common sense, such that our reasoning would allow the world to show itself for what it is, that is to say, without the constructions and distortions that may be products of our attempts at world-and self-understanding but that have nevertheless become impedimenta and obstructions to our coming to terms with the world in its immediacy. In other words, I seek to identify what Ortega y Gasset called "living reason," in order to depart from it and measure ourselves by it in any effort of ours to make sense of ourselves and the world. And this includes, of course, any serious approach enabling us adequately to envisage what living as a universal spectator may be or require.

It could be argued that "vision" is the idea of life itself. And indeed it is, provided that we do not conceive it abstractly or sub specie aeterni. If vision is the essence of life, then it must encompass within itself the very finitude characteristic of life. If vision is the notion of an "activity" coextensive with limited or bounded life, then the highest example of that activity (namely, the effort of self-regard in which we are engaged here) must as well include among its determinants the rejection of absoluteness as ultimate standard of performance. Life is the task of seeing that which discovers itself as fundamentally incommensurate with itself as vision, and it thus constitutes itself as a motor for continual self-correction (which is activated at relevant junctures of self-insight). In other words, if we are essentially seers, we must nevertheless learn how to see. Not every manner of looking at our circumstances at once presents them to us suitably and renders us potentially and genuinely accessible to ourselves. It is this manner of regard that I seek to open up to here -- and in such a way that we may at least have a glimpse as to how a theoretical, contemplative, or speculative understanding of the world is possible

for us. That is to say, I seek to approximate the life form of the universal spectator as one among many, and I wish to do so on the basis of our
ever-forming and re-forming attempts at making sense of our lives -- at
least insofar as such is the required background for the emergence of this
type of humanity.

If we verily may become "friends of looking" (to use Plato's phrase,
which was so dear to Ortega y Gasset),(1) we must then eventually come to
realize what seeing and seeing excellently mean. Should this come to pass,
we can expect not only to live and live well (achieving the eu praxia of
which Socrates and Plato spoke) but as well to transcend or surpass action
in the ordinary sense of the term by grasping the relevant, fitting concepts
of things and events beckoning us at every turn and by achieving the formulation of life in a notion of itself that is adequate to its very inadequacy. This is contemplation or the maximum of vision as the issue of the
life of a universal spectator. And this means -- it seems to me -- not
merely the development of virtue at a given art (i.e., the craft of living
as such) but also the clarification of the idea of the art in question and
its attendant virtue. Here we find a requisite, nay, an urgent task (in
Ortega y Gasset's sense of qué-hacer, not only for the purposes of our self-
completion but also for systematic, freely chosen reasons.

If Ortega y Gasset is fundamentally a philosopher, a true friend and an
all-encompassing lover of wisdom,(2) then it behooves him to determine how
it is possible to become a philosopher, i.e., how it is possible to do so
justifiedly. But this is precisely Ortega y Gasset's own notion of the
philosophical enterprise.(3) In other words, for him the radical wisdom
that is in search of itself (as Aristotle would say) must comprehend as part
of its seeking that inquiry concerned with the roots of its possibility and
legitimacy. But for Ortega y Gasset there is no locus where the motivations
for, and possible answers to, such an investigation could reside, except in
the everyday understanding that is for us the matrix of all reasons.

If our schooling in seeing aims at fulfillment in having us become universal spectators or in enabling us to carry out the performances of a
thoroughly universal and justified contemplation, then we must begin this
new adventure of sense with the analysis of the most humble forms of our understanding experience, namely, at the everyday level of making sense. Only
there, if at all, will we find the grounds prompting and guaranteeing the
possibility of that type of humanity we refer to by the name of universal
spectator. It is to the examination of such grounds that I now turn. In
fact, here I shall limit myself to the analysis of some distinctions seem-
ingly required in order to get on our way towards the life of the universal
spectator as Ortega y Gasset saw it. Nothing short of this should be demanded, but, likewise, nothing more than this ought to be expected. I am
taking only one step in the direction of the clarification of life as
vision.

Living reason, or the basic form of human rationality, consists in the
spontaneous activity of making sense at the level of everydayness. Are we
to infer from this view that reason is an automatic mechanism of the life
process? Or could we perhaps say that reason is a cosmic given or the power
that starts its infallible work at the mere call of unintelligibility in
some area of the world or self? Questions like these constitute the motivation for introducing a distinction that Ortega y Gasset elaborates in the
context of very determinate circumstances. In fact, the situation itself is
the occasion for the distinction.

Ortega y Gasset finds himself teaching an introductory course in metaphysics at the University of Madrid and confronts his students by presenting
for their consideration their most immediate setting, namely, the fact that
they have gathered in a room in order to listen to his lecture. Ortega y
Gasset's question is simple: What is the meaning of being-in-a-room? Or
stated in terms more immediately germane to our topic: May thinking be interpreted to be a manner of being-in-a-room? Our natural reply would be the

denial that thinking could ever be equivalent to that,(4) even if it were to take place at the same time I was bodily present in the room. Being-in-a-room may indeed adopt many modalities, such as getting in and out of the room, staying in it for a minute or an hour, and so on, but it seems that it can never take the form of thinking about it, since being-in-a-room appears to be coextensive with doing something in or about the room,(5) and prima facie thinking does not involve any such activity. Now this interpretation clearly contradicts Ortega y Gasset's own stated opinion, for he contends that "thinking of something is but one of the many ways I have of doing something about it."(6) Accordingly, "being-in-a-room" and thinking about it cannot be different in genus; perhaps the distinction is rooted only in the priority levels at which these activities function in my life, for, as Ortega y Gasset says, "thinking of something . . . can never be our primary or primordial form of doing" something about a thing,(7) although a form of doing it still remains. The grounds for this contention are simple: I cannot enter into that relationship with something that we have called thinking, except if the object of my action was already related to me in a way which "does not merely consist in thinking of it."(8) In fact, the situation described as "thinking about the room" can only exist if I have, at one time or another, done something about the room or at least heard about it.(9) Accordingly, Ortega y Gasset distinguishes between two levels of doing or dealing with something, viz., doing stricto sensu (in a strict sense) and thinking.

The term thinking does not immediately denote for Ortega y Gasset any abstract or complicated style of mental behavior, but only the minimal form which it may adopt, namely, noticing something.(10) In the case of the student who is sitting on his chair as he listens to Ortega y Gasset, for example, we find that he does not think of or notice the chair, for he is not busied or concerned with it but with Ortega y Gasset's ongoing lecture. Accordingly, my immediate way of relating to the chair is that of taking it for granted, that is to say, I spontaneously rely on the functions which, displayed in fact by the chair, allow me to be concerned with something else, namely, my theme or topic (which in the example is Ortega y Gasset's lecture).

Ortega y Gasset, then, clearly differentiates between two conscious forms of living or dealing, i.e., relying upon and noticing. This distinction does not however entail the view that those forms are independent. On the contrary, relying upon is the lived, necessary condition for the possibility of noticing or thinking stricto sensu (at least for the minimal level of such activity). This signifies that thinking does not merely ensue on the basis of a course of events that may be accurately described as "relying upon." What is then the sufficient condition of thinking? To put it bluntly: Whenever a "thing" I am relying on as a means to be concerned with something else stands in the way of noticing the object of my concern,(11) I come to busy myself with the thing in question: For example, when my chair squeaks or is too low or collapses under my weight, or when the room is too dark or too large or its acoustic quality is poor, I cannot pay proper attention to the lecturer. All of these affections change my focus from the speaker's words to the chair or the room: it is now that I think of them.(12)

Ortega y Gasset derives an important conclusion from these observations, since he argues that, unless something becomes an obstacle or a difficulty for my action, I do not think of it.(13) Thinking therefore is the activity of regarding and attempting to solve problems and difficulties. At least, that is its primordial sense. On this basis, we would have to deny that thinking is the manifestation of a mental mechanism that begins functioning automatically whenever there is at hand a situation that is unintelligible simpliciter. Thinking is indeed a function of the prior consciousness of difficulty, but not of any difficulty whatever, for only those problems that are problems-for-me (that is, those which are such in the light trigger the activity of thinking. In other words, genuine thinking can only be conceived or occur as an activity of survival. Can we infer from this, on the other hand, that life is irrational, except for those especially motivated occasions? If reason primordially meant the direct confrontation with, and the examination of, a question at hand, then we would have to conclude that life is not in fact reason, simply because life would not be, in this sense, an ongoing rational process. Such would be the case, however, if there were no distinction between consciousness and self-consciousness and between straightforward concern and reflection. But these need not be our findings and our presuppositions, as a closer analysis will reveal.

Take another example. In my everyday life I do not ask questions about electric lighting, except when I need it for a certain task and it is not available. And yet this way of looking at the situation is misleading, for the difficulty experienced by me does not lie precisely in the opportunity or the time at which I concretely raise the question in my life, but in the attitude of the inquiring ego. Any question qua question, contends Ortega y Gasset, is intellectual in nature, but he qualifies his statement:

> This presupposes that the inquiring ego, the ego who asks the question of his own intellect is not intellectual in nature. And if the non-intellectual ego asks the question of his intellect, it means that for him things are already problems, albeit in a pre-intellectual sense.(14)

Thus, Ortega y Gasset's position clearly indicates that reason, in the special sense of the performance of a delimited function at the level of concern with the problematic, is not a self-contained activity. Moreover, reason qua thinking not only finds the conditions for its exercise beyond itself but also in grounds which are "pre-intellectual." And yet this conclusion does not imply that the pre-intellectual ego is itself irrational, perhaps even a bundle of impulses (conscious or not). This is so for several reasons:

1. It is to be noted that the pre-intellectual ego does not merely behave as a user or relier, much less as a mechanism. The ego who uses X in terms of an implicit interpretation Y also apperceives or reflects(15) on the insufficiency of the interpretation when the occasion arises, i.e., provided that the autobiographical, projective, and worldly-objective dimensions constituting the situation so require.

2. But this point implies that the pre-intellectual ego spontaneously considers other means of handling X when Y fails to serve this purpose.

Obviously the way in which the pre-intellectual ego proceeds is structured, motivated, formed, questioning. These can hardly be grounds to characterize it as irrational. Ortega y Gasset succinctly advances this view when he says that things are already problems at the pre-intellectual level. Being a problem in general means having perceived that the sense of a situation is not yet or not any longer available. Being a problem specifically at the pre-intellectual level signifies this too, but something else as well -- the differentiating characteristic is found in the fact that the interest in the solution is not merely contemplative or postponable, for life's continuity as an ongoing, self-constituting process is precisely at stake. And it is so exactly as an unfolding order of motivated reasons. A pre-intellectual problem is not, then, a situation provoked by the vain curiosity of an onlooker but consists in the presentation of the sense-devoid dimensions of a surrounding world which I must handle and, if necessary, transform, if I am going significantly to survive: If things appear senseless to me, my life is ipso facto paralyzed, since it consists in doing, and in this situation I cannot do. This is why Ortega y Gasset refers to the pre-intellectual problem as a "practical problem."(16) A practical problem is one that arises when we find ourselves in the mental attitude that Ortega y Gasset describes as follows:

> We suddenly sense a need or a desire, the possibility of realization of which would require the existence of a surrounding reality which is different from the one which is available: A rock, say, stands in the way. The practical problem consists in this: A different reality should replace what is actual, namely, there should be no rock in the way; therefore, something should come into being. The practical problem is that mental attitude in which we project a modification of the real, in which we plan to bring into being that which is not as yet but would be to our advantage if it existed.(17)

The practical problem opens life up, so to speak, to the reflective. We must however understand this thesis correctly. Ortega y Gasset does not mean to say that this opening up transcends the level of the pre-theoretical: The using, the breakdown, the noticing, and the reinterpreting that culminates in new forms of doing are all one style of living in different, interconnected phases. Living, or spontaneous reason, involves both using and thinking (and both for the sake of each other). Now thinking consists, to begin with, in noticing and planning, and the moment of planning involves the reviewing of the different alternatives for the situation at hand and the choosing among them in terms of an account or justification (logon didonai). But justifying is indeed a form of reflection. Accordingly, living reason encompasses an intellectual dimension for the sake of doing. To call spontaneous reason pre-intellectual, as Ortega y Gasset sometimes and in this context does, might be misleading, for it may suggest that life at the primordial level is merely irrational and impulsive. But this, as we have seen, is hardly the case. We will accordingly substitute the term pre-theoretical for Ortega y Gasset's and say that life or everyday reason is pre-theoretical.

It is possible that there be occasions or even life styles in which we think in a manner quite removed from the conditions at work at the level of urgency and concern. Although Ortega y Gasset accepts the existence of such contemplative, theoretical, or speculative forms of living, he would emphatically deny that reason functions at such levels in a pure or disinterested fashion. We must however rid these formulations of any pragmatistic or even pathetic overtones. If we take metaphysics as the extreme form of theoretical reason, we have to say that it takes over when all other forms of contemporary rational behavior have failed, and life becomes manifest as pure riddle or enigma. Even metaphysics is then for the sake of life and acquires a sense of urgency, having thus its ultimate motivation in praxis. Hence there is no theoretical problem

> Unless it arises from something which already is or is unquestionably there, and, notwithstanding or for that very reason, is thought of as not being, as if it should not be existing. Theory — it is advisable to stress the extravagant nature of this fact — thus begins by denying the reality of the world or by virtually destroying it.(18)

Although both the practical and theoretical employments of reason find their motives in my needs and desires and ultimately in my vocation, they differ essentially in two respects:

1. The telos of practical thinking always transcends it, but the end

of theoretical thinking is itself. Theorizing would be "actuality becoming
the potentiality of itself, the actuality qua potentiality."(19) And this
is so, despite the fact that its motives lie in the practical sphere and
regardless of its sense of urgency when its performance is most genuine. It
is as if its very bondage and fealty to life's problematicity in its immediacy and everydayness allowed it to soar through a medium of its own.
          2. The directions of the two forms of rational activity are al-
together opposite: In a practical problem we seek to find that which is not
on the basis of what is, but in a theoretical problem or in the frame of
mind corresponding to it we seek to find what is (viz., the logos or ratio
essendi) on the basis of that which is not (namely, the fact, which irri-
tates us in its unintelligibility).(20) Because of this difference and for
no other reason is it, contends Ortega y Gasset, that the theoretical attitude cannot be reduced to the practical. Here lie the grounds for that
freedom into which theory grows.
          Once I have made the basic discovery that no thing in my world (and
thereby my world itself) contains its own justification(21), practical or
everyday forms of reasoning become insufficient for the leading of my life.
And the reason for this event is precisely the fact that I orient myself
from given to consequence in everyday life. The theoretical attitude, on
the other hand, explodes the boundaries of the practical by being more
faithful to concern or life's need for self-understanding: This form of
radical fidelity consists in universalizing the scope of the questioning
activity and the problematic nature of the experienced. It is in terms of
it that I find myself dealing with more and more comprehensive totalities
(for example, the cosmos of biological processes, the cosmos of motion and
multiplicity, the cosmos of quantity and order, the cosmos of relations of
meaning, and so on), until we reach the most comprehensive totality of all,
i.e., the cosmos pure and simple. The direction of this ever-universalizing
questioning attitude is not that of praxis, for the goal sought thereby does
not consist in bringing about or changing to or planning for, but in retrac-
ing the apparently brute and ultimate fact of the "there is" and "it is so"
to its foundation, to its last and perhaps unquestionable ground. The theoretical attitude does not therefore amount to the realization that things
and myself are merely characterized by a misery of fulfillment, but in the
radicalization of the mind that brings about the discovery that the totality
of all there is is in want of arkhe, or principle. This conclusion does not
imply that the theoretical life denies or opposes the need for justified
fulfillment which my practical life is; it simply asserts that the theoretical life is the way of access to the awareness that ultimate accounts proceed from projection to principle. The theoretical attitude discloses that
anything real is, first of all, a latent ontological tragedy: Even if something establishes itself in existence by means of the realization of its
potentialities, it is still fundamentally groundless. If being is the
foundation and metaphysics the endeavor to propose it, then we would have to
say that being is the ultimate or satisfactory structure of the practical,
and metaphysics the most radical form of thinking for life.(22)
          There is a qualitative distinction between the product of thinking and
that which has become problematic within the context of the relied upon.
Our theory or our reflective opinion are interpretations of our lived circumstance but are not the circumstance itself.(23) Even if my theory were
to disclose indubitably that my being-in-a-room consists in dwelling in a
delimited portion of geometrical space or in a system of atoms and void, it
would still be true that the room as lived reality does not appear to be any
such thing. Those are possible or alternative explanations for what I live;
they may even be well-founded products of my systematic reflection, but they
still remain the products of a consequent form of living. This is consistent with the fact that the issue of my reflection may be abandoned but not
the appearance which was its occasion.(24)

Simplifying matters, we could say that "being" is the result of noticing and reflection. If we take being as the universal ground which is the outcome of theoretical reflection, we would have to deny that it is the result of a cogitation of living reason stricto sensu or the working interpretation of things as we live them. In this sense, being is the radical reply to the question that life puts to itself when the lived or believed foundations recede and fade, and life in its entirety appears as "senseless." But at the level of living or everyday reason, we would have to say that "things are nothing but their mere and present action on me. Light (for instance) illumines me, and that is all it is"(25) at the level of spontaneity. When light is no longer available and I need it, I must see to it that I procure it.(26) Part and parcel of such an effort is the inquiry after the reasons why there is no light, but that question leads to the fundamental one, viz., "What is light?" If questioning is carried to the limit, we could find ourselves searching after the essence or nature of light. At the level of using or taking for granted, however, the light, the chair, the room, and so on operate, work, or make sense by ordering themselves in chains of means-to-ends. But being as such is always more than those elementary patterns of action, for it is proposed or sought as an abiding structure that in concealment, accounts for the manifest behavior of things. Things have being only as a function of the question for their being, and this question is not formulated unless our working hypotheses have broken down in praxis.(27) At the level of using or relying upon, things consequently are-not; they are nothing,(28) that is to say, they do not appear as constituted and abiding structures but as actions and responses with reference to my life.

Being is therefore not what I live and have, but rather what is not and is lacking in everyday experience. Being is the radical name for the insufficiency and incompleteness of life, and it is precisely thinking which struggles to remedy this constitutive opacity of life.(29) And, when this is rehearsed, not only have we responded to the needs and desires of living reason or everyday life, but we have also — and by the same token — transcended it and established on its basis the new life form of the universal spectator in its rooted and precarious freedom requiring continual rebirths and justifications.

NOTES

1.   Cf., e.g., José Ortega y Gasset, "¿Por qué se vuelve a la filosofía?" in Obras completas (Madrid: Revista de Occidente, 1957), vol. IV, p. 108.

2.   Cf. Ortega y Gasset, Meditaciones del Quijote in Obras I, pp. 311, 313, 316, 320-22: Julián Marías, "Comentario" in José Ortega y Gasset, Meditaciones del Quijote (Madrid: Ediciones de la Universidad de Puerto Rico, Revista de Occidente, 1957), pp. 223-26, 234, 252, 254-55, 266 ff.; Plato, The Symposium, 209 e - 212 a; The Republic, 474 c.

3.   Ortega y Gasset, ¿Qué es filosofía? in Obras VII, especially chapters 5, 7, and 9.

4.   José Ortega y Gasset, Unas lecciones de metafísica (Madrid: Alianza Editorial, 1966), p. 87.

5.   Ibid., pp. 105-106.

6.   Ibid., p. 105.

7.   Ibid., p. 107.

8.   Ibid.

9.   Ibid.

10.   Ibid., p. 108.

11.   Ibid., pp. 108 and 110. Cf. José Ortega y Gasset, Guillermo Dilthey y la idea de la vida in Obras VI, p. 178: ". . . nothing appears as real to us except to the extent that it resists."

12.   Ortega y Gasset, Unas lecciones de metafísica, pp. 119-20, 144.

13.   Ibid., p. 112.

14.   Ibid., p. 113.

15.   Ibid., p. 77.

16.   Ortega y Gasset, ¿Qué es filosofía?, p. 322.

17.   Ibid.

18.   Ibid. (The emphasis is mine.)

19.   Cf. José Ortega y Gasset, "Prólogo a la Historia de la Filosofía de Émile Bréhier" in Obras VI, p. 413; Aristotle, De anima 417 b3.

20.   Ortega y Gasset, ¿Que es filosofía?, p. 323.

21.   Cf. José Ortega y Gasset, En torno a Galileo in Obras V, p. 118.

22.   Cf. Plato, Phaedo 101 d for the notion of to asphales tes hypotheseos; José Ortega y Gasset, Meditaciones del Quijote, pp. 354ff.; J. Marías, "Comentario", pp. 351ff.

23.   Ortega y Gasset, Unas lecciones de metafísica, p. 97.   Cf. Investigaciones psicológicas in Obras completas, ed. del Centenario (Madrid: Alianza Editorial/Revista de Occidente, 1983), vol. XII, p. 359.

24.   Ortega y Gasset, Unas lecciones de metafísica, pp. 98-102.

25.   Ibid., p. 119.

26.   Ibid., p. 125. The notion of perplexity is discussed here.

27.   Ibid., pp. 141-47.   This must be seen in connection with the notions of withdrawal and chez soi. Cf. Martin Heidegger, Being and Time, trans. J. Macquarrie and E. Robinson (New York: Harper and Row, 1962), p. 103. Vide also J. Ortega y Gasset, Kant in Obras IV; "En el centenario de Hegel," Obras V; El hombre y la gente in Obras VII, chapter 1.

28.   Ortega y Gasset, Unas lecciones de metafísica, p. 115.

29.   Ibid., p. 120.

7.
Historiology and Interdisciplinarity: Ortega's "Basic Discipline" for the "Human Sciences"

JOHN T. GRAHAM

As an outgrowth of the "vital reason" and "historical reason" that together constituted his "philosophy of life"(1), and in connection with Hegel's Philosophy of History, Ortega sketched in bare outline a composite new "way of thinking" in 1928 that he called historiology -- or, previously, metahistory -- a basic "science," or "interdiscipline" (so to speak), that paralleled the "basic discipline" or "fundamental science" for the "human sciences" that Wilhelm Dilthey so long intended but finally abandoned after 1900.(2) To Ortega's mind, historiology was a new way of formulating general concepts for history and for related humanistic disciplines, concepts that would be more realistic and practical than if from the physical sciences or from metaphysics.

Ortega never deserted this project, for he referred to it occasionally for the rest of his life, as when he proposed to make historiology -- along with "historical reason" -- the point of departure for history and for inter-disciplinary projects of his Institute of Humanities from 1948 to 1950.(3) Historiology was, he remarked to one of these groups in 1948, "the hardest science of all" (IX, 74).

> The basis of all this (interdisciplinary effort by specialists among the humanities) is Historiology, a discipline that has never been seriously attempted (by historians), with the result that history books, whatever be their particular virtues and merits, are filled with material so errant and effortless and speak of the past as something foreign to us, when in fact it constitutes our very guts. History has to have reason, that is, narrative reason, a telling that explains and an explanation that consists in narrating. The habitual conduct of history is inadmissible, as it wears itself out in proving, sometimes with needless ostentation in rigorousness, the data it deals with, but it does not prove what it says about that data and it even refuses to consider the questions of human reality that they signify, whence it results that history books, which are the easiest to read, are the least intelligible. (VII, 18)

Historiology, Ortega believed, could make history more comprehensive and instructive by defining as concepts the basic structures of the human reality with which it always worked. And directly through these general concepts and indirectly through the resulting "scientific" history, historiology might reinvigorate the rest of the humanities and social sciences in their historical dimensions -- philosophy itself not excluded.

All of the human disciplines and arts shared in the "historicity" of
man and of human "circumstance" (VII, 63), which was defined at least as
much by the past as by the present. With historiology Ortega promised a new
and more intimately human way of describing clearly the common, general
working concepts without which none of the disciplines could function well,
those leading ideas, "usages", and institutions of our collective life or
"living together" (convivencia), such as right, law, justice, freedom,
state, power, bureaucracy, or family, class, society, the social, language,
etc. He proposed a metahistory or historiology to replace both the outworn
metaphysics of the past and the recently impossible pretension of positi-
vists to elevate the human sciences to the status of mathematico-physical
sciences. This historiology was basically a model-building discipline. By
means of it, Ortega hoped to breach the walls that have grown up between
these specialized disciplines and to promote fruitful interdisciplinary cooperation through a common fund of organizational concepts and a common discipline for developing more of such basic ideas.

Not surprisingly, very few have even tried to investigate Ortega's
historiology in depth and breadth, to relate it to his thought as a whole
after 1920. That is because it was for its time even more abstruse, unprecedented, and undeveloped than his or Dilthey's idea of "historical reason."
Nevertheless, it deals with a potentiality too useful to ignore: unified
cognitive, ontological, and methodological concepts for what we call the
"human studies" -- or what Dilthey described as "the spiritual (or cultural)
sciences." Ortega called them the "new Humanities" (VII, 15, 59, 63), by
which he meant history, and the history of art and literature, as well aesthetics, linguistics, philosophy, psychology, and the several social
sciences.

DEFINITIONS AND USAGES

Why historiology, or why metahistory?(4) Although Ortega did not coin
either word, historians and philosophers have long smiled or recoiled at
such presumptuous terms,(5) but the one has been applied also to Heidegger,
and Hayden V. White uses the other in all seriousness.(6) For Ortega, historiology -- literally "a study of history" -- could imply nothing more specialized than "philosophical" reflection on history, as in Toynbee, whom he
later criticized historiologically. Metahistory might mean nothing more
etymologically than the root "after" or "beyond" history, or even "between"
history and some other discipline(s). More probably for Ortega, both terms
signified something like Dilthey's "propaedeutic" (VI, 208), or "prelude,"
on basic things or principles, yet derived not prior to, nor independently
of, the study of history, but from it, with the purpose to inform it, or to
provide it with appropriate general concepts or forms that it lacked. Although he once equated them as "historiology or metahistory," metahistory
perhaps was included within historiology, which, coming later, was broader
and more complex. Ortega's historiology will therefore be understood as a
"discipline" comprising metahistorical constructs, the cognitive procedure
by which they are derived, and the resulting models that serve as methods.
In short, historiology was intended to be a "science," or discipline, for
the construction of generalizations, or models, out of vital and historical
data. The models themselves might then be described extensively in narrative fashion, as generations theory in El tema de nuestro tiempo (Modern
Theme), as the "mass man" type in La rebelión de las masas (Revolt of the
Masses), as the "historical crisis" schema in "En torno a Galileo" (Man and
Crisis), and a modernization theory in Una interpretación de la historia
universal (An Interpretation of Universal History).

THE SOURCES OF METAHISTORY AND HISTORIOLOGY

Ortega himself found several broad parallels and precedents to historiology in the distant past in fields other than history -- notably in Aristotle's metaphysics, in Descartes' "single science," and in the philological New Science of Vico (I, 341f; II, 675; VI, 178). In regard to specific sources, however, the root of inspiration for Ortega's metahistory in 1923 is diffuse and uncertain. Initially, it could have been from Vico, Hume,(7) Hegel, or Comte, maybe Husserl and other phenomenologists after 1913,(8) even Spengler's "morphological" forms, Weber's "ideal forms," or finally, all of them together, but he did not yet know about Dilthey's "basic discipline." History and historicism were possible general sources for historiology in 1928 (VI, 185), but -- Mommsen excepted (III, 51) -- the Prussian Historical School (IV, 523ff) elicited no integrative, interdisciplinary reflections from Ortega until after he had studied Dilthey -- after 1929, and after Historiology.

If Hegel's Philosophy of History did not directly inspire the essay on historiology in 1928, Ortega nevertheless made him the "captain" over all who had somehow anticipated historiology.(9) As in Dilthey's case, Comte's ideas for a hierarchy and encyclopedia of the sciences, capped by sociology, may eventually have encouraged his aspirations toward a unified and "fundamental science," except that Dilthey substituted "psychology," and Ortega historiology, as the paramount and "basic discipline."(10) As Hegel and Comte were the two philosophers of history that he most admired (VI, 26, 417), certainly the latter had as good a claim as the former to be taken as a forerunner of historiology, and perhaps also Destutt de Tracy.(11)

Everything considered, therefore, Ortega's inspiration first for metahistory, then for historiology, was fragmented, multiple, and cumulative. Since Dilthey finally gave up on the ideas of a "basic discipline," Ortega's project therefore remains, if not unique (because of Weber) then innovative to a large degree, not only because he persevered but because he practiced and preached his new discipline. If Max Weber developed "ideal forms," such as bureaucracy and capitalism, that we still use, Ortega not only constructed his own models but told us how to formulate them for ourselves, something Weber did not do. If Weber was indebted to Dilthey's aspiration to "models," Ortega found there confirmation for his own search for a "basic discipline."

METAHISTORY: ITS METAPHORS AND ANTICIPATIONS

It is plausible that Ortega developed his metahistory and historiology because he needed a more definite "covering" theory, a more systematic procedure, and a more settled terminology to devise and to denote "form," "anatomy," "structure," "schema," "model," and "type" (I, 344, 352ff, 360) -- eventually "paradigm" (IX, 123) and "schematic model" (VII, 220) -- terms that his phenomenological way of thinking about life (Erlebnis; vivencia) both temporally and spatially demanded almost from the first, at least from 1913 onward (I, 256).(12)

"Meditation" itself was a schematic, generalizing operation of thought, already concerned with history (I, 340, 344). Even before his basic Meditaciones del 'Quijote' (Meditations on Quixote) (1914), he spoke of science as theory, or a "system of theories," and of philosophy as "the theory of theory." Further, he described knowledge as construction, and the "unity of knowledge" and being as the "method of methods" -- all of this in connection with Husserl and phenomenology. From no later than 1914, we detect a similar generalizing interest evident in a "science" of aesthetics as related to art and literature, an attempt to view things "from the inside" by a "new way of thinking," objective and realistic but as yet unnamed and only faintly discernible like a "distant coast." This science was to be concerned with the repeatable rather than with the unique that pertains to style.

Assessing feminine beauty in "Estética en el tranvía" ("Aesthetics on a
Streetcar") of 1916, he referred to "model" (either unique or plural) in the
same context as "archetypes," "hypothetical construction," and "ideal types"
of a "generic character" (II,35).

From 1917 a new level of sophistication is apparent in Ortega's efforts
to generalize, as he began to turn more to historical and social problems.
Then, in reference to literature and social history, he mentioned a "working
hypothesis" for characterizing the Spanish national character and life" --
the "lack of solidarity" of Spaniards among themselves -- an idea that he
thought could greatly aid the study and understanding of a very diffuse and
confusing phenomenon (II, 164n). From that conception it was only a step to
describing the "anatomy" of España invertebrada (Invertebrate Spain) of 1921
in terms of indocile masses and nonleading elites.

Soon, in Modern Theme (1923), he was aspiring consciously to establish
"a new scientific discipline that could be called metahistory" (III, 149).
There he added to the metahistorical concepts of elites and masses that of
"generation" as "the most important concept of history" (III, 147). Nevertheless, he continued to employ his now accustomed metaphors for this kind
of generalizing operation. Thus, La deshumanización del arte (The Dehumanization of Art) of 1925, as a "sociology of art," defined the "essential" and
"distinct physiognomy" of "unpopularity" in modernist art and culture as a
phenomenon of "dehumanization" (III, 352ff), while Ideas sobre la novela
(Ideas on the Novel) reflected on "the anatomy and physiology" of a century
of "decadence" (III, 387). Perhaps these works were Ortega's effort to develop a theory of aesthetics to fulfill Comte's proposed "systematization of
the sentiments" (VI, 150, 337), but they also smack of metahistorical exer-
cises, if under the guise of metaphors. Contrary to historic rationalism,
he observed in 1924, all things "have a structure, an order and connection
in their parts distinct from the order and connection that our ideas have"
(III, 279), and the same is true of processes. Lord Kelvin called this ra-
tionalistic conceptualization a "model" in physics, by which he meant a
"mechanical schema" to "explain phenomena" (III, 280).

In Mirabeau o el político ("Mirabeau or the Politician") of 1927,
Ortega distinguished the "archetype" político from the "ideal" -- marking
his "essential structure" in reality. These tentative historical schemas of
aesthetic, psychological, social, and political kinds preceeded his effort
to rationalize more precisely the construction of such models in La filosofía de la historia de Hegel y la historiología ("Hegel and Historiology") of
1928.

Despite his aspiration to become a "Galileo of history" by constructing
"a system of history" consistent with free will, Ortega did little to develop metahistory until 1928. Then, in a study of Ibn Khaldun's cyclic philosophy of history, where he declared that "there is no history without metahistory" (II, 676), Ortega elaborated on its meaning and function. "We need
to know the essential structure of historical reality in order to write his-
tories of it. And while that knowledge is lacking and the type of man capable of possessing and exercising it, it will be useless to speak of 'historical science,'" regardless of all the philological and archival labor.
Centuries ago Ibn Khaldun had proposed such a "new science" in his cycle of
three long generations between great historical changes, Ortega noted, and
in 1725 Vico had offered a rationale, concept, and terminology in his New
Science (III, 676). No one had achieved this basic science as yet, however,
including Hegel and Dilthey, but Dilthey was closer.(13)

HISTORIOLOGY: ITS FUNCTION AND MEANING

"Hegel's 'Philosophy of History' and Historiology" (1928) is Ortega's
only work specifically devoted to historiology.(14) By this time, however,
he had clearly rejected any idea that metahistory entailed an Hegelian
"metaphysics of history," or a "logic of history" (IV, 534, 537). In

contrast to Galileo's physics, which had benefited from a long metaphysical tradition that tried to explain what matter is in its generic structure, unfortunately, he said, "there is no metahistory that defines the historical real in genere, that analyzes it in its primary categories." The history "in use" was interested only in the particular, singular, and concrete -- the individual or species whose genus it knew not. But, he insisted, the concrete "is intelligible only (by) a previous abstraction or analysis."

As physics was (in a sense) the concrete form (concreción) of metaphysics, history ought to be the concrete form of a metahistory. Lack of such a metahistory had long prevented history from becoming an "authentic science" (IV, 537). Without adequate "substantives," history was still being written in adjectives and adverbs. The substantives and "genera" that Ortega wanted, were, of course, the "essential structures," which were objects of the "metahistorical investigations" he had projected in 1923, when he had offered "generations" as the first of these (III, 145ff). Still wanting was most of the rational definition and explanation or justification for this, however.

Among his unpublished papers deposited recently with the Library of Congress, which are unedited and undated but are clearly preliminary to "Hegel and Historiology," Ortega has provided several partial definitions of historiology.(15) "Historiology is not only, nor even chiefly, logic of history (as in Hegel) but ratio rerum gestarum, the logos of the historical, of the reality -- not of the thought -- that is applied to the historical." Further, and rather paradoxically, "History is not rational as logical rationality" but is irrational in that respect, yet it signifies "a specific illogical vital-rationality that is the historiological."

Ortega claimed that Hegel did not really get inside history as such but dealt only with a "unique dimension," "aspect," or "facet" touching the logical and the "suprahistorical," which was properly only an "end product" or final "result" of the "historical process" that actually produces "the historical." In other words, Hegel was after something that was not truly historical, an external reason, logic, or Spirit to be imposed on history -- not a reason that might be discovered in history itself as human life undergoing historical change and development. Rather than Hegel's suprahistorical concepts, which suffocate after stimulating us, "historiology or metahistory" relates to "levels" (planos) of "historical reality" somewhere between Hegel's "absolute" and "mere historiography or philology." Historiological "concepts" concerned the meaning, for example, of religion, state, people, epoch, and "spirit of a people," even spirit of class, caste, family, school, and office -- some of which he granted were to be found in Hegel as "structural concepts."

What Ortega's historiology was about is therefore grasped better by considering terms that he used other than logos, ratio, or "historical reason," such words as "structural concept," "conceptual system," and a priori "categorical structures." In other words, he was searching for a new way to generalize about what he regarded as the basic reality: "human life -- not Spirit" -- or human life as history, and history as human life.(16) "Human life," Ortega stressed, "is indeed essentially temporal and historical," and accordingly it should be studied not from the absolute and idealistic but from the "naturalistic point of view."

It was not so much about the individual life that Ortega wanted to generalize effectively but about collective or social life: "all the forms of socialization" as being equally (with the individual) "concrete realities that live historically a life of their own and are constituted in the particular organism that their spirit animates." The "historical reality of an individual act lies beyond it." In contrast, these different "vital unities" of the social type were the main problem facing the "structure of the historical." "The structure of the individual subject," he said, "is given by psychology, but that of the trans-individual (i.e., social) subject is given precisely by historiology."

With a "historical theme," therefore, one must "start from a generality," for which one needs "a scale or system of conceptual reference" in order to define it. The viewpoint of life represents that system better than Hegel's absolute Idea presiding over universal history. The a priori "categorical structure" that comprises the general entity "defines the possibility of the singular events" and of the individual in history -- as "variable elements contrasting to the constants" that were the social "structure or anatomy." It turns out, therefore, that historical reality is not "a cumulative heap but organic and structural."

To sum up now the significance of those notes on Hegel, it is evident that Ortega's historiology was intended to derive a variety of general concepts defining human structures and life experiences (or processes), both individual and social, from history by an operation of "historical reason," systematic in result and realistic in character instead of abstract and idealistic.

Writing then on the theory of historiology, Ortega attributed to "every science of reality," including "scientific" history, four essential elements that may be described as ontological, structural, methodological, and narrative, that altogether (as a whole) constitute its "anatomy," or structure. These are, consecutively: (1) an analytic a priori "nucleus"; (2) hypothesis, to connect vital nucleus to empirical fact; (3) guided induction, in the search for relevant facts; and (4) empirical description, exemplification, or substantiation, with facts or data (IV, 530) -- which some "scientific" disciplines now call "testing" or "verification," but which also involves chronological or topical narrative organization in historiography. The first two elements are mainly theory; the latter two, praxis. As metahistory, historiology was most concerned with the first two points, with its own "theoretical nucleus" that identified it as a "science" or discipline, and related it to the facts of living and historical reality; with the second two points it was more closely connected with conventional history. In practical implementation, therefore, Ortega stretched historiology to cover the third point and to encroach on the fourth, as in Revolt of the Masses and Man and Crisis, which were not history but were historiological exemplification that freely utilized historical data and narrative to establish a type-model and a process model: mass man and historical crisis.

The a priori nucleus, which is the "ontological texture" of that aspect of reality taken by a particular discipline, is matter for physics and "the historical" for history. But whereas traditional metaphysics had defined matter for the one (in its classical period, at least), the other still lacked a "metahistory" to define "the historical," or what was the "radical structure" of historical reality. This nucleus of the historical a priori, therefore, was the first theoretical interest of Ortega's historiology. "The determination of that categorical nucleus, of the historically essential, is the primary theme of historiology" (IV, 534). Historiology rested on "historical reason" which, in turn, was rooted in "the idea of life." Historical reality in the social and cultural orders was, therefore, not reflections of a material (economic) basis but "consequences or specifications of the radical sensation confronting life" in its "wholeness" in any epoch (III, 146,155). From other contexts, too, we know that he regarded human life (altogether as historical, social, cultural, and psychological) as "the historical," the "basic reality" (VI, 13, 25, 32f, 35), i.e., "the a priori nucleus" of the historically real. Ortega granted that this first purely "analytical" part might not ever come to dominate in history, but otherwise, he insisted, there could be no historical science. In other words, the human sciences, humanities, and "scientific" history need a metahistory, or historiology, to perform better their basic operation of valid and repeatable conceptualization, or model-making.

Besides the type or process models already mentioned -- generations, dehumanization, mass-man, and historical crisis -- Ortega developed a number of others that are not so well known but that could have considerable interdisciplinary interest: e.g., the politician, state and "ultra-nation," colonial man and creole (colonial) woman, frontier theory, and "modernization theory" — besides "beliefs" to supplement Dilthey's "world views." By fully two decades, he anticipated the historians' efforts at model-making with historiology: notably, historical crisis (H. Trevor-Roper, T. Rabb et al.) and modernization theory (C.E. Black, R. Grew et al.)(17) Yet historians still scarcely know anything of Ortega's ideas. Whether or not his historiology and schematic models will finally come to be recognized for what they are in fact, and come to be utilized in the human disciplines more widely than now, one cannot say. Nevertheless, more studies in depth of his different models, such as Julián Marías' exposition of generations theory,(18) would be very helpful for those who might want to try them in practice, in research. We can all benefit from more valid generalization in our several subjects.

NOTES

1. For references by Ortega to the "philosophy of life," which he shared with Dilthey, see: Obras completas (Madrid: Revista de Occidente, 1946ff), vol. VI, pp. 165-213, passim: "Guillermo Dilthey y la idea de la vida" ("Wilhelm Dilthey and the Idea of Life"), especially pp. 175, 185, 196n, 205; also VIII, 45-46 and 373, n. 2; La idea de principio en Leibniz (The Idea of Principle in Leibniz), where he affirms that since 1914 (Medi-tations on Quixote) "the intuition of the idea of the phenomenon of 'human life' (has been) the basis of all of my thought."
His philosophy has most often been defined as a variety of existential-ism or as a Spanish near-equivalent of it ("vital reason") — e.g., by Julián Marías and José Ferrater Mora. However, Philip Silver in Ortega as Phenomenologist (New York: Columbia, 1978) offers a perceptive and chal-lenging interpretation, which fits the earlier stages of Ortega's philosophy from 1913 to 1923 fairly well, and Victor Ouimette's José Ortega y Gasset (Boston: G. K. Hall, 1982) sees his final and decisive stage as "historical reason," without drawing the appropriate conclusion of "historicism," which in fact was part of his dual philosophy of life, the final part.
Note: all subsequent short loc. references to Ortega's Obras completas will appear parenthetically in the text by volume and page. All transla-tions from the Spanish texts are my own, but I have given them the usual translated titles, some of which are not very appropriate: e.g., The Modern Theme for the "post-modern" theme of El tema de nuestro tiempo (1923) and Man and Crisis for the lectures "En Torno a Galileo" (1933), first published as Esquema de las crisis (1942).

2. On Dilthey, see especially: Rudolph A. Makkreel, Dilthey, Philo-sopher of the Human Studies (Princeton, N.J.: Oxford University Press, 1975), notably part III (Hermeneutical Critique of Historical Reason), and Michael Ermarth, Wilhelm Dilthey: The Critique of Historical Reason (Chicago: University of Chicago Press, 1978), pp. 135ff, 169ff, 181ff, and indexed references to "fundamental science" and "Life-Philosophy," or "philosophy of life."

3. On the Institute of the Humanities in Madrid, see Franz Nieder-meyer, José Ortega y Gasset, tr. Peter Tirner (New York: Ungar, 1973), pp. 74ff, 83ff. He states that the Institute's name could be reformulated as "Academy for a Theory of Culture on Historical Foundations" (p. 85) and observes that it did not flourish, despite the high hopes of its founder and of some Germans (p. 77).

4. Because there are only two indexed references each for metahistory and historiology in the Obras completas, one might wrongly assume that those ideas were of little importance in Ortega's thought as a whole.

5.   For example, see Arthur Marwick, The Nature of History (New York: Delta, 1970), pp. 105, 234, and 245, where he applies this term to productions like Spengler's, Toynbee's, and R.G. Collingwood's, of which Marx's was the "prototype" -- in other words, both the old (speculative) and the newer (analytical) "philosophies of history," a designation that does not seem quite to cover Ortega's metahistory. Also see Alan Bullock, "The Historian's Purpose: History and Metahistory," History Today, VII (Feb. 1951), pp. 5-11, where Hegel is seen as a prototype predating Marx, and Wells and Croce are also included under this category of "historical" thought. At least Bullock recognizes that historians too must use hypotheses as generalizations to cope with the multiplicity of fact and event, "to open up a subject and suggest lines of approach . . .," but to be used only as they "fit" and do not force the evidence. This is similar to the warning against letting "models" dictate historical interpretation by Sir Isaiah Berlin, "The Concept of Scientific History," History and theory, I no. 1 (1960), 1-31.

6.   Hayden V. White, Metahistory: The Historical Imagination in 19th-Century Europe (Baltimore: Johns Hopkins, 1973). Where White studies the varying "modes" of expression (rhetoric) for our perception of historical reality, Ortega tried to get at the historical reality itself, behind the relativity of preception, by a new "mode of thinking." By emphasizing irony as the appropriate mode for the crisis of the twentieth-century, White, however, has some common ground with Ortega's metahistory, for the latter regarded vital reason and historical reason as an ironic type of reason. Heidegger never once used either metahistory or historiology in his works, so it is apparent that translators' and interpretors' rendering of his "Historie" are of dubious accuracy.

7.   One page in Ortega's notes specifically on Historiology in the Library of Congress, Reel no. 48, makes reference vaguely to Hume, one of whose works (1741, 1748) was called "Of the Study of History," which is literally Historiology, if Ortega chose to take it that way. Ortega papers, Hispanic Focus, p. 25.

8.   See Philip Silver's collection of Ortega's early works that are relevant to Husserl and phenomenology, Phenomenology and Art (New York, 1975), especially pp. 79f and 88ff, also p. 80 ("theory of theories"), 128, 134, 135, and 149.   Also see Nelson R. Orringer, Ortega y sus fuentes germánicas (Madrid: Gredos, 1979), where "concepts" and "genera" (Schapp, Cohen, and Friedemann) are, however, too narrow in focus to qualify as precedents (pp. 157f, 180), but the post-Husserlian influence of Scheler's anthropology and Pfander's psychology and Verweyen's Der Edelmensch ("the noble type") on Ortega's "characteriology" (p. 268f) is possible.

9.   One possibility linking Hegel to historiology theoretically might be his "phenomenology of the mind," which, Ortega notes (VI, 202, n. 1), was related dialectically to "stages of history," which in Dilthey became concrete as historical-philosophical world views that were not clearly successive in appearance (VI, 203ff).

10.   The historization, rather than Comte's hierarchy, of the human sciences is evident in this exposition of Dilthey by Ortega, and it applies likewise to Ortega: ". . . the science of the human is not only History, in the strict sense, but also Theology, Philosophy or interpretation of the world, Jurisprudence, Sociology, Aesthetics, etc." (VI, 185) -- all the latter fields being related to history (VI, 63), since the basic reality for each discipline is human life, which may be seen in development.

11.   Ortega seems to have overlooked Destutt de Tracy, whose ideology was meant to be a "science of ideas," a "philosophical discipline" that was intended to provide "the foundation of all the sciences," but from a strictly sensate-empirical background with the naive expectation of scientific and mathematical certainty.

12.   "Skeleton," "anatomy," and "schematic image" (III, 38f) -- meaning structure or construct (III, 43) -- are metaphors representing the schematic model in those first years of Ortega's metahistory that were always to be used by him as alternatives.

13.   Ortega seemed on the point of developing the "historiological" side of Dilthey's thought when he broke off the Prologue of 1946, leaving many unanswered questions (VII, 58, 67). Apart from historiology, to read only a little of Dilthey, or about him, is to discover still others of the "parallels" and coincidences that Ortega acknowledged as existing between their ways of thinking: e.g., horizon, situation, self and circumstance, point of view, the ideal of totality (or wholism), structures and types -- even "models," although less formally and perhaps less consciously than in Ortega. The convergence was substantial, therefore, but Ortega felt himself to have come to these points independently and to have proceeded farther.

14.   Dilthey too had studied Hegel before first turning to the "human studies," and Ortega probably meant to include Dilthey in his historiological series (VI, 521).

15.   These notes on Hegel at the Library of Congress, which relate to historiology, are on Reel no. 39 of the Microfilmed Papers of José Ortega y Gasset, Hispanic Division; see Hispanic Focus (index).

16.   Ortega nevertheless believed that the young Hegel had once glimpsed life as the motor of history, prior to developing the triumphal monocausal Spirit, and "the people as a whole" instead of the great historical individual (V, 416f).

17.   Julián Marías, Generations: A Historical Method, tr. H. C. Raley (University, Alabama: University of Alabama Press, 1970); this needs revision to complete it as a "historiological" (metahistorical) method related especially to crisis. Efforts to apply it have difficulty with its mathematical sequences, if taken strictly; see: Robert Wohl, The Generation of 1914 (Cambridge, Mass.: Harvard University Press, 1979).

18.   Since Ortega's death, historians have begun to construct more or less "historiological" models -- descriptive, narrative, interpretative -- out their detailed knowledge of history, and they have tried to apply them in actual historiography to the concrete facts and eras, with due regard to the "variations" and exceptions that which all such "constants" meet in the reality of historical life and change. For example, on historical crisis, see Hugh Trevor-Roper's The Crisis of the 17th Century (New York: Harper and Row, 1968) -- as unique and nonrepeatable -- and Theodore Rabb's modified version of the crisis "model" in The Struggle for Stability in Early Modern Europe (New York: Oxford University Press, 1975), p. 92, which seems to be conceived as possibly repeatable, with suitable variations, for the eighteenth-century. this historical-crisis model in its several forms -- including Eric Hobsbawm's Marxist version -- was, like Ortega's, clearly suggested by the deep crisis experience of contemporary Western man. Another exmple of modeling by historians since Ortega's time is that of C. E. Black, The Dynamics of Modernization (New York: Harper and Row, 1967), which is even more parallel in character with Ortega's mode in Man and Crisis and Revolt of the Masses as a comparative historical essay, instead

being both embodied and exemplified in detailed research, as Black (like Trevor-Roper for crisis) does later with Russia and Japan. My paper, "Antecedents and Alternatives to Modernization Theory," Missouri Conference on History (1981) demonstrated Ortega's development of a similar yet different modernization theory between the 1920s and the 1940s. Finally, historian Raymond Grew, for Princeton University, obtained the cooperation of other historians to "test" and exemplify modernization theory in successive historical crises of modernization (with "variables") over several centuries duration in Crisis of Political Development in Europe and the United States (Princeton, N.J.: Princeton University Press, 1978). Even before these political or general historians, historians of art and literature (for example, Lovejoy, Welek, and Peckham more recently) sought to apply comprehensive "style"-models of romantic, baroque, etc. -- akin to Dilthey's "world views" and Ortega's "beliefs" -- to general and specific phenomena alike. Carl J. Friedrich's Age of the Baroque (New York: Harper and Row, 1952) attempted such an application to general history for the Rise of Modern Europe series, which often reflects a concern for the integrative possibilities of such constructs, or models.

8.
Ortega in Quest of Don Quixote
WARREN HAMPTON

Miguel de Unamuno's 1897 book En torno al casticismo (About Castilian Purism) had doubtless a special impact on young José Ortega y Gasset's spiritual and patriotic development.   But Unamuno was to alter his earlier critical position, particularly after the disaster of 1898, favoring a new isolationism for Spain.   His changed attitude was to be reflected in the seminal book La vida de Don Quijote y Sancho (The Life of Don Quixote and Sancho) of 1905.   It led to a parting of the ways between the younger and the older philosophers.

What is more, Ortega's sojourn in Germany and his studies there under Natorp and Cohen brought him home as a neo-Kantian and further distanced him from Unamuno, who by 1913, in Del sentimiento trágico de la vida (The Tragic Sense of Life), was sarcastically spelling German culture with a capital K.

Even though by that same year the young professor Ortega had surpassed his earlier neo-Kantianism, his return to the preoccupation of Spain was not so much toward the Unamuno of La vida de Don Quijote y Sancho and Del senti-miento trágico de la vida as to the Unamuno of En torno al casticismo.   It is quite likely indeed that Unamuno's publication of Del sentimiento trágico de la vida prompted the hasty appearance of the incomplete Meditaciones del Quijote (Meditations on Quixote) in 1914.   By now Ortega was ready to rejoin such older members of the generation of 1898 as Baroja, Azorín, Maeztu, and even Unamuno himself in the inward look, though not necessarily in their solution for Spain.   For this, and with his eye on Unamuno, Ortega insisted that it was not so much the quixoticism of Don Quixote that mattered as did the quixoticism of the book Don Quixote.

Until Julián Marías' minute explication of the text after the author's death, Meditations on Quixote(1) was perhaps the least understood and least read among Ortega's major efforts to attract the Spanish reading public to matters of public, cultural, and sociological interest.   The overlooked es-say constituted a harbinger of the raciovitalismo (ratiovitalism) of Ortega's maturity.   In it, he pronounces for the first time the oft quoted yo soy yo y mi circunstancia ("I am myself and my circumstance").

Yet, for all the importance that may attach to the Meditations, first as a final response in the polemic with Unamuno and, secondly, as an early insight into Ortega's philosophical development, the essay is to a large extent a metaphysical inquiry into the function of realism within the genre born of Don Quixote in Renaissance Spain.   In the Meditations we may dis-cover three areas of interest: for contemporary philosophic scholarship, an exploration of reality with Don Quixote as model; for literary criticism, a disquisition on realism and its peculiar role in the poesis of a novel; and last but not least, for the preoccupation over Spain and its reality, the search for a national discipline, or paideia(2), in connection with Cer-vantes' ideals.

It is to this third area that our attention is particularly directed in the hundredth anniversary of Ortega's birth. Its theme is the doleful question, "My God, what is Spain?" which iterates and permeates our senses as a tragic national theme, when we view the misfortunes that have befallen Spain since 1914.

Before continuing, we may wonder why, besides desiring a rejoinder to Unamuno's interpretation of Don Quixote, Ortega chose to return at that point to a narrower national and ethnic preoccupation instead of expanding on his Europeanism. In all likelihood the turn corresponded to the perspectivist phase of his philosophic development.(3) To him at that time there existed as many possible interpretations of reality as there were individual perspectives focusing upon it. Thus we might consider Don Quixote's peculiar relation to reality as simply another perspective exercising its right of interpretation. As there exists an individual perspective on life and reality, so may there be a national or exclusively Spanish perspective. No one may orient himself in the universe save through his own race or nationality, to which he belongs as does the atom of vapor within the passing cloud. To Ortega every race meant a different style and sensibility. When that race is able to develop its particular energies, it enriches the world with still another congeries of customs and institutions, architecture and poetry, science and religion; indeed a fresh set of sentiments and aspirations. The problem obviously lay in endowing each particular group and culture with a capacity for self-realization. In Ortega's mind the salvation of Spain meant his own too. After all, his dictum "I am myself and my circumstance" is followed by "and if I do not save it, I cannot save myself."

Since knowledge of self was the key to the ultimate national discipline, or paideia, Ortega discerned it in the profounder aspects of the novel Don Quixote, regarding which he felt that no great critic or scholar until then had analyzed the work properly or in sufficient depth; a statement that must have irritated Miguel de Unamuno if he read Ortega's essay.

Raising his vision from Spain and Don Quixote to a panoptic view of Western Europe, Ortega divided the latter into two cultural poles, one that is Mediterranean and impressionistic, his own, and another that is Germanic and penetrates the essence of things. For Mediterranean culture, what is important in a thing is its presence, its reality, the here and now of it. Realism is a Latin concept. Germanic cultures are more adapted to the view in depth, or escorzo (foreshortening), as Ortega called it; therefore, they have a more complete grasp of the meaning of things. Their imperative is light upon the subject, so that from the depths it may shine and reveal itself more clearly. "More light," Ortega quotes the dying Goethe.(4) Inasmuch as Frenchmen, Italians, and Spaniards are possessed of ancestral stock Germanic as well as Latin, Ortega suggests a measure of return to the latent Germanic element in Spanish culture for a truer understanding of what quijotismo might offer to the Spanish individual and collective destiny. Naturally this statement flew in the face of Unamuno's anti-German sentiment and constituted the most direct response in the essay to the eminent Rector of Salamanca.

From the above analysis, we receive the conclusion from Ortega that the novel Don Quixote, by remaining true to its condition qua novel, makes a mockery of its own potential depth. Another Quixote himself, Miguel de Cervantes, a paradigm of failed heroism, lived of his illusions and lost. But, if Cervantes did mock the pretensions of his culture, it is no less true that he did not reject the aspiration of heroism as a necessary ingredient of life. Don Quixote is both aspiration and realization, as much a symbol of suffering in his quest as was Christ. Ortega saw Don Quixote as the sad parody of a more serene and divine Christ; a Gothic Christ steeped in modern anguish; a ridiculous neighborhood Christ created by a wounded fantasy in quest of a new will and imagination to replace the ones lost.

In Ortega's view, then, Cervantes represents the active side of a national patriotism whose sense of endeavor stands in opposition to a dead

patriotism that fails to discriminate and eliminate the deadwood of the past
from those few experiences that are the essence of Spain and the Spanish
race.

One of those essential experiences is Cervantes, a prime moment in
Spanish culture. "Ah, if we knew with certainty," Ortega exclaims, "what
Cervantes' style consisted of, in the Cervantine approach to things, we
should have it made. For in these spiritual summits reigns an indestruct-
ible solidarity, and a poetic style bears with it a philosophy and a morality, a science and a politics."(5) So then, if only the contour of Cervantes' style were revealed to us so that we might apply its principles to
the collective problems, Spain would have the opportunity of a fresh
beginning.

But the quest in Cervantes for an answer to the problem of Spain leads
to an enigma, since his own creation, the novel Don Quixote, by remaining
intrinsically a novel, as already stated, yields no ready or recognizable
solution to the problem of Spain or, in the greater context of humanity, of
life itself. Cervantes' own example, however, may have contributed to
Ortega's dictum that life itself is radical insecurity.

These thoughts take us through the essay's introduction and the Preliminary Meditation. Then we are abruptly shifted to the main Meditation, the
one and only First. Titled "A Short Treatise on the Novel," it analyzes the
genesis and nature of the genre born of Cervantes' Don Quixote. If it were
to be considered exclusively for its apparent content, it would pose a problem of irrelevance both to the introductory material and to the spirit in
which the essay was undertaken. But here Ortega, without saying so, is himself inviting us to a deeper reading of his treatise on the novel. And for
this we must seek a connection between the treatise and the preceding text.
We suggest that the connection lies, at least in great part, in the interplay of realism and heroism in the light of the realities of the Renaissance, when man, then placing himself center stage as the measure of all
things, grudgingly discovered the diminished role of heroism within his new
circumstance.

So, then, the old Medieval aspirations of heroism, represented by Don
Quixote's hallucinations, are of a nature that fit epic and poetic molds.
Their natural vehicle is tragedy in the classic sense. But opposite to the
tragic stands the comic mode, ready to devastate the poetic aspiration with
ridicule and irony; its weapon, reality. Just like Sancho Panza, whom Cervantes dispatched to guard common reality against the incursions of Don
Quixote's fantasies, realism is dispatched against the poetic aspirations of
heroism. In realism's absorption of these elements, the would-be hero is
reduced to a vulgar, ambitious figure; his gesture, an ironic jape.

Thus we have the dual nature of the genre novel, which is divided into
higher and lower planes. On the higher side, however minutely, which is the
case of the modern novel, it contains the aspiration toward the ideal, the
poetic, and the tragic. On the lower plane, meanwhile, dwells the ironic or
comic intent. Ortega considered the genre born of Cervantes to be tragicomedy. In the reabsorption, then, of the tragic poetic element by realism,
we are afforded an insight into the connection between this First Meditation
and the Introduction, where Ortega states that the reabsorption of his circumstance is the concrete destiny of man.(6)

Now with the individual's desire of heroism reabsorbed by the commonplace realities of everyday life, what is left to modern man today?   In
looking to the novel Don Quixote for inspiration, we realize that to be a
hero a man must want to be himself. Just as every novel carries ingrained
the essence of Don Quixote, so does each of us, man and woman, bear within,
if not the heroic life, at least its gesture. It could be merely an aspiration, or a mindset, or what have you; yet as in Don Quixote, there must be a
will and a desire, which in our time may mean opposing outmoded traditions
and customs, overcoming inertia, being what one wills to be. In modern man

today, just being loyal to oneself and to one's principles constitutes a measure of heroism.

In Ortega's view, nothing created a greater obstacle to heroism as an activity of the spirit than to consider it limited to certain spheres of life, such as perhaps the military or public service. Every man who strikes vigorously the ground on which he stands will discover a spring. "For Moses the hero, every rock was a fountainhead."(7)

And, so, in meditating on the quixoticism of the novel Don Quixote, Ortega discovered another perspective on heroism, one that is silent and runs deep, one that pervades the intrahistoria (inner history), one that is possible not only to every Spaniard who strives but to the rest of us who are so disposed. "All of us, in varied measure, are heroes."(8)

In the final analysis, even though the book Don Quixote does not yield up Miguel de Cervantes' ideology, it does convey a message. From it we gather that we must cope with reality without abandoning our ideals. When Don Quixote abandoned his, he died.

NOTES

1.   For this essay, the following edition has been consulted: José Ortega y Gasset, Meditaciones del Quijote, con comentario por Julián Marías, 2nd ed. (Madrid: Revista de Occidente, 1966).   Hereafter referred to as Meditaciones.

2.   Paideia: Upbringing, training, instruction, in the active sense; the result of the training itself, in the passive.   A Greek Lexicon of the New Testament and Other Christian Literature, 4th rev. ed. (Chicago: University of Chicago Press, 1952), 608.

3.   See José Ferrater Mora, Ortega y Gasset, New Revised Edition (New Haven: Yale University Press, 1963), pp. 5-8.

4.   Ortega y Gasset, Meditaciones, p. 109.

5.   Ibid., pp. 117-18.   Translation ours.

6.   Ibid., p. 51.

7.   Ibid., p. 52.   Translation ours.

8.   Ibid., p. 47.   Translation ours.

9.
Philosophy as Performance:
The Anti-Orteganists
PAUL ILIE

This essay distinguishes between Ortega's philosophy and Orteganism as an historical enactment, between a mode of cognition and its social instrument-alization. It discusses specifically the forms of opposition to that instrument. Therefore I will not address Ortega's philosophy of knowledge per se, but rather how his philosophy "performed," so to speak, both during Spain's social disintegration prior to the Civil War and afterward under the Francoist regime. My discussion thus involves a study of influence on an-other discipline: political thought. The study also involves another coun-try, in a sense, a country still called "Spain" but an anti-Spain as far as its otherness is concerned, its alien and authoritarian mentality vis-á-vis the enlightened Spain ordinarily identified with Ortega.

My real subject, then, is the role of philosophy in the historical pro-cess. The issue stems from the way in which the German phenomenological school gives rise to differentiations like French existentialism. Ortega himself quickly became interested in the pragmatics of cognition as he worked his way beyond transcendental phenomenology to the execution (ejecu-tividad) performed by the knower whose Being-in the world is nonreduc-ible.(1) The root of this pragmatic differentiation may be traced to Scheler, as Philip Silver has suggested. Its ethical thrust is what separates Ortega from Husserl and establishes his independence of Heidegger. This same performative concept of knowing, and of philosophy itself, is also what enables Ortega to write philosophical journalism as well as formal treatises like La idea de principio en Leibniz (The Idea of Principle in Leibniz). This is his major achievement in a nation devoid of both genuine philosophers and theorists of public policy. He contemplates reality by dismantling logical discourse through literary metaphor, and by using the accessible format of the literary essay. As a result, Ortega's voice reaches many sectors of the intelligentsia, including politicians and social planners. His long-term importance may thus be judged not in terms of the history of philosophical thought but the history of philosophy instrumentalized.

Ortega's impact in Spain is strongest where he amplifies his reflec-tions on aesthetics and social anthropology. It is not so much his recon-sideration of vitalism and rationalist idealism in those contexts that in-tellectuals prized as his regenerative concepts of history and human nature. For example, the Meditaciones del Quijote (Meditations on Quixote), although now scrutinized for ontological meaning in the framework of perspectivism, contains one section subtitled "Critical Thought as Patriotism." "In my opinion," writes Ortega, "nothing today is as important as to sharpen our sensibility toward Spanish culture, which is to say, to feel Spain as a con-tradiction. . . . Our meditation must penetrate to the last layer of ethnic consciousness, analyze right down to the last tissues, review every national assumption without accepting any of them superstitiously."(2)

The hostility to Ortega on the intellectual front therefore takes a nationalistic form that originates in ethnic motives and political irrationalism. What Ortega declares about race and nationhood, what his interpreters deduce from his concept of Spanishness, is the Orteganism that stands distinct from the other categories of his formal philosophy. The Orteganists are not simply the second generation of thinkers who constitute the School of Madrid. They are also the self-declared disciples who turn renegade, the admiring pupils who express disappointment with the teacher's conduct after the Republic is born in 1931. Orteganism in this form exists as Anti-Orteganism. It is a posture wholly dependent on the performative consequences of the philosopher's thought, rather than on the substance of that thought. After the Civil War, and after Ortega's return from exile, Orteganism comes to be defined as the political failure of philosophy. The Anti-Orteganists acquire identity in proportion not only to their counter-vision of Spain but also to their refutation of the analytical vehicle producing his national vision.

Thus Ortega is criticized in contradictory fashion. One opponent complains that he is not a metaphysician but contributes mainly to logic, while another opponent complains of his monumental contradictions. Some critics attack his incomplete factual information, and others fault him not on data but the incorrect interpretation of Spanish history. Either Ortega's principles are fruitful but there is no system, or else his general conceptualization is imprecise. Then there is his religious color blindness, say the conservative Catholics. He is dangerous enough for his books to be removed from school libraries, although liberal Catholics rejoice that he died within the Church. One Jesuit cites his "will to noonday light," a phrase referring to material plenitude as well as rational clarity.(3) This critic goes on to indict Ortega's refusal to face death or to contemplate any mystery that defies Cartesian analysis. Even Aranguren, who asks whether Ortega is worthwhile reading as a preparation for a Spain without Fascism, and who concludes that Orteganism can serve to "civilize a liberal-conservative thought" as yet unformed, also criticizes Ortega's philosophical preoccupations for belonging to the establishment culture of the grandchildren of the Generation of 1898, who are "living in complacency and nostalgia."(4)

It should be added that Aranguren defends Orteguian ethics against ecclesiastical enemies like Santiago Ramírez, who accuses Ortega of "situational ethics" that are unstable and infratranscendent.(5) But the point is that such Orteguian values as personal vocation, authenticity, and the task of duty ("quehacer") fail to persuade his right-wing former pupils, no less than their children and apolitical grandchildren of the younger generations under Franco. It is no attack on Ortega, only an observation, to chart the progressive tarnishing of his prestige. His image deteriorates for the very reason that it avoids situational ethics. That is, Ortega prefers an unspoken, private standard of conduct to convenient expediency. After his return from exile in 1945, he disappoints an expectant younger generation by making no pronouncements about politics. Yet he also declines to accept his university chair in metaphysics, and prefers to establish the Institute for Humanities in 1948. But the Institute closes after two years, with Ortega later admitting that he had failed to cement contact with young people or even to attract them to study.(6)

This was an orphaned generation, says Manuel Lamana, a youth whose insecure expectations required the resurrected father to speak in a loud voice and to explain events that the bewildered children of war did not comprehend. They defined his responsibility as a leader who had been both an abstract thinker and a man of action. The irony here is that the defeated Left shows disillusion with Ortega in the very same terms expressed by the Right in 1935, when Falangist leader José Antonio Primo de Rivera announces that "Don José was severe with himself and imposed a long silence . . . when what an unprotected generation needed was his voice, his prophetic and commanding voice."(7) In 1951, when Ortega failed in his Ateneo speech to explain the reasons for his return or to make any comment about the national situation, the young reacted by losing faith in him. (It should be mentioned nonetheless that Ortega's death in 1955 stirred a thousand university students to march in his honor.)

The point is that a certain ambiguity haunts the public image of this philosopher during the historical performance of his ethic, an ambiguity that is mirrored in his philosophy of historical organicism, whose elitist values subvert its potential for resolute democracy. The fact remains that during his exile Ortega never openly states his convictions about the Francoist dictatorship, nor during the Civil War does he make any clear statements about the issues. And from the beginning of the Republican period, he is a controversial and vituperated figure. His 1931 speech on the "Rectificación de la República" ("Rectification of the Republic") walks an analytical tightrope above national disillusion over governmental policy. In this speech, his defense of working class politics should have placated the Left, and his advocacy of a gigantic, single national party should have comforted the germinating Falangist Right. But for the next two volatile years, Ortega is either insulted or accused of placid silence. He defends himself in the 1933 essay "¡Viva la República!" ("Long Live the Republic!") and reminds critics that he had early condemned convent-burning, had spoken out against political leaders, and had run for election. "I take this occasion for the first time to shout, with the bits of larynx that are left to me, 'Long live the Republic.' I had not shouted before because, among other reasons, I very seldom shout."(8) On this occasion Ortega surveys the experiences that the Republic was obliged to suffer: "The first thing that had to happen was that the so-called Left needed to vomit out all the sillinesses (necedades) it had in its belly. Now that this has happened, it is a step forward, a gain and not a total loss. Now the so-called Right will have to go through the same process."

Ortega writes this in 1933, after the Left is voted out of power. By now he has lost favor with both radicals and lukewarm philomarxists. But neither does he enjoy the sympathy of the newly dominant Right. José Antonio publishes what he calls a "Homage and Reproach," which merely acknowledges the master's preeminence as the teacher of an entire generation. The reproach, on the other hand, strikes at the philosophical heart of Orteguian historicism.(9) Our teacher, says José Antonio, is not accustomed to shouting, but then why does he take the political platform at all? The question for this disciple-turned-politician is whether intellectuals should become involved in politics when by definition they seek the absolute truths beyond circumstantiality. José Antonio's answer is yes, a philosopher should engage himself if he feels morally compelled. But then he should not enter into a halfhearted flirtation.

And this is the crux of the reproach. Ortega has given up in disenchantment, and leaders have no right to feel disenchanted. What is worse, says the Fascist intellectual, is that Ortega is really on our side but declines to confess it. His book on España invertebrada (Invertebrate Spain) tells of a nation in need of a "common soul," a soul connected by vertebrae. Despite this need, Ortega does not suggest corrective policy. There is no advocacy in the analysis. His lesson describes the cohesion that makes a nation a nation, the nationalizing power of a society, which consists of force just as much as of moral persuasion. Ortega's book declares against pacifism. It argues that when particular interests block national unity, reasoning will be useless. Only force will be effective. His words declare "the power of force, the great historical surgery."(10)

If what Ortega says about force is philosophically true, if force is a structural principle of history, then its operation does not require Ortega's particular sanction: to implement force successfully will be to confirm the validity of his ideas on history. His critics, in spite of this, demand a public posture. They require of him the advocacy of philosophical ideas in the historical moment, the performance of ideas here and now rather than the persistence of ideas in the timeless discourse of abstraction. The Anti-Orteganists and the right-wing Orteganists both misunderstand their teacher. And here two points are clear. Ortega argues that Spain has always and congenitally been invertebrate, a view that is repugnant to the intellectual super-patriots even though its corollary denies cleverly that any decadence can be possible. Second, Ortega defines the lack of backbone as the lack of a gifted minority that the masses recognize to be superior and thus are willing to obey. And this view delights the totalitarian Right through a misinterpretation of the concepts of "the masses" and "the people" as Ortega intends them.

Ortega follows Husserl in describing the higher order of objectivities like "the people" and the state. This type of objective entity is grounded in a psychic reality that is intersubjective. Common meanings are the basis of community understanding. Nevertheless, a strong web of intersubjective meanings does not guarantee a convergence of subjective beliefs, much less a consensus of socio-political values. Furthermore, perceptions of the state, and especially the language describing the state or any historical entity, pose hermeneutical problems. Even the raw data selected to illustrate a phenomenon, say regional peoplehood, poses an interpretive problem. Thus a description may be intelligible within the paradigmatic meanings of philosophical discourse and still make no sense within the political paradigm. Hence the disciples who misconstrue the master also lose faith accordingly.

At the same time, philosophical description regardless of its comprehensibility enters the historical process and affects events. Thus Dionisio Ridruejo breaks with the Right in the 1940s and teaches socialism to his young followers even while reciting the formula about indebtedness to Ortega: there is nobody working seriously in intellectual matters who does not owe something to Ortega.(11)   Then there is right-wing ideologue Mauricio Carlavilla who tells his readers that Ortega is frothing at the mouth with notions of a moribund Spanish race and its history of decadence.(12) Or else there is Gáspar Sabater, who blames Ortega for deserting the "spiritual" quest that is the essence of the "Spanish style," this blame being justified by a vulgarized understanding of Ortega's idea of the "unitary character" of Western civilization and the threat to it by mass-man. From here it is an unsurprising step to the Anti-Orteganism of the literary generation of 1950, and to the hostility of Juan Goytisolo or the satire on Ortega by Luis Martín-Santos, even though no causality may be involved. The Anti-Orteganist position exists, first as a resentment against intellectual pessimism of the kind propagated by the Generation of 98, and then against all introspection that results in a weak self-image of Spain, which is considered unpragmatic if not unpatriotic. And where the views seem to be Orteganist, they are misconstructions of Ortega's writings produced through the hermeneutics of historical performance.

Misinterpretation at the level of pragmatics comes about because the act of knowing is performed by a knower whose Being-in-the-world is nonreducible. Ortega fully grasped this performative concept of knowing, and it brought glory to his pre-Civil War career. It caused him great harm afterward, for reasons of uncompromising standards as a philosopher, as we will see.

When Ortega writes that Spain is a sorry example of mass contempt for the talented few, his statement resonates in semantically different ways. He declares that conditions are good for Spain's effort at self-renewal. But then he asks whether the nation can muster the will-power. He does not know. He does know that Spanish history is pathological, owing to its regional particularism and impulse to take direct action. Worse still, the disease is just a symptom of national decomposition in the very soul of the Spanish people, whose psychological tonality inheres in its ethnic nature. This description is badly received by the Anti-Orteganists, who react to it with the hermeneutical criteria of praxis. As a result, they misconstrue the concept of "the people." Ramiro Ledesma Ramos identifies the people

with the state: he rejects Ortega's alleged premises of Rousseauvian, revolutionary politics, premises that convert the state into an institution that
serves the people in the way that national values serve a community.(13)
For Ledesma, the state is the people, identified with the masses at the ethnic base and not at the level of historical circumstance. For him, the role
of will-power should not be in doubt, and Ortega must be criticized for
writing political books such as Redención de las provincias (The Redemption
of the Provinces) that ignore models like the iron-fisted Soviet state or
the muscular Fascist states.

However, Ortega is making his analysis from the standpoint of a trans-
historical ideal of truth, and this requires him to renounce a Spanish or
even a European perspective, let alone a praxis. In Meditations on Quixote
he urges Spain to free herself from the superstitions of her national past.
False traditionalism follows from an unhealthy reverence of history. This
idea depends on a semantic paradigm that is not political, contrary to what
the right-wing ideologues would prefer. Ortega's philosophical language
must be gauged by the historiography of Spengler and Frobenius, as his book
on Atlantis shows. Here he tranquilly contemplates the disappearance of
cultures and their rhythmic replacement by new cultures. The human factor
is cosmic and not ethnic. Thus the categories of Spanish, European, and
Occidental dissolve in philosophical discourse. They serve the discourses
of politics within the limits of immediate national history. But history is
defined as the relinquishment of historical limitations.

In the end, Ortega listens to his inner voice rather than to the call
of those who would become, in their disillusion, the Anti-Orteganists. His
sense of his destiny is already foreshadowed in Atlantis, where he writes:

> We have lost our penchant for seeking at all costs the
> continuity among things. . . . This becomes plain in
> the current state of historical science. . . . After
> one hundred years of dithyrambic concern with Ancient
> Greece, we feel today . . . that we don't understand the
> Greeks. At first sight, this realization would seem a
> negative achievement. But it is not: to recognize
> having suffered an illusion is to achieve a new truth.
> Disillusion is only painful in life. In theory, disil-
> lusion is a rebirth and burst of light.(14)

NOTES

1. "Essay in Esthetics by Way of a Preface," cited by Philip Silver,
Ortega as Phenomenologist (New York: Columbia University Press, 1978), p.
114.

2. Ortega y Gasset, Meditaciones del Quijote (Madrid: Revista de
Occidente, 1958), p. 78. All translations here and elsewhere are mine.

3. J. Iriarte, S.J., "Ortega y su circunstancia última," Indice
(Octubre, 1955).

4. La cultura española y la cultura establecida (Madrid: Taurus,
1975), p. 14.

5. La ética de Ortega (Madrid: Taurus, 1958), pp. 53-56.

6. Letter of 22 June 1953, cited by Manuel Lamana, Literatura de
posguerra (Buenos Aires: Editorial Nova, 1971), pp. 120-21.

7. José Antonio Primo de Rivera, "La política y el intelectual,"
Obras completas (Madrid: Revista de Occidente, 1950), pp. 373-76.

8.   "¡Viva la República!," Rectificación de la República (Madrid: Revista de Occidente, 1973), pp. 251, 257.

9.   Obras, pp. 373-76.

10.   España invertebrada (Madrid: Revista de Occidente, 1959), p. 34.

11.   Dionisio Ridruejo, "En los setenta años de Don José Ortega y Gasset," Casi unas memorias (Barcelona: Planeta, 1976), pp. 319-21.

12.   Mauricio Carlavilla, Anti-España 1959 (Madrid: Nos, 1959), p. 198.

13.   Ramiro Ledesma Ramos, La conquista del Estado (Barcelona: Ediciones Fe, 1939), pp. 85-87.

14.   Las Atlántidas y Del imperio romano (Madrid: Revista de Occidente, 1960), pp. 49-50.

10.
José Ortega y Gasset and His
Three Visits to Argentina
JESÚS MÉNDEZ

In any discussion of Argentine intellectual history, a special place has to be set aside for the visiting foreign observer. Beginning with the Spanish conquistadores and continuing with the English travel writers of the nineteenth-century -- W. H. Hudson, R. B. Cunninghame Graham, and Sir Francis Bond Head -- Argentina, as part of a broader American context, has been a fruitful source of inspiration for foreign observers. The visits of José Ortega y Gasset to Argentina fit into that tradition of guests who recorded their impressions of the great South American nation and who were profoundly affected by the experience.

The late nineteenth-century saw a period in Argentina of economic prosperity and increasing agricultural exports, mainly beef and wheat, that would last (with only minor interruptions) until the Great Depression of 1930. Partly as a result of the internationalization of the Argentine economy through agricultural exports, European intellectual thought began to appeal to a native Argentine aristocracy that had emerged as a result of the prosperity and that had become a patron of the arts. European ideas, art, and architecture became models to be copied. An immigration policy, implemented in the latter half of the nineteenth-century to racially "Europeanize" the country with white settlers, increased Argentina's emotional ties to Europe.(1)

With the dawn of the twentieth century, a cultural phenomenon arose -- the visiting professional writer from Europe who came to Argentina on a contractual basis. Beginning with the visits by the Spanish novelist Vicente Blasco Ibáñez and the French novelist Anatole France in 1909, the paid foreign lecturer made his appearance. By 1910, the centennial of Argentine political independence from Spain, the Argentine population was becoming more prosperous, literate, and sophisticated, and it was able to support a modest, yet at the same time ambitious, amount of literary activity.

Argentina, however, underwent changes in the six-year period from 1914 through 1919 that seemed to signal the dawn of a new age -- the end of social and political hegemony by the aristocratic elite and a reappraisal of the "Europeanization" of the country. The election in 1916 of Hipőlito Yrigoyen to the Argentine Presidency as the candidate of the middle-class Radical Party brought into question oligarchical political rule. In addition, the disruptive effects of World War I focused attention on Argentina's dependence, both financially and culturally, on Europe. The elite class in Argentina became disenchanted with aspects of their development program for the country. The outbreak of the war had proven the fallacy of blindly accepting the so-called progressive aspects of positivistic European culture, while, on the political front, the Radical Party owed in large measure its electoral victory to a middle class swollen by years of European immigration to Argentina. Support began to erode among the upper classes for continued

accelerated modernization, and, instead, Argentina's traditional Spanish
roots began to gain a new, appealing dimension, particularly if this
Hispanismo left open the possibility of authoritarian repression of unstable
social elements in the old Spanish colonial tradition.(2)

An important event in the development of Argentine thought was the
arrival in Buenos Aires in 1916 of the Spanish philosopher and writer, José
Ortega y Gasset. His visit was sponsored by the Institución Cultural Española, founded in March 1914, to honor the memory of the Spanish critic
Marcelino Menéndez y Pelayo, who had done so much to foster interest in
Hispanic American Literature with the publication in 1895 of his Antología
de poetas hispano-americanos (Anthology of Hispanic American Poets).(3) In
1914 the Institución began sponsorship of an academic chair of Spanish
culture at the University of Buenos Aires, which brought to Argentina Ramón
Menendez Pidal to lecture at the university for two months. Ortega y Gasset
was chosen to occupy the post in 1916.(4)

The first visit of Ortega y Gasset to Argentina had a profound influence on the country's intellectual scene. His knowledge of contemporary
German philosophy, acquired during his years of study at Marburg and Berlin,
introduced many Argentines to German philosophy and reawakened interest in
intellectual circles in Immanuel Kant. During his stay in Buenos Aires,
Ortega conducted a university seminar on Kant and gave a series of public
lectures on philosophy. Coriolano Alberini, who became a professor of philosophy at the University of Buenos Aires in 1918 and was the dean of its
Facultad de Filosof{a y Letras from 1928 to 1940, viewed Ortega's visit as
follows:

>   Sometimes the artist overshadowed the thinker but
> from the Argentine point of view, that was an advantage
> in a medium so reticent to philosophical speculation
> . . . and he (Ortega) was successful in awakening a
> great interest for philosophy.(5)

Alejandro Korn -- a medical doctor by profession who became, in his antipos-
itivistic fervor, one of Argentina's leading philosophical minds -- viewed
Ortega's visit as an even more momentous event. According to Korn:

>   The presence of Ortega y Gasset in the year 1916 was
> an event for our philosophic culture. Autodidacts and
> dilettantes had the occasion to listen to the word of a
> teacher; some awakened from their dogmatic lethargy and
> many discerned for the first time the existence of a
> less pedestrian philosophy. Since then the love for
> studies increased, and the sway of positivistic doctrine
> decreased.(6)

In his lectures, Ortega emphasized the need for Argentina to cultivate
philosophical speculation with an emphasis on human matters. He charged
that an enormous disproportion existed in Argentina between the economic
activities of the society and other activities. He labeled as a defect this
economic exclusivism -- a defect that must be corrected by dedicating more
energies to superior cultural activities.(7) Ortega's exhortation to Argentines to concentrate on humanistic endeavors generally found a welcomed reception in Argentine elite circles.

Ortega y Gasset returned for a second visit to Argentina in 1928. That
year was also very important in Argentine politics. It was a time when the
populist, Radical Party policies seemed to have reached the pinnacle of success. After the first Radical presidency of Yrigoyen from 1916-1922, populist policies had suffered a setback in 1922 when Marcelo T. de Alvear, a
member of the aristocratic wing of the party, was elected president. Many
of the popular measures of the Yrigoyen administration were rescinded by

Alvear, in spirit if not in fact. Yrigoyen, however, returned to the
political arena and in 1928 was reelected president by a wide popular
margin. Confrontation politics against the entrenched social and economic
elite returned to Argentina, and Ortega was there, just as in 1916, to
witness the taking of political power by the Argentine masses.

Ortega had kept in close contact with Argentina in the 1920s through
private correspondence with friends and through his newspaper column, which
appeared regularly in La Nación, one of Buenos Aires' leading elite newspapers. Already highly regarded in Argentine intellectual circles, Ortega had
cemented his reputation with España invertebrada (Invertebrate Spain) published in book form in 1921, with an expanded version following in 1922, and
La deshumanización del arte (The Dehumanization of Art), first published as
articles in 1924. In addition, he had founded in 1923 the Revista de Occidente, a publication that increased his prestige among Argentine intellectuals.(8) The Revista published books and articles in Spanish by leading German philosophers -- including Hegel, Diltney, Husserl, and Brentano. Using
the Revista as a forum, Ortega introduced many German philosophers to a
Spanish-American intellectual world shockingly ignorant, at that time, of
the German language.

On a personal level, Ortega had maintained close relations with members
of the Argentine social elite. One of the friends he had made during his
1916 visit was Victoria Ocampo, the future grande dame and patroness of
Argentine letters. Victoria (as she was widely called by friends), born into a wealthy family that traced its ancestry back to Spanish colonial times
in the Río de la Plata area, served gladly as an influential and sensitive
link between Argentine intellectuals and some European writers. She became
the friend of many of the world's leading minds of the 1920s and 1930s, and
she made her European acquaintances aware of the intellectual climate in
Argentina. Victoria epitomized the Argentine social elite of the 1920s and
its role as the tie between foreign intellectuals and the mass of Argentine
society.(9)

On his visit in 1928, Ortega came to Buenos Aires at the invitation of
the Amigos del Arte. Founded in July 1924, the Amigos del Arte became in
the 1920s the chief aristocratic sponsor for new artists on the Argentine
scene. The organization's board of directors and its commissions included
many of the aristocratic names in Argentine society. The various commissions of letters, sculpture, decorative arts, music, public relations, and
publications boasted a curious mixture of socially prominent people and intellectuals, among them Victoria Ocampo. The best of the Argentine social
elite came to participate in the functions of the Amigos del Arte.(10)

Ortega's lecture schedule, perhaps betraying his leisurely Spanish manner, was not crowded. The first in a series of talks at the Amigos del Arte
was not scheduled until the evening of September 11, almost three weeks after his arrival. When the day came, however, the lecture hall at the Amigos
del Arte was filled with the organization's members (the only ones allowed
to attend), and expectations ran high.

The lecture, entitled "Preámbulo sobre qué es nuestra vida" ("Preamble
on the Meaning of Our Lives"), began on time, but Ortega, who was visibly
nervous, became dizzy within a few minutes and stopped in midsentence.
Whispers swept the auditorium. As Ortega stepped off the dais, he fainted
and had to be carried offstage. Though he regained consciousness shortly
afterward, the lecture was postponed indefinitely.(11) The next morning all
of Buenos Aires was talking about the incredible turn of events of the night
before at the Amigos del Arte. Ironically, Ortega's reintroduction to
Buenos Aires became the object of mass attention in an incident filled with
theatrical potential, and the reaction elicited from the press and the general population underscored the relevance of his later lectures on the rise
to predominance of the masses. The Argentine masses, on this occasion,
turned Ortega, the academician, into an instant celebrity, a public figure,
in the Buenos Aires of 1928.

Ortega resumed his lecture two weeks after his first appearance, and, on October 15 and 28, he closed the cycle of talks at the Amigos del Arte with the two most memorable lectures of his visit. The lectures, entitled "El nivel de nuestro tiempo" ("The Level of Our Times") and "El peligro de nuestro tiempo" ("The Danger of Our Times"), formed the nucleus for what would become his most famous book, La rebelión de las masas (The Revolt of the Masses).

Significantly, the first of the two conferences came just three days after the inauguration of Yrigoyen for a second term as President of Argentina. Consciously or unconsciously, the topic of the looming threat from the masses seemed to be on the minds of many people in Argentina in that month of October 1928, after the landslide electoral victory of Yrigoyen.

Ortega has admitted the debt La rebelión de las masas owes to those two final conferences he gave at the Amigos del Arte.(12) At the conferences, as well as in the book, Ortega discussed the rise of the masses in the political and social arena and his belief that the masses had taken over the leadership role that the enlightened minorities had once exercised. He added that one characteristic of the masses was their disrespect for the rights of minorities.(13) Ortega was more explicit in his last conference on the revolutionary aspect of the growing influence of the masses. He made the point that

> never have the masses been able to triumph when the mi-
> norities were firm in their positions. When they impose
> themselves, it is because the minorities have not been
> sufficiently strong or capable to defend their posi-
> tions.(14)

One of the solutions, according to Ortega, was the creation of new guiding minorities with different principles to replace the weakened former elite leadership and to forestall the ascent of the amorphous and undisciplined masses. It would be up to the intellectuals, Ortega added, to create the principles which would guide the rising new minorities.(15)

Ortega's impact on Argentina in 1928 cannot be underestimated. All his lectures, including the more technical ones he gave at the University of Buenos Aires, were published in La Nación as well as in other newspapers. As a result of his trip, there flowed from his pen a series of articles on Argentina and the Argentine mentality.(16) His personal friends, including Victoria Ocampo, were influenced by his ideas.(17) His aristocratic, aloof manner proved to be curiously attractive to many Argentine intellectuals uncomfortably aware of their own elite position within a burgeoning Argentine mass society. Ortega became so popular that his initially projected stay of one-and-a-half months stretched into four months, with an intermediate trip to Santiago de Chile where he addressed the Chilean Parliament. He departed Buenos Aires in January 1929.

Intellectually, Ortega's 1928 visit had a profound long-term impact on Argentina. He continued a life-long friendship with Victoria Ocampo, becoming a member of the board of editors of her new elite magazine Sur in 1931.(18) Ortega also wrote many articles on Argentina and the Argentines as a regular contributor to La Nación. His elitist views concerning the phenomenon of the masses and their relationship to a ruling class would certainly color much of Argentina's elite intellectual thought in the 1930s. In addition, the logistics of his visit showed the cooperation of the oligarchical-intellectual coalition at its best. The humanistic and elitist interests of Ortega, the social elite, and many of the Argentine intellectuals were in agreement during the visit. The newspaper coverage, the university lectures, the conferences at the Amigos del Arte were all essential components of the visit. Another aspect was the almost token participation assigned to the Radical government. The social elite were in virtual control of the visitor's itinerary, lecture sites, and social functions. In

addition, implicit in all of the elitist rhetoric bandied about by the intellectuals and their followers was a veiled criticism of the semi-populist
Radical government of Yrigoyen.

The years between Ortega's 1928 visit and his third, and final, stay in
Buenos Aires from 1939 to 1942 are filled with important political developments in Argentina. A military revolt led by General José F. Uriburu over-
threw the constitutionally elected government of Yrigoyen on September 6,
1930, and opened, in the opinion of many, the era of political and social
instability that Argentina has suffered during the past 50 years. To place
too much emphasis on the coup itself, however, is to neglect the social,
political, and cultural conditions in Argentina prior to the developments of
the 1930s. The coup -- a great departure from the democratic political
tradition Argentina had developed since the middle of the nineteenth-century
-- made possible the continuation of several elitist intellectual trends,
which, we have seen, had already appeared in Argentina prior to 1930. At
that time, however, most observers would not have foreseen that many of
those trends would later lead to the birth of a semi-Fascist ideology.

The 1930s also saw the beginning, and the end, of the Spanish Republic
and Ortega's unfortunate experiences in that ill-fated enterprise. On August 31, 1936, Ortega left Spain and sought exile in France. During his
stay in Paris, Ortega was persuaded by Argentine friends to go to Buenos
Aires and make it his new temporary home.(19) At the end of August 1939,
Ortega, his wife, and their daughter Soledad arrived in Buenos Aires.
Ortega's final stay in Buenos Aires would be his longest, two-and-a-half
years.

Ortega's last visit to Argentina was a bitter experience. His personal
health was not the best. In addition, he came to Buenos Aires under sharply
different circumstances from earlier visits. Before, he had come as a spiritual conqueror; now he was an intellectual exile. But Ortega was not
alone. Américo Castro, Claudio Sánchez-Albornoz, Ramón Gómez de la Serna,
Francisco Ayala, Ramón Pérez de Ayala, María de Maeztu, Rafael Alberti, and
others spent portions, or all, of their exile in Argentina. The phenomenon
is significant in underscoring the growing importance of Argentina as a mar-
ketplace for Spanish-language intellectuals. Yet, in the absence of an official and sympathetic government program to lend support to the exiled
Spanish intellectuals -- in sharp contrast to the Mexican case, for example
-- many of the exiled Spaniards eventually resettled elsewhere in Hispanic
America and in the United States.(20)

Most of the exiled Spanish intellectuals in Argentina quickly became
disillusioned. To many of the men and women who had been politically active
in the Spanish Republic, the Argentine intellectual and political conservatism ushered in by the 1930 military coup seemed to symbolize the negation
of much of the social and political progress the world had undergone in previous decades.(21) Among those expressing discontent was Américo Castro,
who by 1942 had settled down to a teaching career at Princeton in the United
States. In a private letter dated that year, Castro wrote: "If Argentina
does not assume leadership as a stable and functioning democracy, who in
hell is going to assume charge of the destiny of the Hispanic world?"(22)
Ortega himself, in 1941, confessed to Victoria Ocampo that he was going
through the most anguished stage of his life.(23)

Ortega seemed merely to exist during his two-and-a-half years in Argentina. He lectured at the University of Buenos Aires and at the Amigos del
Arte, and he continued to publish widely including his usual articles in La
Nación. But all this he had done before. He seemed to lose interest in
developments in Argentine intellectual circles, a fact commented upon by
close acquaintances.(24) He also resented the fact that extreme conservatives (some would say Fascists) in Argentina were expropriating Hispanismo
as their banner, particularly after the victory of the Franco forces in the
Spanish Civil War. After Victoria Ocampo's liberal journal Sur issued a
blanket indictment against those hispanophilic, reactionary forces, Ortega,

who as a Spaniard resented being placed in the same category, resigned from his honorary post on the consulting board of the magazine.(25)   On February 9, 1942, Ortega and his family left Buenos Aires by ship for Portugal, never to return to Argentina -- his third visit a sharp contrast to his two earlier triumphant stays.

In conclusion, it must be noted that the perdurability of the reputation Ortega y Gasset enjoys in Argentina can be explained not only by his three visits and the many friends he left behind in Buenos Aires, but also by the fact that, although a foreigner, he and the Argentine intellectuals voiced similar concerns.   It was this commonality of humanistic and elitist interests and perceptions that assure him a permanent place in the history of twentieth century Argentine thought.   Ortega, the prestigious foreign visitor, verbalized and, because of his reputation, intellectually legitimatized in Argentine society many of the concepts already held by a certain segment of Argentine intellectuals and the social elite.   The tragedy in Ortega's life lies in the fact that similar developments in Spain and Argentina led towards authoritarian political solutions, and events left Ortega a stranger in his native country of Spain as well as in his adopted homeland of Argentina.

NOTES

1.   One of the best studies of the Argentine aristocracy ruling the country at the end of the nineteenth-century -- the so-called Generation of 1880 -- still remains Thomas F. McGann, Argentina, the United States, and the Inter-American System (Cambridge, Mass.:   Harvard University Press, 1957).

2.   Fredrick B. Pike, Hispanismo, 1898-1936; Spanish Conservatives and Liberals and Their Relations with Spanish America (Notre Dame, Ind.:   University of Notre Dame Press, 1971), p. 4.   For an excellent general history of the Argentine Radical Party, see David Rock, Politics in Argentina, 1890-1930; The Rise and Fall of Radicalism (New York: Cambridge University Press, 1975).

3.   Marcelino Menéndez y Pelayo, Antología de poetas hispano-americanos publicada por la Real Academia Española (Madrid: Est. Tip. "Sucesores de Rivadeneyra," 1893-95).

4.   Ironically, Ortega was not the first choice to occupy the chair of Spanish culture at the University of Buenos Aires in 1916.   The Institución Cultural Española originally wanted Miguel de Unamuno.   Ortega was paid 2,500 dollars (6,000 pesos) for his services with all expenses paid, including round-trip sea voyage from Europe and lodging in Buenos Aires.   For details surrounding the finances of Ortega's 1916 trip to Argentina, see the minutes for the board meetings of the Institución Cultural Española held on March 15, March 30, June 17, and September 14, 1917, in the Libro de Actas no. 1 in the Archive of the Institución Cultural Española, Buenos Aires. For a summary of Ortega's conferences in Argentina in 1916, see Institución Cultural Española, Anales: Tomo primero, 1912-1920 (Buenos Aires: Institución Cultural Española, 1947), pp. 13-59.

5.   Coriolano Alberini, Problemas de la historia de las ideas filosóficas en la Argentina (La Plata, Argentina: Universidad Nacional de La Plata, 1966), p. 71.   All quotes in this article have been translated from the Spanish into English by the author.

6.   Quoted in José Luis Cosmelli Ibáñez, Historia cultural de los argentinos, 2 vols. (Buenos Aires: Editorial Troquel, 1975), vol. 2, p. 397.

7.   Institución Cultural Española, Anales: Tomo primero, p. 201.

8.   Out of a press run of 3,000 copies, more than half were acquired by Espasa-Calpe for distribution to Latin America, and most of those issues went to Argentina. See Evelyne López Campillo, La Revista de Occidente y la formación de minorías (1923-1936) (Madrid: Taurus, 1970), pp. 60, 66.

9.   For a good biography of Victoria Ocampo, see Doris Meyer, Victoria Ocampo: Against the Wind and the Tide (New York: George Braziller, 1979).

10.   Asociación Amigos del Arte, (Estatutos) ((Buenos Aires): no publisher, (1924?)), pp. 3-8.   The annual dues for active members was 20 dollars (50 pesos). Patrons paid 41 dollars (100 pesos) a year, and life membership was 416 dollars (1,000 pesos). According to Elena Sansinena de Elizalde, the guiding force of the Amigos del Arte throughout most of the organization's existence, Ortega was brought to Argentina in 1928 for 7,700 dollars (18,500 pesos) by the Amigos del Arte, with his lodging bill at the Plaza Hotel paid for by the Argentine government. See letter from Elena Sansinena de Elizalde to Rafael Vehils, president of the Institución Cultural Española, dated March 24, 1939, at the Archive of the Institución Cultural Española, Buenos Aires.

11.   La Nación (Buenos Aires), September 12, 1928.

12.   In a "Prefatory Note," Ortega acknowledges his past treatment of the theme of the masses in his book Invertebrate Spain (1922), in an article in El Sol of Madrid, entitled "Masas" (1926), and in the two lectures given at the Amigos del Arte in 1928. See José Ortega y Gasset, The Revolt of the Masses (New York: W. W. Norton and Company, Inc., 1932), p. 9.

13.   La Nación, October 16, 1928.

14.   La Nación, October 29, 1928.

15.   Ibid. A detailed summary of Ortega's 1928 conferences in Argentina may be found in Institución Cultural Española, Anales: Tomo tercero, segunda parte, 1926-1930 (Buenos Aires: Institución Cultural Espaqola, 1953), pp. 185-248.

16.   Among the most famous of Ortega's essays on Argentine themes are: "La Pampa . . . promesas" in Obras II, 4th ed., (Madrid: Revista de Occidente, 1957), pp. 635-643; "El hombre a la defensiva" in Obras II, pp. 643-666; "Por qué he escrito 'El hombre a la defensiva'" in Obras IV, pp. 69-74; "Meditación del pueblo joven" in Obras VIII, 2nd ed., (Madrid: Revista de Occidente, 1965), pp. 389-406.

17.   In an unpublished letter to the North American writer Waldo Frank, Victoria Ocampo praises Ortega's The Revolt of the Masses. See letter from Ocampo to Frank, July 13, 1931, in the Waldo Frank Papers at the Rare Book Room, University of Pennsylvania, Philadelphia.

18.   For the founding of Sur, see Jesús Méndez, "The Origins of Sur, Argentina's Elite Cultural Review," Inter-American Review of Bibliography 31:1 (1981): 3-16.

19.   Ortega was invited jointly in 1939 by the Amigos del Arte and by the Institución Cultural Española to give a series of conferences and to participate in the festivities celebrating the twenty-fifth anniversary of the founding of the Institución Cultural Española. The two institutions shared the cost of paying Ortega's fee of 5,000 dollars (20,000 pesos -- the

peso had been devalued during the depression of the 1930s). See letter from Sansinena de Elizalde to Vehils, March 24, 1939, in Archive of the Institución Cultural Española. For Ortega's remarks at the ceremonies marking the twenty-fifth anniversary of the Institución Cultural Española, see "En la Institución Cultural Española de Buenos Aires" in Obras completas VI (Madrid: Revista de Occidente, 1958), 4th ed., pp. 234-244.

20.   Patricia W. Fagen, Exiles and Citizens; Spanish Republicans in Mexico (Austin: Institute of Latin America Studies, The University of Texas, 1973); José Luis Abellán, Filosofía española en América (1936-1966) (Madrid: Ediciones Guadarrama, S.L., 1967).

21.   Many historians have used the term "década infame" to describe the 1930s in Argentina because of the economic and political graft and corruption of the period carried out by the restored conservative order. The term was first used by José Luis Torres, La década infame (Buenos Aires: Editorial de Formación "Patria," (1945)).

22.   Américo Castro to Avelino Herrero Mayor, March 28, 1942, in Archivo y Museo del Escritor, Sociedad Argentina de Escritores, Buenos Aires.

23.   Ortega to Ocampo, December 12, 1940, in José Ortega y Gasset, Epistolario (Madrid: Revista de Occidente, Colección "El Arquero," 1974), p. 168.

24.   Máximo Etchecopar, Historia de una afición a leer; Ortega, nuestro amigo (Buenos Aires: EUDEBA, 1969), p. 79.

25.   Ibid., pp. 84-85.

11.
Ortega y Gasset and the Limits of Conservatism
VICTOR OUIMETTE

In the early years of his public career, Ortega made many ringing declarations of his sincere faith in intellectual and political liberalism, as a truly European value, as a generous emotion, and as a guarantee of scientific and cultural progress within a social atmosphere that stimulated individual fulfillment. Between 1906 and 1913 in particular, he presented such liberalism as a moral obligation that the contemporary, thinking man could not shirk, and he urged his intellectual colleagues to participate in revivifying the liberal commitment.(1) At this time he did, in fact, consider liberalism much as other European intellectuals did, although within Spain such a stance offered much that was new.

In the years leading up to the formation in 1913 of the Liga de Educación Política, Ortega stressed his awareness that liberalism was not a political ideology, but an ethical stance, often quite unrelated to partisan political affiliation, and certainly separate from the established political parties that still attempted to define themselves with outdated rhetoric that was as much out of step with the times as it was with the needs and aspirations of a world in flux. He viewed liberalism as an attitude that could be associated with much more than politics, for only the liberal approach could engender the new solutions that Ortega considered indispensable in all aspects of European life as the continent moved into a profoundly new stage in its development. Moreover, he still identified liberalism with the politics of the left.

After this youthful insistence on liberalism as a moral imperative, and a period during the First World War when he explored more deeply the theory and philosophy of liberalism, Ortega began to move towards a truly coherent definition. During the Dictatorship of General Miguel Primo de Rivera (1923-1930), when censorship made genuine political commentary almost impossible, Ortega expounded in general terms upon both the benefits and the limits of liberal political attitudes, while avoiding the traditional association of such attitudes with parties of the left.

The fall of Primo de Rivera in January 1930 and the months leading up to the declaration in April 1931 of the second Republic provided Ortega with an opportunity to attempt to put his principles into practice by setting the tone for the political changes that had now become imminent. He could see that Spain had become an important test area for the future of European nations and that, while learning from the experience of those nations that were politically more developed, Spain must simultaneously point the way ahead for the entire continent. Conservative ideologies were gaining much ground in Europe by promoting exclusivistic notions of social intolerance, statism, and exaggerated nationalism. Spain, however, had just experienced the collapse of more than six years of rigid conservativism that, by often drawing its inspiration from Italian Fascism, had provoked not a renewal but rather the death by exhaustion of a centuries-old political and social system.(2) New ideas were now needed, and it was Ortega's judgment that the prevailing conservative ideologies had nothing to offer in the way of a dynamic and effective framework that would guarantee the country's future as a truly modern Western nation.

Such a commitment would seem to call for renewed declarations of political liberalism, and while Ortega did indeed supply them, it is of some interest to note his way of doing so. Between 1930 and 1933, and even after, he wrote as a true liberal intellectual, very much in tune with the times, despite repeated partisan accusations that he was drifting gradually toward the right.

It now seems evident that, in fact, Ortega's political attitudes remained as liberal as ever, but that in a moment of heated partisanship he knew that reliance upon still more doctrinaire pronouncements would have diminished the visible seriousness of his thought. His aim was not to set forth any dogmas, but rather to prod the country into reflecting upon its choices. As a result, not until after the Civil War did he again employ the term liberalism with any frequency, preferring instead to practice what he saw as a new liberalism, free from notions of left and right, but in clear opposition to the futility of conservatism. He encouraged the nation to reject the simple solutions, dead ends, and historical evasions that were being offered by the intolerant left and the regressive right. By discrediting those options that could not serve, he left Spain free to redefine itself from among the nearly limitless wealth of worthy, contemporary solutions that remained. To speak of liberalism in such highly-charged times, when the terminology itself had become suspect and contaminated, would have been restrictive and, as he hinted, "illiberal," however paradoxical that might seem.

If liberalism, then, was an attitude, a mental cast that affected a man's, or a nation's, way of coping with life, Ortega insisted that true politics, on the other hand, had to be determined above all by a specific human and historical reality. It could not be seen as the idealistic application of abstract goals to that reality, in the hopes of seriously altering or deflecting it, nor could it be seen as an effort to return to a vanished and probably mythical past. Historical evolution, he warned, is as inexorable as it is capable of offering surprises, since on occasion it occurs, not as smooth gradualism, but in sudden leaps that require swift new ideas.

This means that politics must be ever alert, rooted in a vibrant awareness of the immediate state of the country, yet in relation to the realities of the historical circumstance and the direction that it is likely to take. A truly liberal perspective, brought to political thought, can enhance the possibility that politics may strike that sensitive balance between national aspirations and the historical moment. Any politician can hope to succeed only if he learns to open himself to an indescribably more varied reality than that already encompassed in his theories. As Ortega was to observe in 1930, when Spain was in the midst of such a historical leap:

> There does not begin to be any politics, then, until the
> man who feels these or those desires comes out of himself and, by analyzing like a zoologist the society in
> which he lives, discovers its new organic needs, that is
> to say, the shape of the new State that the new society
> carries germinant and preformed within itself. . . .
> Only he who articulates his intimate desires with public
> needs is a politician.(3)

Ideals, however noble, have a secondary, or "adjectival," role in politics, which has to deal with what is and can be, if it is to be effective. In Ortega's judgment, nineteenth-century political liberalism had fallen victim to excessive idealism.(4) Its undeniable success within its circumstance had eventually become petrified and resulted in a failure to continue to assess perceptively. As it failed to adapt, it had gradually detached itself from those newly-emerging social realities that demanded attention throughout the West in the first decades of the twentieth-century.

Especially in such a time of sudden change, of severe crisis, effective political thought had to distinguish between how the politician felt things ought to be and how they had to be. As Ortega said in 1933, when he had finally ceased his own political activities, ". . . I do not believe that to think politically is to do what may seem right, or what may please or amuse, but rather to go in search of the underground truth, the truth of the times."(5) Only an open mind could detect this underlying truth and coordinate it with the historical possibilities. The early twentieth-century was already seeing new social groups -- especially the workers and the young -- emerge into political existence and any political ideology that failed to take them into account and incorporate them into the new state that must be created was condemned to failure. Ortega in his maturity saw the struggle as taking place between the old and the new, between the archaic and the vital, and not necessarily between the left and the right. Both political liberalism, and its most important instrument, parliamentary democracy, had been allowed to deteriorate into hollow rhetorical terms. As he wrote in 1924, "For a long time the 'liberals' have reduced their political action to expressing enthusiasm or indignation. This habit has led them to defeat."(6) When the old values had become static, and showed no promise, contemporary man was left without political faith. Into the resulting vacuum flowed such aberrational concepts as Fascism and Communism.

Ortega dismissed Fascism and Bolshevism as ideologies of despair that owed their existence and temporary success in other parts of Europe to the failure of politics to create genuine reforms to meet the changes in contemporary needs. Spain's unique historical situation did not seem to him to offer naturally fertile ground for such solutions unless her political leaders refused to be part of a boldly imaginative new breed. In 1930, Fascism and Bolshevism were still dangers that Spain could avoid. Conservatism, however, was less an ideology than an enduring human trait, and had to be addressed in a different way.

Although Ortega's attitude towards conservatism had become greatly refined since his youth, in its essence his analysis remained unchanged. Earlier, he had contrasted liberalism and conservatism, and concluded that "liberalism is generous politics par excellence,"(7) whereas "The conservative direction ignores ideal demands, denies their ethical value, and attends on this point to what has already been achieved, when it is not fomenting the return to forms of political constitution that have been superseded. Liberalism believes that no social regime is definitively just: always the standard or idea of justice demands something beyond, a human right that has not yet been recognized and which, therefore, transcends, overflows the written constitution."(8) Conservatism embodies stasis, he believed, while liberalism offers and seeks change.

This was the time when he accused conservatism of "torrid materialism,"(9) in contrast with the progressive cultural aspirations of liberalism.(10) Ortega always saw conservatism as an "instinct of preservation," characteristic of a defensive, bourgeois concept of life in which the special virtues of the individual -- the guiding impulse of nineteenth-century liberalism -- were subordinated to the usefulness of relationships to the entire social fabric, which must be preserved intact at all costs.(11)

Such a posture was antihistorical, he claimed, because it permitted the triumph of the undifferentiated and irresponsible mass over the individual. Individual talents, especially from the still disenfranchised social classes, were thus seen as subservient and even unrelated to social usefulness. As a consequence, adaptability to inevitable historical evolution was impeded, precisely because it meant change. Ortega insisted that social change, however, is neither good nor bad, but simply an unavoidable part of

the historical process. Since it cannot be denied, evaded, or ignored, it
becomes the duty of responsible politics to find ways of responding to it.
Therefore, by the beginning of the 1930s, he could declare unequivocally
that "today nowhere is conservative politics possible."(12)   The conservative instinct, of course, would always endure, but in times of profound
change, conservative politics could not prevail. In most of the continent,
with the exception of England, Ortega accused conservative ideology of remaining resolutely immobile, bereft of constructive policies, able to define
itself only as anti-Marxist.(13)

The years between the resignation of General Primo de Rivera and the
outbreak of the Civil War (1930-1936) provided Spain with the opportunity
not only to rise to the highest level of contemporary European nationhood —
therefore, some sort of liberal democracy — but they also obliged the country to confront its immediate historical reality. New institutional structures had to be devised and daring innovations had to be attempted in order
to incorporate all facets of the Spanish populace into the governance and
direction of the nation. The conservatives, whatever their party affilia-
tions, could offer only immobilism, and those crucial months merely proved
that Ortega was right when, as he looked back to the example offered by
Julius Caesar and his imaginative approach to the expansion of the Roman Em-
pire, he observed the "confusionism and frivolity into which, not always,
but almost always, the conservative classes of a country fall when the inevitable hour of the great innovations arrives."(14)

An important distinction was made here by Ortega, for while he believed
that the conservative sectors of any society normally consist of those who
benefit from, and are therefore content with, its existing structure, simple
nostalgia for the ancien régime in times of change did not in fact seem to
him the decisive element. Rather, he believed that the most historically
significant characteristic of conservatives was the preordained failure of
their efforts to "sustain the unsustainable"(15) in the face of inescapable
change. The secret of political success lies in learning how to assess
change, how to turn it to best advantage, and how to live fruitfully with
it. Conservatism is, by definition, complacency, a desire to seek safety in
the herd, and as he warned Spanish university students, whose lot it would
be to build on the new national realities, "The peoples who feel safe in
History are those who fail most."(16)

The liberal stance offers the ever renewed possibility of revolution,
but, more than a desire to return to the past, Ortega saw in conservatism
throughout history the eager conviction that change can be denied, that history's imperatives can be resisted by an act of the will, a refusal to make
concessions. Despite the repeated pattern of conservatism, he knew that
nothing else could be expected now: "What can we do! Everything has its
limits, and the limit of the conservative temperament lies in radicalism.
It cannot be radical even about itself. Nonetheless, it can be observed
that this constant experience does no good, and the conservatives do not
give up trying to conserve everything."(17) Echoing his own long-held conviction, he could conclude only that "I believe that it is simply a question
of an imaginative inability that is joined on to the type that is the conservative man."(18)   Societies and their politicians need imagination to
rise to the challenge of change by establishing coherent systems that will
permit the full flowering both of individual capabilities and national aspirations, within the inescapable realities of the moment. The purely defensive response of the conservative mind will always hinder progress, he
argued, but it becomes a dangerous liability when history takes one of its
great leaps: "Rather than recognize that present reality is itself authentic chaos, they think that if institutions are modified, chaos will come.
But chaos does not have to come; it is already there."(19) Such is the
dramatic nature of human life that tests man's mettle as he flounders towards new answers.

To Ortega, no social institution, however large and however well-estab-
lished, was immune to change. At its most successful, nineteenth-century

liberal democracy had demonstrated an inspiring ability to adjust its institutions so as to accommodate the evolving needs of a growing middle class.   In the process, the traditional aristocracy, the conservative segment at the time, had also been obliged to adapt.   By the early decades of the twentieth century, and especially in Spain, still more fundamental adjustments were required as the proletariat claimed its rights.   The middle class, however -- the new conservatives -- shrouded itself in complacency and cultivated a belief that minor refinements of the great social structures, themselves creations of the liberal imagination, could suffice to keep history at bay.   Most important was the preservation of the intangibility of the overall structure, the state.   Conservative notions of reform, Ortega said, reveal a perverse sort of utopianism as inappropriate as that espoused by extremists at the other end of the spectrum.

When historical reality itself had dramatically reshaped itself, as it had so clearly done in the Europe of the early twentieth-century, the very type of man whom governments had to serve also changed and must be attended by means of nothing less than a new state.   Spain had undergone such a sea change in the period between about 1909 and 1930, and Ortega's unshakeable conviction that politics must always flee facile abstractions and address itself to present realities caused him to warn against the sterile abstrac tions of both extremisms: "And in fact, the conservative is usually as much a Utopian as the radical.   Both are prey to two opposing chimeras: the former believes that, <u>fundamentally</u>, society never changes; and the latter, on the contrary, <u>believes that it</u> can change on a whim."(20)

As is well known, Ortega foresaw the continued gradual disappearance of small political units into larger federations that would still respect their cultural and spiritual integrity.   Such was one of the principles enunciated in <u>España invertebrada</u> (1920-1922), and it also moved him in his call for a <u>federated Spanish Republic</u> a decade later.   The future, he insisted, would certainly bring about a European union, yet he observed that, true to their nature, conservatives would continue to oppose and ignore all such likelihoods.(21)   Although conservatism would be unsuitable for either the changes or the future, "archaic" liberalism was no less guilty of failing to adapt, and Ortega did not hesitate to point out that it, too, suffered from a similar lack of imagination: "The old liberals extended the rights of the individual to groups and associations, but they had not imagined that society could organize itself into huge corporations as powerful as the State itself."(22)   Such reorganization was already well underway, and it was incumbent upon a renewed liberalism to serve again as a stimulus; it must once more represent the possibility of revolutionary, dramatic change.   In the present circumstances, Ortega insisted that a conservative political posture could neither deal with evolving forces nor offer leadership, and must be resisted: ". . . today a politics that is simply a defense of interests is inevitably stillborn, because it has neither the consent of the masses nor, consequently, the strength to shock.   A politics that defends interests can neither warm hearts nor fix illusions, and without this one cannot count on incorporating that new shock force that is youth."(23)

The future had arrived.   Like any form of thought, archaic liberalism had ceased being a vital attitude and had become another exhausted ideology that would vanish, as it should.   The static quality of conservatism, however, the instinct to preserve when one's imagination cannot encompass fundamentally new realities, will always offer its seductive charm.   Yet such an attraction is a drag on human vitality, and Ortega was categorical in his insistence that those who must live in the present and with their sights set on the future must always gird themselves for the struggle that is human life.   Only the truly liberal imagination provides them with the necessary tools.

NOTES

1.   See, for example, "Reforma del carácter, no reforma de costumbres," El Imparcial, Madrid, 5 October 1907; in Obras completas, 12 vols. (Madrid: Revista de Occidente, 1966–1983), vol. X, p. 21. Except where otherwise indicated, all references are to this edition, and all translations are my own. I have discussed at greater length Ortega's early liberalism in my José Ortega y Gasset (Boston: G. K. Hall, 1982), pp. 39–41.

2.   For the influence of Mussolini's new Fascism on Primo de Rivera's Dictatorship, see Shlomo Ben-Ami, Fascism from Above: The Dictatorship of Primo de Rivera in Spain 1923–1930 (Oxford: Clarendon Press, 1983). An important work for understanding the intellectual context of Ortega's politics is Robert Wohl's The Generation of 1914 (Cambridge, Massachusetts: Harvard University Press, 1979).

3.   "César, los conservadores y el futuro, II," El Sol, Madrid, 6 July 1930, p. 3.

4.   See Ortega's important comments regarding Guizot and the doctrinaire liberalism of the nineteenth-century in the "Prólogo para franceses" (1937), La rebelión de las masas, Obras IV, pp. 122–27.

5.   "Don José Ortega y Gasset traza un análisis hondo y sutil de la situación del mundo," Luz, Madrid, 1 June 1933, p. 11.

6.   "Ideas políticas, I," El Sol, Madrid, 29 June 1924; Obras XI, p. 32.

7.   "El momento político," El Sol, 26 June 1919; Obras X, p. 555.

8.   "Ideas políticas, I," pp. 34–35.

9.   "La solidaridad alemana," El Imparcial, Madrid, 9 February 1908; Obras X, p. 26.

10.   "Imperialismo y democracia," El Imparcial, 12 January 1910; Obras X, p. 130.

11.   "La resurrección de la mónada," El Sol, 12 February 1925; Obras III, pp. 342–43.

12.   "Rectificación de la República," 6 December 1931; Obras XI, p. 404. See also "Discurso de D. José Ortega y Gasset sobre la necesidad de una República mejor," Luz, 5 February 1932, p. 5.

13.   "En nombre de la nación, claridad," El Sol, 9 December 1933; Obras XI, p. 536.

14.   "César, los conservadores y el futuro, I," El Sol, 22 June 1930, p. 3. Part of this article was incorporated into section VII of "¿Quién manda en el mundo?," chapter XIV of La rebelión de las masas, Obras IV, pp. 253–56.

15.   Ibid.

16.   "Actos de la F.U.E. Conferencia de don José Ortega y Gasset," El Sol, 10 October 1930, p. 8.

17.   "César, los conservadores y el futuro, I."

18.   Ibid.   Cf.   "Lerroux, o la eficacia," El Radical, 22 July 1910; Obras X, p. 157:   ". . . the conservative — that is, the man without imagination . . ."

19.   Ibid.

20.   "César, los conservadores y el futuro, II."

21.   See "Peligro en Europa," La Nación, Buenos Aires, 20 August 1930, p. 8; incorporated into section IX of "¿Quién manda en el mundo?," pp. 272-275; Harold C. Raley, José Ortega y Gasset: Philosopher of European Unity (University, Alabama: University of Alabama Press, 1971), chapters 5 and 6.

22.   "En su segunda conferencia D. José Ortega y Gasset estudia los movimientos políticos del presente," Luz, 3 June 1933, p. 11.

23.   "Discurso de D. José Ortega y Gasset sobre la necesidad de una República mejor," loc. cit.

12.
The Real and the Ideal:
Two Europes in the Thought
of Ortega

HAROLD C. RALEY

In a general sense, the theme of Europe in Orteguian thought has been discussed and substantiated to such a degree that it hardly needs further
elucidation. From the time of his earliest writings Ortega was clearly and
irrevocably one of the so-called europeizantes. Unlike Unamuno, for instance, who went from being an early proponent of Europeanization of Spanish
culture to standing as an ardent defender of Spanish casticismo, Ortega did
not waver in any essential way from his first position. As late as October
1954, exactly a year before his death, Ortega reiterated his view of Europe
with these words: "The idea of Europe, especially a unitarily organized
European economy, is the only shape we find on our horizon that could be
converted into a dynamic ideal. It alone could cure our peoples of the de-
moralizing incongruity between the international breadth of their problems
and the provincial narrowness of their national states."(1)

Nevertheless, although Ortega's enthusiasm for the European ideal does
not wane during the course of his intellectual life, there is a gradual
shift of emphasis. Whereas in 1910 he saw Europe as the possible salvation
of Spain (and vice versa, i.e., Spain as a possible saving dimension of
Europe), by the end of his life Europe had become the salvation, the only
salvation for him, of the several European states themselves.(2)

The comparison of Ortega to Unamuno in relation to the theme of Europe
was not merely fortuitous. Recent research has revealed that the young
Ortega reacted vigorously to Unamuno's position on such topics as irration-
ality and the prospect of Europeanization.(3) But it would be a mistake to
view Ortega's interest in Europe as a derived topic offered solely in opposition and reaction to the notions of Unamuno. Rather we find that it
stands with his metaphysical theories of human life as radical reality, circumstance, historical perspectivism, and social reality as an integral part
of his thought throughout his life. But with this difference: Europe functions in his thought not as an abstract schematic series but as a particular
and concrete manifestation of his notion of circumstance. To put it another
way, Europe is the testing ground for Ortega's theories of human reality.
In my book on Ortega, I have tried to show that Ortega's philosophy of Europe is so integrally a part of his general system that there is a risk of
misunderstanding both unless both are taken together as formal and concrete
dimensions of the same manner of thinking.(4)

I sustained such arguments more than a dozen years ago, and I find no
reason to state otherwise now. Yet there are a few points about his notion
of Europe that were not sufficiently clarified in my earlier work; nor to my
knowledge has anyone else shed much light on them. These I should like to
outline in the present study.

To begin with, we need to acknowledge that Ortega had certain geopolitical notions about his Europe that did not coincide with the geographical

delineations on a map. On one occasion he wrote: "Europe is to be understood above all and properly as the trinity of France, England, and Germany.
In the region of the globe that they occupy, there has matured a module of
human existence according to which the world has been organized."(5) But he
was not completely rigid in his definition. In 1953 he wrote: "The West
(meaning Europe) has always been the articulation of two great groups of
peoples: the Anglosaxons and Germans on the one hand and the Latins on the
other."(6) And he goes on to observe somewhat whimsically in the same context that the West, or Europe, could be divided by dietary habits into two
groups: ". . . on the one hand the peoples who drink wine, use oil, and eat
honey; and on the other, those who drink beer, use lard, and eat sauerkraut."(7)

   This is the context wherein Ortega's real or supposed "Germanism" has
been discussed, explained, and often condemned. It is an argument that I
propose neither to raise nor resolve, except insofar as it relates tangen-
tially to the theme of this study. And I do so in a purely negative way so
as to point out that the two Europes he speaks of, Latin and Germanic, are
not what I have chosen to elaborate. Were this the case, an argument could
also be made for an East-West dichotomy. In 1934 Ortega stated: "The three
capitals that form Eastern Europe, Moscow, Rome, and Berlin, have been discussed too much already. Opposed to them and their confused and barbarous
politics, we hope that the vertical, authentic Europe of the West prevails,
the Europe of London, Paris, and Madrid."(8) Therefore, Ortega's Europe
does not include the Slavic East, most certainly it does not include Russia.
Paraphrasing Ortega's ideas on Russia, Julián Marías states:

> Russia does not belong to Europe, because its structure
> consists of its not belonging, of the elimination of the
> presence of other nations, the presence in which resides
> . . . the essence of the nations of Europe. A society
> is a system of common vigencias (binding usages); Rus-
> sia, as of today, has a completely different repertory,
> and what is more, this prevents the osmosis by means of
> which such usages undergo transformation, transmission,
> extension, or implantation. In this sense, Russia lies
> at an enormous social distance from Europe. . . .(9)

   Nor does Ortega include the United States in the European orbit, and he
goes on to reject the notion of American leadership for Europe. In La
rebelión de las masas he suggests among other things the following points:
(1) that the United States is strong not primarily because of its technology
but because of its youthful vigor, just as Russia is powerful not because of
communism but in spite of it; and (2) that the real history, and consequently the period of leadership for both countries, lies in the future, possibly
in the distant future. Both cultures, he notes, are related to Europe, but
neither can function under present circumstances as its successor.(10) I
shall have more to say on this exclusivity but for present purposes it
serves to set the ideological boundaries of Europe as Ortega saw them.

   Even by the late 1920s the Europe to which Ortega had devoted so much
attention was both fragmented and demoralized. Commenting on the threat of
"mass-man," Ortega warns:

> If this human type continues to be master and unques-
> tioned trendsetter of Europe, thirty years will suffice
> for our continent to retreat to barbarism. Juridical
> and material techniques will vanish with the same ease
> with which manufacturing secrets have so often been
> lost. Life will be reduced. The present-day abundance
> of possibilities will give way to a real scarcity, an
> anguished powerlessness, a true decadence. For the

rebellion of the masses is one and the same thing with
what Rathenau called "the vertical invasion of the bar-
barians."(11)

Although mass-man stands in direct relationship to such mass movements as
Communism and Fascism, these phenomena are not the only threats to European
civilization in Ortega's view. Regressive nationalism not only has contributed directly to two great wars in this century alone but also impedes progress toward a more productive European structure. In Ortega's words:
". . . all these nationalisms are but blind alleys. When we attempt to project them into the future, their limitations are evident. They lead nowhere."(12) Elsewhere he comments on the peculiar psychological nature of
contemporary nationalism: "Today no people admires any other; on the contrary, each frowns on and reproves any peculiarity of any other people,
ranging from the way they walk to the way they write and think. This fact
means that 'open nationalism' has become a cowardly 'closed nationalism' or,
to use a fine French expression, a nationalisme rentré (withdrawn nationalism)."(13)
    Given this demoralized, uncooperative mood in Europe, Ortega came to
believe by about the year 1930 that it was possible for communism to triumph, an eventuality he had rejected some years earlier. Bluntly he warns:
"Provided he may serve something that gives meaning to his life and allows
him to flee from his own existential emptiness, the European may not find it
hard to swallow his objections to communism and feel himself impelled not by
its substance but by its moral thrust."(14)
    Summing up Ortega's views of Europe over a twenty-five year period,
1930-1955, we can say that they show his growing concern and even alarm over
the increasing state of demoralization of European civilization and his almost apocalyptic vision of what its collapse would bring. Consider, for example, one of his more pessimistic assessments written near the end of his
life: "I do not believe that the general lines of collectivism can be
avoided or modified to a sufficient degree; but it is possible to salvage
within those tendencies certain aspects of life, of an individual nature. . . ."(15)
    Such is the Europe over which Ortega claimed intellectual custody for
much of his life. Yet in its actual form it is not the Europe that from his
earliest years captured his imagination and stirred his enthusiasm and which
in his last years became almost his only stated hope of collective salvation. There is yet another Europe in Ortega's writings that deserves commentary because it stands somewhat in contradistinction to what we have so
far discussed.
    Ortega's "other" Europe might be called a gestalt theory of European
civilization, for insofar as it functions as an ideal it exceeds the sum of
its parts. As a specific example, Ortega notes that contemporary economic
problems despair of solution so long as they are subject to purely national
policies. There is no hope, in other words, for the economic problems of
France, or Germany, or Italy when viewed over a long term. But there is, or
could be, a "European" solution (which not fortuitously has happened in the
form of the Common Market.) Similarly, it remains doubtful whether there is
a purely German policy of national scope that can satisfy the German's deep
need for purpose in his life.
    Nationalism has run its course, in Ortega's opinion, and as with all
realities that have done so, it now reveals only its negative, ugly aspects.
On the other hand, a United States of Europe could satisfy that need by
providing an ample future horizon that in turn would instill in men a new
sense of duty, purpose, and patriotism. This other Europe, this gestalt
union of the European states is for Ortega the only real hope for Europe
because it is the only structure that offers a viable future. There is
nothing mystical in Ortega's argument for a kind of United States of Europe.
Rather it existed prior to the emergence of nations and it has continued to

be the reality that informs their existence: "The unity of Europe is not a fantasy but realty itself.   The other is the fantasy: the belief that France, Germany, Italy, or Spain are substantive, and therefore, complete and independent realities."(16) Statements of this kind abound in his works and taken together reveal that Ortega believes the unifcation of Europe to be both logical and historical, the pathway of its natural development. Europe, he argues, has evolved through out decisive stages.   The emergence of nations as historical realities represented an enormous advance over the feudalism of an earlier age.   Likewise, the spectacular combination of liberal democracy and technological innovations in the nineteenth century (stemming from earlier industrial and philosophical advances) allowed the European masses to assume for the first time an active role in history.

The phase of supranationalism inherent in a united Europe would be equally or more spectacular, but unlike the advent of mass intervention, which Ortega views with consternation and uncertainty, the idea of a supernation is for him the road toward the eventual salvation of European civilization.   Yet he was not convinced that Europe could or would make the leap to unification.   Increased communication and contact among nations appears to have hindered rather than helped the process.   In analyzing the effect that rapidly transmitted opinions have on other countries, Ortega observes somewhat gloomily: "This would suffice to explain why, just when the European nations seemed close to achieving a higher form of unification, they have begun suddenly to withdraw into themselves, to seal themselves off from one another, encased within their national boundaries as though they were in hermetic diving suits."(17)

The scope of this study does not permit us to examine the many occasions on which Ortega made allusions to his notion of a European superstate. In any case he offers few specific details of how union would be accomplished, except to express the wish that it would include the British system as a model of political checks and balances, thereby obviating the threat of a monolitic state that would stifle individual and national initiative.(18)

Because of the tentative nature of the concept in his thought insofar as detail is concerned, any criticism of his ideas must be provisional and in any case should stop short of insistence on real or imagined weaknesses in his arguments.   Still one might point out that precisely because his concept is an outline and not a blueprint or procedural schematic, it is perhaps a bit too pat and wistful.   We cannot doubt Ortega's sincerity and probably would be hard pressed to refute his historical analysis leading up to this hoped for metamorphosis in European culture.   But at the moment of ideal transition we are left with mere generalities, so that for all its grounding in history, the emergence of the supernation itself is highly problematic and makes us wonder whether it could come about by any other process than something bordering on mutation or calamity on a grand scale.

But there is perhaps a more serious objection that could be raised to his theory from another perspective.   It seems that Ortega (and others, for he is by no means alone) chooses to define Europe not only in selected geopolitical terms but also according to its more desirable ideological traits. Hence the East is dismissed because it is given to heavy-handed politics and ideology and is a bit suspect in its historical development.   This seems to me to be a serious error, one that has led to a multitude of misconceptions and dangerous confrontations.   Ortega loathes Communism as he detests Fascism, for they epitomize the mass mentality and therefore threaten to annihilate the achievements of European genius.   The error, I would suggest, lies not in this opposition but in his rejection of such phenomena as being alien to the real spirit and history of Europe.   For it could be argued that were they truly alien, as say, animism or Buddhism are to the European ethos, then it is unlikely they would appeal as they have.   Rather it might be more accurate to label them as European "alter egos," as other examples in the long line of European notions that have swept imperialistically over the world, usually to mankind's benefit but sometimes to its harm.

Not everything European is positive. It has its darker side, its un-
happy creations, its oppressive modes, and these have their adherents as
surely as do other ideologies and ways of life.(19) Ortega does not recognize these alter egos of European genius and so does not believe that Communism, like its extremist brother Fascism, is a genuine European creation
with an appeal similar to that of other European ideals of recent centuries.
Perhaps this is another way of saying that in Ortega's view whatever is
flawed in the European ethos can be discarded in the quantum leap to the
status of a supernation. But most of us have learned from Ortega himself
that man does not escape shortcomings by setting off in search of utopias,
and he also taught us that truth ignored has a way of taking its revenge on
our fondest schemes. The apparent inability of Europe to approach anything
resembling Ortega's ideal of unification may be an indication that European
civilization is burdened by more imperfections that he would care to admit.

NOTES

1.   "La idea de Europa, y especialmente la de una economía europea
unitariamente organizada, es la única figura que hallamos en nuestro hori-
zonte capaz de convertirse en dinámico ideal.   Sólo ella podría curar a
nuestros pueblos de esa incongruencia desmoralizadora entre la amplitud
ultranacional de us problemas y la exiguidad provinciana de sus estados
nacionales." Obras completas (Madrid: Revista de Occidente, 1961-64), vol.
IX, p. 741.   Following references are to the Obras.   This and subsequent
translations are mine.

2.   "Europa, cansada en Francia, agotada en Alemania, débil en Inglaterra, tendrá una nueva juventud bajo el sol poderoso de nuestra tierra.

España es una posibilidad europea.
Sólo mirada desde Europa es posible España."

(Europe, tired in France, exhausted in Germany, weak in England, will have a
second youth under our land's powerful sun.

Spain is a European possibility.
Spain is possible only when seen from Europe.)

(Obras I, p. 138). The question of Spain does not figure prominently in
Ortega's final works, most of which were first given as conferences in Germany, England, and Switzerland. Of Spain itself he notes: "Yo también he
callado — y muy radicalmente — durante todo ese tiempo, porque en España
no podía hablar y fuera de España no quería hablar." (I have also kept
silent — and very radically so — during all this time, because in Spain I
could not speak and outside of Spain I did not wish to speak.) (Obras IX,
pp. 73-74).

3.   I have attempted to trace in a general way Ortega's indebtedness
and reaction to Unamunean thought. See my La visión responsable: la filosofía de Julián Marías ("El legado de Unamuno") (Madrid: Espasa Calpe,
1977) pp. 57-87.

4.   See José Ortega y Gasset: Philosopher of European Unity ("Toward
Authentic Morality") (University, Alabama: University of Alabama Press,
1971), pp. 168-187.

5.   "Por Europa se entiende, ante todo y propiamente, la trinidad
Francia, Inglaterra, Alemania. En la región del globo que ellas ocupan ha
madurado un módulo de existencia humana conforme al cual ha sido organizado
el mundo." (Obras IV, p. 239).

6.   "Occidente ha sido siempre la articulación de dos grandes grupos de pueblos: los anglo-sajones y germánicos de un lado, los latinos de otro." (Obras VIII, p. 449).

7.   ". . . de un lado los pueblos que beben vino, usan aceite y comen miel; del otro los pueblos que beben cerveza, toman manteca y comen sauerkraut." (Obras VIII, p. 449).

8.   "Ya han hablado demasiado de las tres capitales que forman el Oriente europeo, confuso y bárbaro en política: Moscú, Roma, Berlín. Frente a ellas deseamos que prevalezca la vertical de la Europa auténtica, de la Europa occidental, atlántica, formada por Londres, París, Madrid." (cited by Luis Recasens Siches, "Sociología, filosofía social y política," Cuadernos Americanos, 15, I, pp. 118-19).

9.   "Rusia no pertenece a Europa, porque su estructura consiste en su no pertenencia, en la eliminación de la presencia de las demás naciones, en la cual estriba . . . la esencia de las naciones de Europa. Una sociedad es un sistema de vigencias comunes; Rusia, hoy por hoy, tiene un repertorio completamente distinto y, lo que es más, impide la osmosis en virtud de la cual se operan las transformaciones de las vigencias, su transmisión, extensión o implantación. En ese sentido, está a enorme distancia social de Europa." (Julián Marías, Obras (Madrid: Revista de Occidente, 1961), p. 452).

10.   "No importaría que Europa dejase de mandar si hubiera alguien capaz de sustituirla. Pero no hay sombra de tal. Nueva York y Moscú no son nada nuevo con respecto a Europa." (It would not matter if Europe ceased to command, provided there were someone able to take her place. But there is not the faintest sign of one. New York and Moscow represent nothing new, relative to Europe.) (Obras IV, pp. 239-40).

11.   "Si ese tipo humano sigue siendo dueño de Europa y es definitivamente quien decide, bastarán treinta años para que nuestro continente retroceda a la barbarie. Las técnicas jurídicas y materiales se volatilizarán con la misma facilidad con que se han perdido tantas veces secretos de fabricación. La vida se contraerá. La actual abundancia de posibilidades se convertirá en efectiva mengua, escasez, impotencia angustiosa; en verdadera decadencia. Porque la rebelión de las masas es una y misma cosa de lo que Rathenau llamaba 'la invasión vertical de los bárbaros.'" (Obras IV, p. 174).

12.   "Pero todos estos nacionalismos son callejones sin salida. Inténtese proyectarlos hacia el mañana y se sentirá el tope. Por ahí no se sale a ningún lado." (Obras IV, p. 273).

13.   "Hoy ningún pueblo admira a otro; por el contrario, se toma a mal y reprueba toda peculiaridad del otro pueblo, desde la manera de moverse hasta su modo de escribir y de pensar. Este hecho significa que el 'nacionalismo hacia fuera' se ha transformado en un acobardado 'nacionalismo hacia dentro' o, para usar una feliz expresión francesa, en un 'nationalisme rentré.'" (Obras IX, p. 743).

14.   "Con tal de servir a algo que dé un sentido a la vida y huir del propio vacío existencial, no es difícil que el europeo se trague sus objeciones al comunismo, y ya que no por su sustancia, se sienta arrastrado por su gesto moral." (Obras IV, p. 275).

15.   "No creo que las líneas generales del colectivismo puedan ser ni evitadas ni modificadas en grado suficiente, pero si es posible salvar

dentro de ellas ciertas formas de vida, de actuación individual. . . ."
(Obras IX, p. 699).

16.   "La unidad de Europa no es una fantasía, sino que es la realidad
misma, y la fantas[a es precisamente lo otro: la creencia de que Francia,
Alemania, Italia, o España son realidades sustantivas, por tanto, completas
e independientes." (Obras IX, p. 295).

17.   "Esto bastaría a explicar por qué, cuando las naciones europeas
parecían más próximas a una superior unificación, han comenzado repentina-
mente a cerrarse hacia dentro de sí mismas, a hermetizar sus existencias,
las unas frente a las otras, y a convertirse las fronteras en escafandras
aisladoras." (Obras IX, pp. 312-13).

18.   See Obras VII, p. 229.

19.   In a work that never attracted the attention it deserved, Eugen
Rosenstock-Huessy argues that each "world revolution" picks up where another
had left off and that none is absolute and all-persuasive. He goes on to
argue: "Man can neither bear to be cut off from his roots in the past, nor
to have all his highest beliefs confined within the bounds of one nation or
continent." He also observes: "Democracy has no surer approach to the
masses of men than the other three forms of government (monarchy, aristocracy, and dictatorship). Each form seems, strangely enough, to express a
popular longing. The German civil law, the English Common Law, the French
laws of nature, the Russian laws of Lenin, were all welcomed with fierce
enthusiasm." Out of Revolution: Autobiography of Western Man (New York,
1938; Norwich, VT., 1969), pp. 459, 479).

13.
From Ortega to Jaspers: Thoughts on Situating Vital Reason

ERLING SKORPEN

Vital reason is essential to Ortega's espectador universal in his or her wide-ranging curiosity, observation, and effort in making sense of existence. If adequate to this task, it is hardly surprising that conceptualization of vital reason itself is no simple matter. The difficulty is moreover compounded if, as it seeks to comprehend everything, it must recursively include itself like an eye hoping to see itself seeing. Nevertheless, when stating that "life cannot tolerate being supplanted either by revealed faith or by pure reason," Ortega does not hesitate to distinguish vital reason from such arch uses of the latter as geometrical, physical, economic, or political reasoning.(1) These uses have more than marginal utility for the universal spectator, but not vital reason's indispensable role, as when it now must rescue itself from its disabused faith in pure reason's various uses to satisfy all our wants.

Vital reason can save itself from itself because of its signal differences from pure reason. First of all it is fundamentally narrative in character: "The collapse of physical reason," Ortega observes, "leaves the way clear for vital historical reason."(2) It is more than this, however, and of course much more, Ferrater Mora agrees, than merely a synonym for "living reason" or "life as reason." Indeed: "As our guiding principle in our search for the 'system' of being," Ferrater Mora says it is insistently methodological, such that it must ultimately be viewed as "reason at large" determined "to penetrate (life's) own structure and significance."(3)

If in our own terms we think of vital reason as "reason in the essential service of life," we can also agree with Ortega's criticism of the "cynical refusal to use reason." Such refusal accompanies historical crises in the late Greco-Roman era and fifteenth-century Renaissance Italy, but as a phenomenon "of desperate monotony and repetition" he says it cannot long endure:

> But when men find themselves happiest in that apparent
> -- and so easy -- liberation, so do they feel themselves
> most hopelessly prisoners of that other and irremediable
> reason; of that from which -- whether you like it or not
> -- it is impossible to escape because it is one and the
> same thing as living: vital reason.(4)

If, then, vital reason is at once historical, methodical, protective of, indeed even identical with, human life, what are its actual tools? Silver concludes that it is essentially "systematic phenomenological thought," thus that it functions by intuition and analysis, yet is also dialectical and synthetic.(5) However, to this should be added imagination, inasmuch as Ortega finds and goes on to insist that "that program of life which each person is, is clearly the work of his imagination. . . . The stone, in order to be a stone, has no need to construct in fancy what it is going to be; but man has. . . . In one of its essential dimensions, then, human life is the work of imagination."(6) A man of 50, for instance, considers the possibility of yet another romantic involvement. But he concludes that he has already experienced the "excellences" and "limitations" of that form of life known as "loving a woman." It has, for him, become "an absolute reality" to be put behind in order "to advance upon himself."(7) So to advance with no loss of drama to his life clearly calls for imagination; he must concoct for himself more not less enthralling adventure than before.

This is the existential rather than scientific use of imagination. The latter may abstract reproductively from observed correlations to the uniform laws of physics, or it may project creatively from such data to the morphological images of genetics, a difference illustrated by Boyle's gas laws versus Crick and Watson's double helix for genes. Or, contrary to anything observed at all, scientific imagination can even depict mechancial motion in vacuo. "Only when he has his imaginary reality well in hand," says Ortega admiringly of Galileo, "does he note the facts, or rather, does he observe what relationship obtains between the facts and the imagined reality."(8)

But such specialties of natural reason cannot perform the nurturing function of vital reason. Science can, of course, investigate the body's physical chemistry along with the person's cognitive psychology. It is unable, however, either to put humpty-dumpty back together again or to account for the Orteguian drama of a person's life, as in the case above of the man who forsakes romantic involvement for, say, sagacious spectatorship. No such acts of imaginative self-transcendence can be found among the "conceptual" discoveries, including standard deviations, of the physical chemist, genetic biologist, or cognitive psychologist. They would, in fact, only be viewed as "contaminants" of the "purity" of scientific findings.

Yet the drama of once having been a Christian may owe much to science, as when anthropology today further discredits Holy Writ on human origins. That shows how pure reason still skirmishes against residual medieval faith in continuation of its general charge from vital reason since the Renaissance. Ortega ignores such mopping-up, but neither does he note the key role of "moral reason" in this process. Today this is practical reason expressed by civil libertarian criticism of fundamentalist Christian opposition to women's equality, criticism rooted in respect for all persons whatever their race, color, or sex. With the possible exception of medical science, moral reason thus seems much closer to the heart of life than natural reason. Medicine may be necessary for human health, but morality is essential to human worth. Both therefore merit vital reason's special attention, the latter more so since it ultimately upholds the value of human life, consequently its care by physicians.

To develop moral reason's relevance further, we must supplement Ortega's system of history. In its first incarnation, vital reason does not, pace Ortega, pursue only Eleatic ontology for Plato, say, or Aristotle. It also fastens upon such basic human virtues as wisdom, courage, temperance, and justice. In the discrimination of values, endurance of hardships, moderation of appetites, and distribution of deserts, respectively, these constitute cardinal strengths of the animal rationale, that is, reasoning life itself.

In a much later incarnation, vital reason again is not satisfied with the Cartesian ontology of mind-body dualism alone. To the antiqua virtus it adds moral precepts derived from the exercise of Kantian autonomous reason. These range from specific imperatives to tell the truth and keep promises to broader obligations to think for oneself and advance human rights including those of women. Both sets of principia ethica, ancient and modern, are appropriate to any form of human existence premised upon reason, as historically empowered by the arts of Socratic dialectic and Kantian criticism practically applied.

However, if Ortega slights vital reason's reliance on moral reason, he is not insensitive to its effects. In The Revolt of the Masses, he laments the average person's ignorance of history and consequent lack of standards other than today's "false life" of sports mania, art nouveau, sunbathing, and political violence.(9) Such dehumanizing values have in fact only become more prevalent, as illustrated at present by the physical violence and blatant sexuality on television and film and in literature and the media. But also in Revolt, Ortega defends the values of strong individualism and scientific ingenuity promoted by the Enlightenment. If the values of new political and economic institutions should transcend those of liberal democracy and industrial technology, these are not for Ortega likewise to be transcended. For no one can aspire to universal spectatorship without them; he or she must always think independently and rely on science to replace untested belief with researched fact.

The future would be bleak, however, without other permanent values, from Aristotelian habitual moderation to Kantian principled truthfulness. Are there better safeguards, in fact, against the human tendencies towards extremism and deception as marked by Ortega in times of historical shipwreck? The present is for him such a time because of our diminishing faith in science and technology to satisfy our every need and desire, notwithstanding the impassioned and influential defense of this faith by C. P. Snow not long ago in terms of applied science's capacity to provide not only for all of life's "primal" necessities, but its "jam" as well.(10)

Faith in science can therefore remain strong. But all faith for Ortega, not only in revealed religion, is expressive of vital reason. Classical philosophy, Christian revelation, and Cartesian rationalism successively illustrate vital reason's promotion of life. Each reacts dialectically to and transcends what went before. Each represents a form of life providing salvation from its predecessor's demise. It does not matter that Christian revelation is theistic and otherwordly and that philosophical naturalism both before and after is pagan and of this world.(11) Each in its time constitutes a hermeneutical triumph in making and giving both meaning and direction to human existence; each plays its part, therefore, in Ortega's imaginative reconstruction of history.

So for Ortega a new expression of vital reason deserving of faith is needed to transcend scientific faith and reality. Politically, he foresees the future in terms of a European nation-state whose vitality would exceed Communism's while ending nationalism's "exclusionary" mischief on the Continent.(12) He refuses, however, to become an existential seer and tell shipwrecked individuals how to fill the void created by their disillusionment in the omniscient and omnipotent claims of science.(13) That would merely stifle calls from within themselves to fashion their own separate destinies — as happens nowadays when they eagerly submit to gurus from the East or would happen were they to succumb to cynicism's repudiation of vital reason noted earlier.

Is it contrary of Ortega to outline a political strategy for Europeans while offering no existential remedy for their despair? The former is an exercise of pure reason aimed at "a plan of action and a programme of collaboration" by the French, English, Germans, Italians, etc.(14) The latter is a challenge to vital reason for which "the problematical thing (is) the very self of the subject. And if the answer to a partial problem is called a solution, the answer to this absolute problem of the personal being is called salvation."(15) (The European Economic Community may be a logical step toward eventual political unification of its members; but Ortega is right, no such solutions will work for the existential plight of Europeans, or anyone else, once faith in the scientific world view is abandoned.)

Related to his reticence, moreover, Ortega leaves to vital reason paradoxical labors. One is to provide for both the individual's salvation and a

form of life suitable for everyone.   In other words, "the problematical
thing" is not just the self-transcendence of the single self, but a fresh
transcendent reality clarifying the future for all.   This is not, however,
an impossible or unprecedented task. Vital reason has done it before, most
recently with the varied paths of numerous self-directing heirs of Enlightenment faith in the promises of science, from Diderot and Franklin early on,
say, to Einstein and Dewey in our own time. But what of vital reason's duty
to rise anew to this demand, yet Ortega's unwillingness to lead the way? Is
he unnecessarily or unconscionably coy?
     Ortega's fellow centenarian, Karl Jaspers, is altogether sympathetic.
His counterpart to the universal spectator is the "true human being," and
such a person, Jaspers says, does not want to be "recognized as a prophet,
but remains hidden." And as if describing Ortega himself, Jaspers explains:

>   Were he known as a prophet, he would become a demogogue,
>   an ephemerally idolized and then dismissed leader of the
>   masses, or one who, for a time, would set the fashion
>   for a worshipping group. . . .   He does not want dis-
>   ciples, but companions. . . .   His essence works indi-
>   rectly, he does not become a plastic figure; he does not
>   lay down any laws. Nor merged in the enterprise of the
>   coming and going of idols of the life-order, he works as
>   self-existence on behalf of self-existence; for he cre-
>   ates life as a demand through influencing others out of
>   their own sources. . . .   He does not predict the fut-
>   ure, but describes what is. . . .(16)

     Perhaps, then, the universal spectator we take Ortega himself to be
prefigures the life-form of future man or woman in response to vital reason.
But so to situate him or her requires that we look again at those who have
brought us to this point in human self-awareness.   As remarked earlier,
Aristotelian civic virtues combine with Eleatic ontology to index mankind's
aspiring rational animality, as do Kantian moral principles along with Cartesian dualism later for our aspiring rational autonomy.   Behind the earlier
synthesis is vital reason's classical discovery that we human beings are not
just featherless but rational bipeds, behind the latter its Cartesian finding that we individuals possess not just different talents but distinct
cogitos.
     Between these two great advances in human self-knowledge is knowledge
of oneself as one of a kind. We owe this discovery to the Renaissance and
all those Vasari writes about, from Giotto, say, to Michelangelo. Ortega is
not as clear about this as well he might. On the one hand, the Renaissance
is for him an extended period of crisis, restless and without form, between
the collapse of medieval faith and the rise of modern science.   On the
other, he recognizes that modern science is preceded by a "dimension of
art," but since he sees each new stage of human history to be anticipated by
art, he leaves the "explanation to another day."(17)
     From Burckhardt on, however, it is widely accepted that the Renaissance
marks the rise of singular individuals who aspire to become universal human
beings, l'uomo singolare and l'uomo universale.(18) These related aims call
for the exercise of eccentric prerogatives from artistic license and true
dilettantism to multiple achievement and cosmopolitan freedom.   Together
such aims and prerogatives constitute a novel and definable form of life
showing that one need not be a discarnate angel thinking only individual
ideas to become, as Aquinas thought, an infima species, that is, one of a
kind. A human being can, in fact, know what he or she and nobody else is
through singular vision exhibited in all the material ways employed by Vasari's subjects, from brush and canvas and chisel and stone to forge and met-
al. For such individuals, then, vital reason is not "restless and without
form," as Ortega says, but expresses the faith that the human artificer

aware of his or her singularity can "endeavor to create something perfect," as Michelangelo affirmed, "striving for something divine."(19)

To backfill the history of human self-understanding in this way is to add important lineage to Ortega's universal spectator and Jaspers' true human being. Both descend from those who first know themselves as an animal rationale, then as an infima species, then as a res cogitans. But what as now? In post-Cartesian philosophy Ortega finds that the cogito becomes firmly established as the "proto-thing, the Urding . . . (which) identifies, thing-ifies -- verdinglich -- all the rest."(20) That is, the individual cogito, which each of us essentially is, now takes itself to be the sense-maker, object-construer, and indeed reality-constructor of everything it experiences, from the everyday world to the most recondite realms of science and metaphysics.

For Ortega this is the "idealist thesis." It is not, however, the true voice of vital reason since it virtually imprisons the cogito in phenomena of its own making and remaking. Vital reason wants, realistically, to speak otherwise:

> The 'I' is the innermost being, it is that which is within us, it exists for itself. Nevertheless, it must, without losing our innermost character, find a world which is fundamentally different from itself and go forth, outside itself to that world. Therefore the 'I' must be intimate and exotic, withdrawn and free, a prisoner and at liberty. The problem is startling.(21)

Vital reason is nevertheless not at a loss to deal with this problem. As before, it has the dialectic of history at its disposal: "For the ancients, being meant a 'thing;' for the moderns, being meant 'innermost subjectivity;' for us being means 'living,' therefore intimacy with ourselves and with things."(22) And if such intimacy is extended to our social world, we find that even our self-existence in all matters great and small depends on it, not, pace idealism, vice versa:

> Your strong will shows that I am a milksop. Obviously the reverse is also true; your faults reveal my virtues to my own eyes. Thus it is the world of you's and by virtue of them, that the thing I am, my I, gradually takes shape for me. I discover myself, then, as one of the countless you's, but as different from them all, with gifts and defects of my own, with a unique character and conduct, that together draw my genuine and concrete profile for me -- hence as another and particular you, as alter tu. And now we see why . . . we must, I think, reverse the traditional doctrine. . . .(23)

In such incisive ways vital reason affirms its present faith in "'living' as the basic datum, the primordial and indubitable reality of the Universe."(24) This is not, of course, the meaning of "living" we find in such expressions as "making a good living" or "living is easy." For Ortega the concept carries all the ontological weight existenz does for Jaspers, viz. "Existenz finds itself in the world. It wants to learn what is. It wants to experience it, by itself, in the world."(25) But Ortega adds that we must strive to become fully transparent to ourselves as well, and that this cannot be done "by playing the stock market or by winning battles."(26) Instead, we must confront our being thrown into life in serious yet sportive sense-making of it. This becomes Ortegan "preoccupation," which is entirely different from the "humble desire to be like everybody else, to renounce the responsibility of their own destiny, and dissolve it amid the multitude."(27)

Ortega is indisputably his own best example of such preoccupation in his jovial, often teasing display of vital reason with his listeners and readers. On its more serious side, however, his modus operandi also illustrates Jaspers' further characterization of true human beings. They form an

> anonymous chain of friends from among whom, here and there, and through the subjectivity of individual activities, one selfhood is revealed to another and perhaps distant selfhood. In this immaterial realm of the mind there are, at any moment, a few indwellers who, entering into close proximity, strike flame out of one another by the intimacy of their communication. They are the origin of the loftiest soaring movement which is yet possible in the world.(28)

Few can doubt that Ortega's universal spectator and Jaspers' true human being would, if "in close proximity, strike flame out of one another by the intimacy of their communication." But when Jaspers likens the "anonymous chain of friends" to an "Invisible Church of a corpus mysticum," the universal spectator might well demur. For Ortega does not hide his disdain of mysticism:

> My objection to mysticism is that out of the mystic vision no intellectual benefit redounds to mankind. . . . If mysticism is keeping silent, philosophizing is saying, discovering in the great nakedness and transparency of the world the very being of things -- ontology. Compared to mysticism, philosophy would prefer to be the secret which is shouted aloud.(29)

So if there is a parting of the ways for Ortega's universal spectator and Jaspers' true human being, it is here. The latter for Jaspers is someone whose "frankness of an unlimited will to see becomes in him a silence, not because he wishes to conceal what he knows and might say, but because he does not wish to drag into the realm of the spoken what in existence would be obscure owing to this inveracity."(30) Undergirding such frankness is what Jaspers calls "philosophical faith" in principled opposition to faith in revealed religion. It also contrasts, however, to vital reason's insistence upon the "great nakedness and transparency of the word" to reveal "the very being of things," not only by resorting to silence when saying would be untrue to one's perceived reality, but also by recourse to "ciphers of transcendence." Such ciphers include those works of art, poetic metaphors, religious myths, and philosophical speculations that for Jaspers "light up the roots of things" without idolatrous or dogmatic intent.(31)

Ortega himself may fall back on such ciphers, when, for instance, he finds the Egyptian myth of the eye of Horus to be a mnemonic image for "the first attribute of Providence; the seeing of oneself, the first essential attribute of life itself."(32) For Jaspers, however, this complex and openended image is more than just an aid to memory. It invites sustained reflection on the mystery of self-conscious existence, thereby to "touch transcendence" on the way to "fulfilled silence."(33) Again, it is profound appreciation for such language and silence that sets philosophical faith apart from revealed religion, and not just vital reason, in the knowledge that ciphers that orient us toward Transcendence are not final for us and perhaps never can be. As Jaspers elsewhere says: "Reason moves toward rendering all Being transparent only to experience the shock of the absolutely opaque. . . ."(34)

As it seeks to "clarify" this limit, existential reason turns to philo-sophical faith, not unmindful, however, of its own predilection for "the secret which is shouted aloud." For in close communication with the univer-sal spectator, Jaspers' true human being would hope for agreement:

> the silence at the limit of cipher thinking is realized, not by refraining from thought and speech, but by carry-ing them to the extreme where they revert to silence. In time, (however), they will shortly make us speak again.(35)

Quite possibly, then, the mythical image of the eye of Horus is a cipher of transcendence spoken if not quite shouted aloud by Ortega. But so, too, are the philosophical expressions "living" and existenz remarkably alike in intersubjective utterance by Ortega and Jaspers. They are ciphers for the transcendent mystery of our being-in-the-world, as still are animal rationale, infima species, and res cogitans. Denoted by "living" and existenz is a form of life still to be fully sounded by adherence to the precepts of existential preoccupation. Minimally these are the pursuits of authentic selfhood, intimate companionship, indirect communication, and transcending imagination of equal concern to Ortega and Jaspers however they differ over mystical silence and transcendent cipher. Such goals histori-cally complement moral reason's earlier but still vital virtues of rational animality, prerogatives of singular individuality, and principles of autono-mous agency. No rational animal can do without wisdom, no singular individ-ual without eccentricity, no autonomous agent without truthfulness, anymore than can any existential self do without imagination.

Fidelity to all such imperatives, again, is perhaps the best armor against the solipsism Ortega warns against: "When man is left, or believes himself left, alone with no other reality than his ideas to impose its stern limits on him, he loses the sensation of his own reality, he becomes an ima-ginary, spectral, and phantasmagoric entity."(36) But in large measure they also comprise the "human tasks in the world" Jaspers assigns to those whose differing philosophical and religious faiths do not prevent them from work-ing together.(37) To cultivate not just wisdom but justice in civic life, not just singularity but artistry in cosmopolitan life, not just truthful-ness but equality in Kant's universal kingdom-of-ends, and not just imagina-tion but centeredness in Jaspers "immaterial realm of the mind," all are illustrative of such tasks.

These tasks also constitute keys to our very survival as a species. For no one can doubt that they would help to make "life worth living," such in this way:

> To achieve a life that is worthy of him, man must sur-vive -- but he will survive only if he achieves that life. This is a circle that we cannot break out of merely to stay alive. Now, at the brink, mere life de-pends on worthy living. This alone leads to actions that would bar atomic doom.(38)

If the foregoing imperatives of moral reason are thus necessary for our survival, what could be more proof of their genealogy in vital reason also? For both Ortega and Jaspers, however, that is one and the same as saying that they are products of our historically evolving self-understanding, which includes the depth of human self-awareness that allows us to assess our present if parlous situation in precisely these terms. But on this programmatic note for our survival on a plane of worthy living, let the espectador universal have the final word:

> We can be sure that we have reached a higher spiritual
> level because if we look down at our feet, at our point
> of departure which is "living," we find that in it the
> ancient and the modern are conserved, integrated with
> one another, and superseded.(39)

NOTES

1.   José Ortega y Gasset, En torno a Galileo (Man and Crisis), trans. Mildred Adams (New York: Norton Library, 1963), p. 84.

2.   José Ortega y Gasset, Historia como sistema (History as a System), trans. H. Weyl, W. C. Atkinson, E. Clark (New York: Norton Library, 1962), p. 183.

3.   José Ferrater Mora, Ortega y Gasset (London: Bowes & Bowes, 1956), pp. 41–46 (parentheses added).

4.   Ortega y Gasset, Man and Crisis, p. 84.

5.   Philip W. Silver, Ortega as Phenomenologist: The Genesis of "Meditations on Quixote" (New York: Columbia University Press, 1978), pp. 99ff.

6.   Ortega y Gasset, Man and Crisis, p. 179.

7.   Ortega y Gasset, History as a System, pp. 205ff.

8.   Ortega y Gasset, Man and Crisis, pp. 14–15.

9.   José Ortega y Gasset, La rebelión de las masas (The Revolt of the Masses), trans. anonymous (New York: Mentor Books, 1950), p. 135.

10.   C. P. Snow, The Two Cultures and A Second Look (Cambridge: Cambridge University Press, 1964), p. 44. But see, also, I. Bernard Cohen's long awaited Revolution in Science (Cambridge: The Belknap Press of Harvard University Press, 1985), for yet another enthusiastic avowal of radical faith in science.

11.   Cf. Peter Gay, The Rise of Modern Paganism, Vol. I of The Enlightenment: An Interpretation (New York: Knopf, 1967).

12.   Ortega y Gasset, The Revolt of the Masses, pp. 131ff.

13.   Ortega y Gasset, Man and Crisis, pp. 138ff.

14.   Ortega y Gasset, The Revolt of the Masses, pp. 120ff.

15.   Ortega y Gasset, Man and Crisis, p. 134 brackets added.

16.   Karl Jaspers, Die geistige Situation der Zeit (Man in the Modern Age), trans. Eden and Cedar Paul (New York: Doubleday Anchor Book, 1957), p. 190.

17.   Ortega y Gasset, Man and Crisis, p. 88.

18.   Cf. Jacob Burckhardt, Die Kultur der Renaissance in Italien (The Civilization of the Renaissance in Italy), trans. S. C. G. Middlemore (New York: Harper Torchbook, 1958), Part II. Colin Morris places the development of the individual earlier in France, in The Discovery of the Individual 1050–1200 (New York: Harper Torchbook, 1973).

19. Betty Burroughs, ed., Vasari's Lives of the Artists (New York: Simon & Schuster, 1946), p. 301. This should make clear that Ortega's "rebarbarized" Renaissance man of action, Man and Crisis, p. 96, is but one aspect of the period, one that does little or no justice to his contemporary, the many-sided man of arts.

20. Ortega y Gasset, History as a System, p. 198.

21. José Ortega y Gasset, ¿Qué es filosofía? (What is Philosophy?), trans. Mildred Adams (New York: Norton Library, 1964), p. 182.

22. Ibid., p. 206.

23. José Ortega y Gasset, El hombre y la gente (Man and People), trans. Willard R. Trask (New York: The Norton Library, 1963), p. 170.

24. Ortega y Gasset, What is Philosophy?, p. 207.

25. Karl Jaspers, Der philosophische Glaube angesicht der Offenbarung (Philosophical Faith and Revelation), trans. E. B. Ashton (New York: Harper & Row, 1967), p. 283. Heidegger's notion of "Dasein" in Sein und Zeit (Being and Time), trans. J. Macquarrie and E. Robinson (London: SCM Press Ltd, 1962) is virtually identical: "We are ourselves the entities to be analysed. The Being of any such entity is in each case mine . . . . Being is that which is an issue for every such entity. This way of characterizing Dasein has a double consequence: ((1) existence and (2) mineness)," pp. 67-68, parentheses a summation of Heidegger's consequences.

26. Ortega y Gasset, What is Philosophy?, p. 216.

27. Ibid., p. 215.

28. Jaspers, Man in the Modern Age, p. 211.

29. Ortega y Gasset, What is Philosophy?, pp. 110-111.

30. Jaspers, Man in the Modern Age, p. 190.

31. Jaspers, Philosophical Faith and Revelation, pp. 92ff. It is interesting how in his own way Ortega respects the risks of "saying." In Man and Crisis he offers this aside: "It has not been hidden from me that I could have had almost all the youth of Spain behind me, as one man; I would have had only to pronounce a single word. But that word would have been false, and I was not disposed to invite you to falsify your lives." He relates this refusal to his fear of fomenting any extremism that "consists in excluding, in denying all but a single point of the entire vital reality" (p. 152). This means that he did not wish to become a demagogue, but if a "single word" can "falsify the lives" of many in this sense, why might it not also falsify the "vital reality" of a mystic's experience?

32. Ortega y Gasset, What is Philosophy?, pp. 216-217.

33. Jaspers, Philosophical Faith and Revelation, p. 125.

34. Karl Jaspers, Die Vernunft und die Existenz (Reason and Existenz), trans. William Earle (New York: The Noonday Press, 1955), p. 93.

35. Jaspers, Philosophical Faith and Revelation, p. 125 brackets added.

36.   Ortega y Gasset, History as a System, p. 228.

37.   Cf.   Jaspers, Philosophical Faith and Revelation, pp. 356ff.

38.   Karl Jaspers, Die Atombombe und die Zukunft des Menschen (The Future of Mankind), trans. E. B. Ashton (Chicago: Phoenix Books, 1961), p. 331.

39.   Ortega y Gasset, What is Philosophy?, pp. 206-207.

Part II

Aesthetics, Language, Art

14.
Ortega and the Aesthetics of Metaphor
ANTONIO F. CAO

José Orteqa y Gasset's aesthetic ideas constitute an important portion of his philosophical works and are second to none in the sphere of twentieth-century Spanish thought. But Ortega was not only a theorist, but a writer, a stylist, as well. In the opinion Juan Marichal, it is in this latter capacity that he will be better known to posterity.(1)

As a constant spectator, observer, and critic, Ortega was atuned to the artistic and literary activity that characterized the first quarter of this century. Especially the post-World War I years were rich in experimentation within the arts, and poetry was no exception. The successive waves of the avant-garde: cubism, expressionism, ultraísmo and creacionism in Spain, and finally surrealism had had in common the exaltation of the poetic image. Thus, Ortega's studies on metaphor should not surprise us, particularly when one also considers his fondness for this device throughout his writings. As Angel Rosenblat points out: "His prose appears before us filled with constant sparks of metaphors and similes, which constitute that undying charm of Plato's Dialogues. . . ."(2)

Rosenblat also stresses the aforementioned double nature of Ortega as a writer and as a philosopher.(3) This situation implies a tension that is more evident in Ortega's theoretical considerations about the metaphor than in his writings. Nonetheless, Julián Marías, Ortega's disciple, has remarked how at times the metaphoric expression has implicitly predated important ideas, later on explicitly couched in philosophical discourse. Thus in "Adán en el paraíso" ("Adam in Paradise") (1910), the important concept: "I am myself and my circumstance,"(4) conceptualized later on in 1914, appears as a metaphor.(5)

The object of this study is to trace the evolution of Ortega's theoretical writings on the metaphor bearing in mind the tension between Ortega the writer and the philosopher.(6)

Ciriaco Morón Arroyo, one of the most important critics of Ortega, considers four basic texts in which the Spanish philosopher deals with the metaphor:

1. "Renan" (1909)

2. "Ensayo de estética a manera de prólogo" (1914)
    ("Essay on Aesthetics in the Form of a Prologue")

3. "Las dos grandes metáforas" ("The Two Great
    Metaphors") (1924)

4. La deshumanización del arte (The Dehumanization of
    Art) (1925)(7)

In addition, I shall include "El amor en Stendhal" ("Love in Stendhal") (1926) and Idea del teatro (Idea of Theater) (1946) with the aim of giving a more complete picture of the evolution of the Spanish philosopher's ideas on metaphor.

In discussing "Renan", Morón Arroyo sees an attitude of disdain on the part of Ortega towards verisimilitude and metaphor, pointing out that for the Spanish philosopher "verisimilitude is precisely the synthesis of science and myth attempted by Renan."(8) Ortega illustrates this theory with the example of a painting by El Greco, "The Gentleman with the Hand on his Chest". In this figure we take for granted "a human presence that deviates from the laws of Anthropology, and underneath this feigned skull we can only surmise the existence of an imaginary psyche. However, we are completely certain that we are facing a Spaniard."(9) For Morón Arroyo these words corroborate Ortega's disdain towards both El Greco's painting and the feigned skull of the Spaniard supposedly painted by the Cretan artist.(10) In essence, he is stressing Ortega's intellectually rigorous view of verisimilitude as opposed to truth.

At another point in "Renan", Ortega establishes the difference between these two terms:

> Verisimilitude is the similarity to that which is truthful, but it must not be confused with that which is probable. Probability is a truth with little weight, but a truth nonetheless. Verisimilitude, on the other hand presents itself simultaneously as neither true nor false. The more verisimilitude approaches strict truth the more its energy will increase, as long as it is never fused with truth. By way of a graphic formula we may have recourse to a polygon circumscribed in a circumference: its sides may indefinitely multiply themselves, embracing closer and closer the circumference without ever becoming one with it. (I, p. 452)

The Spanish philosopher defines the world of verisimilitude as being the same of that of real things with a "metaphoric interpretation" (I, p. 454), and exalts it:

> That unlimited universe is built with metaphors. What richness! Starting with the modest comparison that gave rise to almost every word to the huge cosmic myth, such as that of the divine cow Hathor of the Egyptians, nourishing an entire civilization, there is almost nothing else in the history of mankind other than metaphor. If everything metaphoric were to be supressed from our lives, we would be diminished ninety per cent. (I, p. 454)

Here Ortega, the writer, the creator of metaphors, eulogized the metaphoric world, albeit different from truth.

In his "Ensayo de estética a manera de prólogo" ("Essay on Aesthetics in the Form of a Prologue"), Ortega analyzes a metaphor of a poet from the Spanish Levante, López Picó: "a cypress tree is like the specter of a dead flame". In it, he defines the metaphoric object "as being neither the cypress, nor the flame nor the specter, but rather the new composite object 'cypress tree-specter of flame.' However, each of these elements lose their reality" (VI, p. 257). Ortega adds:

> We witness a process whereby first things are annihilated as real images and then we are pushed towards a new world where cypress trees are flames. . . . If the

cypress is to become an object of my perception, my activity, I must ignore the object called cypress and look
in the opposite direction toward myself and witness the
derealization of the cypress while it transforms itself
into an activity of my "self". . . . We call this act-
ing-self image a feeling. . . . In our example we are
expected to see the image of a cypress through the image
of a flame, we see it as a flame, and vice-versa. But
if we consider them opaque images, then they exclude
each other, and yet we realize the possibility of the
perfect fusion of both images while still preserving
their individuality. As a feeling they become transparent. The feeling of a cypress tree becomes identical to
that of a flame. Why? We do not know; it is the irra-
tionality of art. . . . Each metaphor discovers a law
of the universe. And even after it has been created, we
still do not know why. (VI, pp. 259-261)

From the above we may conclude that the dichotomy between verisimilitude and truth stated in the essay on Renan is resolved by the real and true
fact that verisimilitude becomes part of the self. This integrating solution is in line with what José Ferrater Mora has termed the "perspectivistic" phase in Ortega, expostulated in his Meditaciones del Quijote (Meditations on Quixote) also written in 1914. Its famous central phrase "I am myself and my circumstance" (I, p. 322) is "far from being a trivial tautol-
ogy," according to Ferrater, for it involves a "double assumption" indicat-
ing it is impossible to conceive of the self without its own circumstances
and, conversely, no circumstance can be conceived of without the self as its
"dynamic centre."(11)

In his next essay, "Las dos grandes metáforas" ("The Two Great
Metaphors"), Ortega goes on to differentiate between the scientific metaphor
and the poetic metaphor:

Poetry is metaphor; science only uses it (II, p. 387)
. . . Science states the identity between the abstract
portions of two different objects, whereas the poetic
metaphor proposes the total identification of two concrete objects. . . . It utilizes the partial identity
of two objects to state, falsely, their total identity.
Such an exaggeration of identity beyond its truthful
limits conveys the poetic value. The poetic metaphor
starts to irradiate beauty precisely at the point where
its truthful dimension ceases to exist. But, vice-versa, there is no poetic metaphor without a discovery of
effective identities. Let us analyze any poetic metaphor and within its bosom we would clearly find a positive identity, that is to say a scientific one, between
the abstract element of two objects. Science utilizes
inversely the metaphoric device. It starts with the total identity between two concrete objects, knowing that
it is overall a false identity to end up with that portion of the identity that is truthful. Thus when a psychologist talks about the "bottom of the soul"(12) he
knows that the soul is not a barrel with a bottom to it,
but he wishes to suggest to us the existence of a psychic layer which plays within the structure of the soul
the same role that the bottom of a container would.
Contrary to poetry, the scientific metaphor goes from
more to less. First it affirms a total identity only to
deny it later on, leaving only a sediment of truth. (II,
pp. 392-3)

The dichotomy between reality and verisimilitude -- formerly intrinsic to the metaphoric device -- is now resolved along parallel lines, depending upon the realm within which the metaphor operates. Both the scientific and the poetic metaphors contain false and true elements: in the case of the former, we dismiss the false one; in the latter, the untruthfulness acquires an aesthetic charge. It becomes the poetic element. Notice, however, that Ortega does not dismiss the element of truth contained in the poetic metaphor, which always advances knowledge in the natural world. Although in La deshumanización del arte (The Dehumanization of Art) Ortega exalts the metaphor calling it "probably the most fertile power of mankind" (II, p. 373), he now sees in metaphor a desire to evade reality: "Metaphor circumvents an object by masking it with another one, and it would be completely meaningless unless we consider underneath the metaphor an instinct that leads man to avoid reality." (III, p. 373) Metaphor then becomes "a lyric weapon that turns against natural things wounding or altogether killing them." (III, p. 374)

Whereas only a year before (1924), Ortega saw in every poetic metaphor a means of advancing the knowledge of the natural world, the latter now perishes in the hands of its previous discoverer. Why this change? Perhaps Ortega is reacting against a basically antirealistic ludic element in much of the art and literature of his time. Let us not forget, however, that the most important movement of the avant-garde, surrealism, had from its very inception in 1924 a very serious aim, that of changing man and society. Despite the objectivity that Ortega claims in La deshumanización del arte (The Dehumanization of Art), we sense a dislike on his part for anything that is untrue and unreal, as well as for the metaphoric device leading to it. Ortega's disapproval of the process of evasion is further accentuated a year later in his essay "El amor en Stendhal" ("Love in Stendhal") (1926). In it he considers mysticism as a process of evasion, of annihilation: "Once the mind has been emptied of everything, the mystic insists in convincing us that he is in the presence of God, that he is filled with God."(13) However, according to Ortega, "Any theology communicates more about God, more notions about divinity than all the ecstasies of all the mystics put together. Because instead of approaching the mystic with skepticism, we must take his word at face value, we are forced to accept what he brings us from his transcendental immersions and later on we must assess if this is of any worth."(14) Ortega then concludes: "And the truth is that after accompanying him in his sublime journey, what he succeeds in communicating to us is of little importance. . . . I doubt that the enrichment of our ideas about divinity may reach us through the underground route of mysticism rather than through the luminous ways of discoursive thought. Theology, not ecstasy," he exclaims.(15)

It is curious that in his indictments against the unreal, the unnatural, Ortega's vehemency is more akin to the subjectivity of the lyrical world than to the objectivity of philosophical discourse.

Finally, it would be relevant to consider Ortega's Idea del teatro (Idea of Theater) (1946) where he discusses anew the nature of metaphor:

> Stage and actor are the universal metaphor incarnate, and this is the theater: the visible metaphor (VII, p. 459). . . (Upon uttering a metaphor such as a cheek is like a rose) it is necessary for the cheek to cease being a cheek and for the rose to cease being a rose. When the two realities are identified in a metaphor, they collide, they annul each other, they neutralize each other. . . . Metaphor becomes a mental atom bomb. The results of the annihilation of these two realities are precisely that new and marvelous . . . unreality. (VII, p. 460)

Likewise in the theater, when an actor interprets Hamlet, "it is necessary for the actor to cease being the real man as we know him and it is also necessary for Hamlet not be the real man that he was. It is necessary that neither is real and for both to derealize themselves continuously, to neutralize themselves, so that only the unreal as such survives, the imaginary. (VII, p. 461) . . . The role of the actor is thus to create a farce" (VII, p. 465). . . . However, "farce as such has existed since the beginning of mankind . . . and human life cannot be exclusively 'serious,' it has to become at times a farce and that is why theater exists (VII, p. 466). . . . Distraction, diversion is consubstantial with human life, it is not an accident or something to be dismissed or done without" (VII, p. 469) Nonetheless, Ortega now does not think that diversion is a frivolous activity, but rather reserves this adjective for the person who considers diversion unnecessary (VII, p. 469).

In Idea del teatro (Idea of Theater) Ortega enthrones metaphor once more as a necessary part of life. It is no accident that he alludes in this essay to the aforementioned metaphor of the cypress tree that is a flame (VII, p. 461) dating back to his perspectivistic phase. But, whereas then the integration took place in each instance or circumstance with a total fusion of the self with the reality of the cypress tree metaphorized into a flame, now we are faced with an "unreality" independent from and opposite to "reality." Furthermore, since the mid-twenties Ortega had been focusing the emphasis of his essays on life itself.(16) Thus emerged his concept of "vital reason," which in a way was a corollary of "perspectivism," for there was a necessity on the part of man to "know himself and his circumstances," and, as such, "vital reason" became "our guiding principle in our search for the system of being."(17) During the thirties Ortega had accentuated the notion that life is inherently problematic, having compared it in several instances to a shipwreck, as Ferrater has pointed out, adding in his interpretation of Orteguian thought that "insecurity is not everything in human existence. Together with man's perennial state of uneasiness, we must take into account his perpetual craving for security."(18) Thus, as a respite from this vital anguish and as a complement to it, Ortega warrants the wonderful world of unreality a deserving and necessary place in our lives. With this aesthetic principle, Ortega the writer and creator of metaphors and Ortega the philosopher and proponent of rational discourse are again reconciled.

NOTES

1. Juan Marichal, "La singularidad estilística de Ortega," La voluntad de estilo (Madrid: Revista de Occidente, 1971), pp. 217-18.

2. Angel Rosenblat, "Ortega y Gasset: Lengua y estilo," Homenaje a Ortega y Gasset (Caracas: Universidad Central de Venezuela, 1956), p. 70.

3. Ibid., p. 68.

4. I have translated from the original Spanish into English all the quotations from primary and secondary sources, with the exception of the study by José Ferrater Mora published in English.

5. Julián Marías, Ortega: Circunstancia y vocación (Madrid: Revista de Occidente, 1960), p. 352.

6. For a detailed analysis of some of the most important images and metaphorical clusters used by Ortega in his writings and for a classification of same, see Ricardo Senabre Sempere, Lengua y estilo de Ortega y Gasset in Acta Salmanticensia (Salamanca: Filosofía y Letras, 1964) Vol.

XVIII, No. 3, particularly chapters 4 and 5, entitled, respectively, "Metaphor" and "The World of Images," pp. 125–211.

7.   Ciriaco Moró Arroyo, El sistema de Ortega y Gasset (Madrid: Ediciones Alcalá, 1968), p. 387.

8.   Ibid.

9.   José Ortega y Gasset, Obras completas.   First edition (Madrid: Alianza Editorial, 1983) Vol. I, p. 451.
All the quotations from Ortega are taken from this edition, unless otherwise specified.   From now on, I shall indicate in parenthesis the volume and page numbers.

10.   Morón Arroyo, op. cit., p. 387.

11.   José Ferrater Mora, Ortega y Gasset (London: Bowes and Bowes, 1956), p. 27.

12.   I am aware that "depth of the soul" would be a more idiomatic translation, but then the metaphor that Ortega is attempting to explain would weaken considerably or disappear altogether.

13.   José Ortega y Gasset, Estudios sobre el amor, 15th edition (Madrid: Revista de Occidente, 1964), p. 118.   This essay alluded to is included in this volume.

14.   Ibid., p. 116.

15.   Ibid.

16.   Mora Ferrater, op. cit., p. 38.

17.   Ibid., p. 41.

18.   Ibid., p. 54.

15.
The Ludic Element in Orteguian Aesthetics

RAFAEL E. HERNÁNDEZ

José Ortega y Gasset develops his aesthetic theory after the First World War. At that time, European intellectual circles had started a comprehensive cultural analysis that challenged the values of the past that were held responsible for the catastrophe of war. Ortega, always striving to be abreast of what was taking place, also started his own cultural analysis. According to Enrique Lafuente Ferrari,

> The context in which Ortega's analysis took place was a concrete one: the year 1925. In which direction? In the direction showed by cubism and fauvism in painting, by the dada movement . . . and by the ultraísta poets. Surrealism . . . and other abstract directions were just starting around 1910 and were just being noticed by the general public at the time Ortega was writing.(1)

These movements advocated that the modern artist, unlike the classic one, does not pursue any truth; instead, he/she pursues those interpretations (whatever they might be) that allow the artist to obtain the most desired results. His/her art is the expression of values felt (whatever they might also be) in the process of creating the artistic work, which, in turn, is the embodiment of the values of the author who conceives, selects, enriches, and objectifies them into a synthesis. In turn, the modern spectator does not depend only on the artist's values in order to appreciate the work of art. Just as the work of art is only a version of the artist's values at a given moment, it is also just a starting point for many interpretations; it is a reality open to the emotional and imaginative world of the observer. This is the artistic context within which Ortega elaborates his aesthetic theory.

In this context, art is not a search for absolutes. For Ortega, then, art is "una cosa sin trascendencia"(2) (something without transcendence), which for him is not the same as something without importance. Precisely because art is "artificio . . . farsa."(3) (artifice . . . farce), it offers the individual the only alternative beyond everyday reality. For the artist, art is the great opportunity to conceive a "mundo virtual"(4) (a virtual world) structured as a totality. Unlike science, which dissects everything and makes each thing into a case, art is the synthesizing activity par excellence. Ortega says:

> Science breaks the unity of life in two worlds: nature and spirit. In the process of looking for totality, art has to fuse those two faces of life.(5)

The synthesis, the artistic form, is a new world, internally structured, "una totalidad ficticia"(6) (a fictitious totality) that the artist offers to the multiple points of view of the spectators. Each way of appreciating and interpreting this world constitutes an individual aesthetic perspective.

According to Ortega, the aesthetic activity cancels ordinary reality. He says that "el objeto artístico sólo es artístico en la medida en que no es real."(7) (The aesthetic object is artistic only to the point that is unreal.) That is, in order to exist as artistic object, its components and form do not have to reflect the conditions under which things exist normally. The artistic object exists on a level in which anything is possible. In this context, the classic principle of verisimilitude ceases to be valid, and any artistic canon is senseless beyond any individual perception, be it artist or spectator.

At the same time, as a synthesis the work of art is not only negation of a reality, but also affirmation of another. The aesthetic components that affirm it are the metaphors, visual, auditive, or in combination. According to Ortega, "The metaphor is probably the most productive tool that a person possesses. Its efficiency touches the boundaries of magic. . . ."(8) In a passage directed to the heart of his aesthetics, he affirms:

> The aesthetic object finds its elemental form in the metaphor. I would say that aesthetic object and metaphoric object are the same; that is to say, that the metaphor is the basic aesthetic element.(9)

In the process of canceling or destroying ordinary reality, the metaphor becomes an evoking image of what the artist supplants and, at the same time, an evoking image of other realities in the inner world of the observer. The innumerable interpretative possibilities that the metaphor offers make it the key element of Orteguian aesthetics. That is why as, Ortega states:

> Every image has . . . two faces. One face is an image of one thing or another; the other face is . . . something personal, mine . . . it is a moment of myself.(10)

The interpretative multiplicity of the metaphor and the validity of each individual aesthetic perspective relativize Orteguian aesthetics. Now art does not have to be a product of serene reflection; it does not have to be controlled or made step by step according to certain norms; it can be born spontaneously as a fruit of the artist's genius from whom no explanations or justifications are required. This new art, as Ortega calls it, does not distinguish between real and unreal, logic and illogic, useful and altruistic; it actualizes forms that defy gravity and harmony, and it does not have limitations, except those impossible to feel or imagine. The patterns of proportion and equilibrium that serve classic harmony give way now to the evoking force of the metaphor, no matter how disturbing or distorting it might be. The important thing now is not the serene pleasure but the repercussion of the image in the inner world of the observer; this, in turn, leaves the artist in total freedom to use innumerable sensory resources or visual effects, no matter how much they might contravene, for example, the old unities of time and space, symmetry, the equilibrium of the masses, and tonal, mimetic or musical gradations.

Since this aesthetics does not have pretentions to transcendence, both the artist and the spectator can dedicate themselves to aesthetic play. This ludic activity (from the Latin ludere: "to play") is equivalent to a process of metaphorical unrealization with no goal other than carrying out itself. Unlike classical aesthetics, which had to serve the principle of docere et delectare, that is, "teaching while pleasing," Ortega's aesthetics leaves both the artist and the spectator in complete freedom to ignore such

ulterior ends. Consequently, the new art does not have to serve any specific human need other than offering the artist and the spectator an opportunity to play. Ortega affirms:

> At this point it is important that we arrive at a clear
> understanding of the issue at hand. To feel happy or
> sorrowful about the human destinies that, perhaps, the
> work of art presents before us is something very differ-
> ent from true artistic enjoyment. Furthermore, that
> preoccupation with the human part of the artistic work
> is, on principle, incompatible with strict aesthetic en-
> joyment.(11)

Ortega explains this idea even more in a famous paragraph. He compares
human needs with a flower garden, and the artistic work with the sight that
the spectator gets upon focusing, not on the garden per se, but on the glass
panel of a window that overlooks the garden:

> The reader is asked to imagine that we are looking at
> the garden through the glass panel of a window. Our
> eyes will accommodate in such a way that the ray of
> vision would penetrate the glass without focusing on the
> glass itself but on the flowers and branches of the gar-
> den. Since our goal . . . is looking at the garden
> . . . we will not see the glass panel. . . . But now,
> let us make an effort; let us disregard the garden and
> focus on the glass panel. Then the garden disappears
> before our eyes, and we only see diffused masses of co-
> lor that seem to be attached to the glass panel. There-
> fore, seeing the garden and seeing the glass panel are
> two incompatible operations: one excludes the other,
> and both require different ocular accomodations.(12)

The representation of the garden with its plants and flowers was the classical and realistic art of the past. The vague chromatism that one perceives
upon focusing on the glass panel is the new art, which destroys the objective reality of the flower garden and supplants it with metaphoric play.
    Now, since the characteristic of the new art is not the reality that
lies behind the glass panel, then any reality, chromatic nor not, serene or
chaotic, can be the subject of the aesthetic vision. The important things
are the metaphors that appear on the glass panel. In this way Ortega gets
rid of the tranquil and harmonic themes of the classical locus amoenus and
advocates a risky, creative and open-ended artistic adventure. All of this
means that the artist and the spectator of the new art are totally free to
create and interpret the artistic forms. They do everything: they create,
develop and transform any artistic values. In this context, Professor
Harold Raley affirms:

> One cannot forget that Ortega's opus, including his es-
> says on art, was, to a certain extent, a gigantic effort
> to overcome the culture of the 19th century. Nineteenth
> century art had pretended to monopolize nothing less
> than reality as a whole and, therefore, got excessively
> loaded with transcendences. . . . That art wanted to
> speak sub specie aeternis to all people and forever.(13)
> Ortega turns back the aesthetic order of the 19th cen-
> tury. . . . The new art . . . strips itself of all
> transcendence. It is more a sport or farce and requires
> only a display of energy. . . . The human element is
> not its terminus ad quem or the finality of this art

since it does not pretend to achieve any final goal; the human element is its terminus a quo, that is, the source from which the artistic flow freely comes.(14)

Play, then, reigns supreme in Orteguian aesthetics. Beauty, as an ideal notion to be discovered, disappears as an objective and gives way to pure personal expression; pleasure, as a required indication of beauty, loses its aesthetic necessity; and the disproportionate and even the repugnant can have aesthetic value if they reflect the subjectivity of the artist. The aesthetic key becomes the ludic way in which the artist transforms his or her subjective reality, whatever it might be, in pure expression. Kandinsky, for many the precursor of abstract art, said at the beginning of this century: "The artist should be blind to the spectacle of the world in order to pay attention to his inner music."(15) In turn, Ortega, almost paraphrasing Kandinsky, adds: "The artist has become blind to the exterior world and has turned his eyes toward inner and subjective chambers."(16)

In sum, Orteguian aesthetics is innovative; it rebels against any normative intellectualism, against a timid aesthetics, and against the logic of classical rationalism and aesthetics that pretended to be the ideal. At the same time, the new art is a ludic reality; it does not owe anything to the old aesthetics, and it does not have any limits.

NOTES

1.   Enrique Lafuente Ferrari, "Cuarenta años de deshumanización del arte," Revista de Occidente III (Octubre, Noviembre, Diciembre, 1963), p. 314. This and all subsequent quotations have been translated from Spanish by the author.

2.   José Ortega y Gasset, "La deshumanización del arte," en Obras completas (Madrid: Revista de Occidente, 1962), vol. III, p. 383.

3.   Ortega y Gasset, "Elogio del 'Murciélago'," en Obras II, p. 326.

4.   Ortega y Gasset, "Adán en el paraíso," en Obras I, p. 484.

5.   Ibid., p. 485.

6.   Ibid., p. 484.

7.   Ortega y Gasset, "La deshumanización del arte," p. 358.

8.   Ibid., p. 372

9.   Ortega y Gasset, "Ensayo de estética a manera de prólogo," en Obras VI, p. 257.

10.   Ibid., p. 260.

11.   Ortega y Gasset, "La deshumanización del arte," p. 357.

12.   Ibid., pp. 357-358.

13.   Harold C. Raley, "La deshumanización del arte: Aclaraciones sobre una posible contradicción en Ortega," Revista de Estudios Hispánicos, VII (Enero, 1973), p. 147.

14   Ibid., p. 153.

15.   Lafuente Ferrari, "Cuarenta años de deshumanización del arte," p. 317.

16.   *Ibid*.

16.
Ortega's Phenomenology of Language Versus Linguistic Philosophy

WILLIAM T. LAWHEAD

Twentieth-century philosophy is marked by the overwhelming attention that it has given to language and meaning. Concern with these themes is usually associated with the linguistic philosophies of the leading Anglo-American philosophers of this century. However, not enough attention has been paid to the contributions to these topics that have come from outside the borders of England and America. Accordingly, in this paper, I would like to present a few remarks on the outlines of a philosophy of language that José Ortega y Gasset sketched out for us.

I consider Ortega's position to be a "phenomenology of language" even though he did not identify himself with this movement. However, he was in intellectual dialogue with philosophers such as Husserl, Scheler, and Heidegger, and many of his essays, such as "A Few Drops of Phenomenology," show his affinities with the movement.(1) Furthermore, his position bears striking parallels with those of "card-carrying" phenomenologists such as Maurice Merleau-Ponty. Ortega was not in a position to directly address the linguistic philosophies that began gaining prominence toward the end of his life. Therefore, I have chosen to juxtapose his phenomenology of language with the perspective of the linguistic-analytic movement in philosophy.

Two of the most influential figures in early twentieth-century philosophy were Bertrand Russell and Ludwig Wittgenstein. Though there are differences between their philosophies, they held in common the belief that language could be adequately understood as a logical system of propositions. However, it was Wittgenstein who later came to discover the inadequacies of his own position for reasons similar to those found in Ortega's critique of the linguistic sciences. In his later work, Wittgenstein confessed that the "crystalline purity of logic" was a requirement he imposed upon his subject rather than a result of his investigation.(2) Hence, he proposed a new form of investigation that would treat language not as a logical system but that would bring into prominence the fact that "the speaking of language is part of an activity, or of a form of life."(3)

Similarly, Ortega's solution is to call for "a linguistics that should have the courage to study language in its integral reality, as it is when it is actual living discourse, and not as a mere fragment amputated from its complete configuration."(4) Hence, he proposes that we study language "not as an accomplished fact, as a thing made and finished, but in the process of being made . . . in the very roots that engender it."(5) One way of doing this, of course, would be through a historical study, going back to the mist-shrouded dawn of human linguistic development. Ortega proposes instead what I will call "phenomenological archaeology." This is an inquiry into the origins of language, not through a historical study, but by way of uncovering the various strata of language as we find it until we get to the most fundamental level. If it is true, as Ortega claims, that "language is always being made and unmade," then this process will be fruitful in illuminating the origins of language.(6)

Ortega's phenomenology invites us to explore the regions of language below the level where it appears as an abstract system. Hence, a more fundamental level is that one which he labels as "speaking." Speaking is the use of words in concrete contexts by flesh and blood human beings. As Ortega puts it, "The reality 'word' is inseparable from the person who says it, from the person to whom it is said, and from the situation in which this takes place."(7) Language as a system is abstracted from and derives whatever reality it has from the phenomenon of speaking. Here, words are more than lexical tokens.   Instead, they function as gestures.   They are the linguistic embodiment of actions, intentions, thoughts, and feelings.   Ortega says that "to speak is to gesticulate,"(8) and in one bold phrase sweeps aside all the centuries-old Cartesian dualism between our mental life and our bodily life.   To speak is to be an embodied being immersed within my circumstances.

In a brief exercise in linguistic analysis paralleling the project of the Wittgensteinians, Ortega discusses the utterance "my love."(9) By itself, in the abstract, it is in fact merely a sound, subject to phonemic analysis.   However, when it is said concretely by a mother to her child or by a specific man to a woman, it becomes a verbal action.   In different circumstances it will carry or (perhaps create) different though related meanings.(10)

Ortega goes on to point out, however, that linguistic activity does not stand alone but is integrated with all the other aspects of human life.   It is woven into that total set of circumstances that Wittgenstein called our "form of life."(11) Ortega says that a word, when spoken, "enters into sudden coalescence with the beings and things around it which are not verbal."(12)

With each child who struggles to become a verbal organism, language is recreated and born anew.   However, when we deal with any human phenomenon, there are never any absolute beginnings.   Though the child must struggle to reenact the birth of language for himself, he is still born into a world that is already dissected by words.   From the very first, the language of our society is a framework that filters and molds the mute and fluid content of our experience.   For this reason, Ortega refers to language as a "paradigmatic example of the social."(13)   Hence, speaking always arises out of the context of that-which-is-spoken.   Through our speaking we shape language, but our language, in turn, also shapes us.   This latter movement Ortega refers to disparagingly as "linguistic coercion."(14)   Through the language of our culture we are socialized, the collectivity takes up residence in us, and we become a functioning member of a linguistic community. Though this process is inveitable and, in fact, necessary, Ortega presents it with a tone of regret for it can diminish our freedom.   Though we may be able to escape a particular society, we can never fully escape our mother tongue.(15)   The problem with this process is that a language provides us with a fertile but never adequate "index of realities."(16)   It consists of more than simply words and meanings but also suggests ways of approaching and appropriating the world.   Language guides our perceptions into preestablished channels and provides us with unquestioned interpretations of the world.

Once again, Ortega's philosophy speaks to our contemporary philosophical situation.   In the past three to four decades, we have seen the rise of a movement known as "ordinary language philosophy."   It was brought to birth by the later writings and insights of Ludwig Wittgenstein, some of which we have discussed.   While he rejected his earlier attempts to make language conform to the logician's model of an ideal language, in his later period he established a new norm for language.   This norm was drawn from the paradigms of functioning speech found in ordinary language.   However, this sort of approach inaugurated a linguistic conservativism within philosophy.   All innovative ways of speaking became immediately suspect, if not ruled out of court a priori. Philosophy's role was demoted to that of a housemaid, organizing and tidying up language as it was spoken. This denied to philosophers their historic role of being critics of their culture and heralds of new visions.

Though he would agree with Wittgenstein's emphasis on the concrete speaker and the assertion that linguistic activity must be understood within the larger context of our human "form of life," Ortega would take issue with the priority that Wittgenstein gives to ordinary language. Hence, Ortega (with Wittgenstein) rejected the logician's norms as an adequate model to understand language. However, he also rejected the sort of notion we find in Wittgenstein that the accumulated linguistic practice of a community should function as a rigid norm for the speaking subject.

Though he did not directly encounter it, Ortega would find three problems in the highly influential ordinary language of philosophy. First, he denies that ordinary language is some sort of neutral instrument in terms of which philosophical speech is a deviant, unjustified practice. Though words present the world to us, they present it to us as already interpreted. Hence, language can not only reveal reality, it can distort it. As Ortega puts it, "Language is in itself theory -- perhaps theory that is always archaic, mummified, in some cases completely outdated."(17) If our ordinary expressions reflect the ways in which our words are given meaning by their use in our life together, they also reflect all the confusions, stresses, strains, impurities, and changes in human life and culture. Through speaking we may hope to resolve these conflicts (as did Socrates), but in speech as it is given, we cannot expect to find the solution ready-made.

Second, (and this is implicit in the first criticism), ordinary language lacks vitality. Ortega refers to it as a "gigantic repertory of worn-out words."(18) He uses his most disparaging metaphors to refer to the usages and words of our ordinary linguistic commerce. For example, he refers to it as "drained of meaning," "mineralized," "soulless."(19) Again, he says that it is "antiquated," "unintelligible,"(20) "fossilized,"(21) and a collection of "mere, mechanical counters."(22) It is clear that at this point, Ortega's philosophy of language feeds into his social philosophy and his contempt for the collectivity. The established meanings and ways of speaking that operate in the linguistic realm, have a stifling effect on what people think and thus narrow the horizons of the culture's intellectual vision.(23) The taken-for-granted ways of speaking in a culture are the antithesis of the examined life and of the cultural renewal Ortega sought for in his native land.

His third criticism is that ordinary language is too impersonal. To be sure, it is not as impersonal as language viewed strictly as a logical system. Nevertheless, it imposes upon the individual the anonymous and confining perspectives of the established social order. Ortega says of a usage (and this would include a linguistic usage) that is has a "strange power" in that it "does not live or exist except in individuals and by virtue of individuals, and that nevertheless hangs over them like a mechanical, impersonal power, like a physical reality that manipulates them, moves them this way and that as if they were inert bodies."(24)

Though we are all subject to the "linguistic coercion" of ordinary language, it is possible for the creative speaker, the person with vision, to take command over his or her language and use it as a wedge to open up new horizons of meaning. This possibility is the source of our freedom. Unfortunately, it is only those rare individuals in an age who are aware of their freedom and are able to employ it effectively. Most people are condemned to confirm Wittgenstein's thesis that "The limits of my language mean the limits of my world."(25) It is, however, the act of creative speaking that enables language to be born anew and that has been ignored in the linguistic and philosophical approaches that Ortega's philosophy incisively corrects.

Wittgenstein's analysis stops at the level of what Ortega calls "speaking," that is, the established linguistic behavior of a community.   For Wittgenstein, the final justification for any usage was to say that, "This is simply what I do."(26)   However, it is at this point that Ortega's phenomenological archaeology takes us one further stratum deeper.   Below "speaking" as a process of social intercourse is the activity of "saying." Ortega says that saying is "the desire to express, to manifest, to declare."(27)   Saying is an existential act born out of that deeply human need to express.   Literally, this means to "ex-press, to press outwards." In other words, through capturing our experience in words, we insert ourselves within the world.   We appropriate our world through words and give it human value and meaning.   Also, through the process of saying we get a hold of ourselves and give our experience, feelings, values, and thoughts a verbal body.   We speak not only to present our innermost being to others but also to present it to ourselves as well.

In Ortega's analysis, the origins of language are to be found in this fundamental activity of saying.   Thus, he criticizes what he appropriately calls "zoological utilitarianism."(28)   This is the theory of language that presents it as a sophisticated form of animal communication.   However, human speaking is more than simply the sending and receiving of useful signals to accomplish the practical needs of social communication concerning the immediate environment.   Instead, Ortega is among those who argue that speaking grows out of saying and represents a human being's "incoercible need to make clear to the other what was secretly seething in its own 'inwardness.'"(29)

Ortega correctly points out that speaking is surrounded by two kinds of silence, each of which affects the way in which language functions.   First, there is a kind of silence that is below language.   This consists of "all that goes without saying."(30)   If everything had to be spoken to be understood, we could never carry on a conversation.   Hence, speaking is always preceded by, and takes place against, a shared background of common understanding.   Unfortunately, this common background, that which is so obvious it does not need to be spoken, often consists of cultural prejudices.   Too often what is not spoken, and therefore not critically examined, are the tacit values and beliefs that most desperately need scrutiny.

A second form of silence consists of that which is above language. Though first and foremost a man of words, Ortega had a healthy respect for the limitations of language.   It is too often assumed that what is commonly spoken is an adequate representation of what is experienced.   Hence, the linguistic coercion Ortega has referred to causes us to pour our experiences into verbal categories that may not fit them.   For this reason, he mentions the need to "determine whether this instrument invented for saying is adequate and in what measure it is or is not so."(31)   Though words can never perfectly appropriate their object, it is the task of the poet and the philosopher to push them to their limits and to embark upon raids into the terrain of silence to win over for language whatever wealth it can capture.

There is a dialectical process at work here.   People have new things to say and, hence, discover new ways of speaking.   If a happy combination of a fruitful insight and a creative use of words has occurred, a new way of seeing and speaking the world may find its place within the cultural horizon and the originally innovative expression may eventually become a standard usage.(32)

However, there is a problem here as to how this can occur.   Ortega says that for the individual, conventional speech is like a "series of phonograph records that he plays in accordance with what he wants to say."(33)   But what if the available "phonograph records" do not contain the message that he wants to speak?   In other words, what if the language and the cultural modes of expression are impoverished?   What if there is no concept and no words in a society's inventory that will adequately capture the individual's insights?   This poses a dilemma for the creative speaker who must, in the words of philologist Owen Barfield, "either mean what was meant before or talk nonsense!"(34)   Ortega expresses this problem as a tension between "personal expression and collective cliche" or between "individual 'saying' and 'what people say.'"(35)

Ortega has answered this question in his 1924 essay, "Las dos grandes metáforas" ("The Two Great Metaphors").(36)   Through the skillful use of metaphor, those truths that have not yet been spoken can be brought to light and verbally appropriated.   The conceptual and linguistic categories of a culture may not be able to present a radically new insight.   However, the metaphor is a device for bending and stretching the given categories so as to encompass and present that which is genuinely original.

Ortega is uninhibited in his discussion of the importance of metaphorical language.   He says that the metaphor is "an indispensable mental tool"(37) and that it is "an essential means of intellection."(38)   Furthermore, he compares the role of metaphor to that of scientific exploration in its function of discovering truth and obtaining knowledge of reality.(39)

Conventional speech follows well-worn paths, whereas what an individual seeks to express may lie between these habitual routes or, perhaps, in a field which has not yet been transversed by speech at all.   However, new ideas can't come naked into the world, but must be "clothed" with available words.   For this reason, Ortega says that through the metaphorical aspect of language, "the term acquires the new meaning through and by means of the old one, without abandoning it."(40)

The domain of established linguistic usages, or what Ortega calls "speaking," is freighted with acquired conventions and dominated by traditional perspectives.   It seduces us into accepting the taken-for-granted views of the world.   However, through the use of metaphor a writer can engage in what Ortega calls "saying" and give verbal and communal expression to his private vision and in that way break through the sediment of a culture.

The linguistic conservatives who follow Wittgenstein are correct in claiming that language has its life in the concrete speaking of a linguistic community.   They are wrong, however, in making established linguistic usages some sort of inviolable norm.   As Ortega has suggested, creative speech need not result in linguistic anarchy or a verbal solipsism.   In fact, to refuse to accredit novel uses of language would be to freeze conception and perception, requiring us to deal with a changing world and developing experience in ways that are no longer adequate.

Allow me now to briefly summarize the philosophical significance of Ortega's position.   First, he fully realizes the role of language and the importance of understanding it if we are to carry out the Socratic task of self-examination.   Moreover, he understands both the dangers and the riches that given language presents to a culture.   Here he is very contemporary, and his insights have been underscored by work in Anglo-American philosophy and sociology in the last few decades.

Second, Ortega's approach avoided some of the failings of linguistic philosophy.   His phenomenological leanings made him appropriately critical of the abstract norms imposed upon language by the logician-philosophers of this century.   He also provided the rudiments of a critique of the Wittgensteinian philosophy, a philosophy that almost became an unquestioned orthodoxy in some philosophical quarters in the past few decades.   Though his philosophy of language is admittedly sketchy and was not his primary concern, his position does present a model of faithfulness to the subject matter under consideration.

Third, though we have not had the opportunity to discuss this point, Ortega's philosophy of language provides an admirable case study of consistency.   When a philosopher writes about language, he or she is, of course, using language.   Thus, the philosophical position serves as its own judge.   Too often, as Wittgenstein found out in his early work in the Tractatus, the claims a philosopher has made about language destroy any possible theoretical foundation for making those very claims.   I believe that a careful study of Ortega's use of language, particularly of his own use of philosophical metaphors, would show that all that he has said about the nature of language is confirmed by his own use of language. I would not go so far as to say that "the medium is the message," but certainly Ortega's medium is consistent with his message.(41) Surprisingly, philosophers too often have failed to achieve this consistency. Furthermore, Ortega's outworking of his philosophical mission illustrates how an intellectual can achieve the delicate balance of going beyond the given horizons of one's culture while still maintaining communication with it. He has shown us how that which is new can be spoken through, and by means of, that which is old.

NOTES

1.   José Ortega y Gasset, The Dehumanization of Art and Notes on the Novel, trans. Helene Weyl (Princeton, N.J.:   Princeton University Press, 1948), Chapter III.

2.   Ludwig Wittgenstein, Philosophical Investigations, trans. G. E. M. Ascombe (New York: Macmillan, 1953), No. 107.

3.   Ibid., 23.

4.   José Ortega y Gasset, Man and People, trans. Willard R. Trask (New York: W. W. Norton, 1963), p. 241.

5.   Ibid., p. 242.

6.   Ibid., p. 243.

7.   Ibid., p. 235.

8.   Ibid., p. 253.

9.   Ibid., p. 235.

10.   Ibid., p. 236.

11.   Wittgenstein, No. 23.

12.   Ortega y Gasset, Man and People, p. 239.

13.   Ibid., p. 252.

14.   Ibid., p. 251.

15.   Ibid.

16.   Ibid., p. 181.

17.   Ibid.

18.   Ibid., p. 190.

19.   Ibid., p. 198.

20.   Ibid., p. 211.

21.   Ibid., p. 212.

22.   Ibid., p. 262.

23.   Ibid., p. 90–91, 262–63.

24.   Ibid., p. 209.

25.   Ludwig Wittgenstein, Tractatus Logico-Philosophicus, trans. D. F. Pears and B. F. McGuinness (London: Routledge and Kegan Paul, 1961), No. 5.6.

26.   Wittgenstein, Philosophical Investigations, 217.

27.   Ortega y Gasset, Man and People, p. 243.

28.   Ibid., p. 250.

29.   Ibid.

30.   Ibid., p. 244, 246.

31.   Ibid., p. 245.

32.   Ibid., p. 252.

33.   Ibid., p. 258.

34.   Owen Barfield, "Poetic Diction and Legal Fiction," in The Importance of Language, ed. Max Black (Englewood Cliffs, N.J.:   Prentice-Hall, 1962), p. 67.

35.   Ortega y Gasset, Man and People, p. 252.

36.   José Ortega y Gasset, "Las dos grandes metáforas," in Obras completas, 6th ed. (Madrid: Revista de Occidente, 1963), vol II, pp. 387–400.

37.   Quoted from Julián Marías, José Ortega y Gasset: Circumstance and Vocation, trans. Frances M. López-Morillas (Norman, Oklahoma: University of Oklahoma Press, 1970), p. 271.

38.   Ibid., p. 274.

39.   Ibid.

40.   Ibid., p. 273.

41.   See Nelson R. Orringer, "Ortega y Gasset's Sportive Theories of Communication," Modern Language Notes 88 (1973):   207–34.

17.
Between Antitheses: Subject and Object in the Landscape Essays of Ortega y Gasset

R. LANE KAUFFMANN

Juan Marichal has argued that Spanish intellectual history during the century prior to the Spanish Civil War was virtually tantamount to the conflict between society and the individual. Four successive generations of intellectuals, from Larra to Ortega y Gasset, were concerned exclusively, claims Marichal, with "delimiting the domain of the self."(1) There is some truth in this claim, but it overlooks the preoccupation with external nature, and with the Spanish landscape in particular, which marked the writings of the last two generations on Marichal's list -- the generations of Unamuno and Ortega. Nor was the landscape a mere topos for the writers of their time. In the hands of Unamuno, Azorín, and Ortega, the landscape essay became a minor genre deserving a chapter of its own in modern Spanish intellectual history. Concentrating here on Ortega's landscape writings, I will argue that they afford a glimpse into the stylistic and ideological mainsprings of his thought.

If, as the German critic Theodor W. Adorno maintained, the proper theme of the essay is the relationship between nature and culture,(2) the landscape essay is that species of the genre in which nature is constantly being transformed rhetorically into culture, in which an encounter with a natural scene engenders at once a cultural interpretation of that scene. Despite its referential aspect, the landscape essay is not primarily a mimetic genre, for what concerns it is not nature as an immediate datum or thing-in-itself, but rather a mediated experience of nature, a particular relation between subject and object, viewer and scene. "I am myself and my circumstances," Ortega wrote, and he might have added: in the process of representing my circumstances, I will inevitably represent myself as well. The central issue is of course the relation between these two poles of experience, as projected in the essay. Ortega's landscape writings fetishize neither the subject nor the object, but focus instead on their cognitive interaction. This was consistent with his perspectivism, which always brought into play not only the object but also the angle of vision, or point of view -- not just the thing perceived but the way in which it was perceived. This foregrounding of the cognitive process was Ortega's most original contribution to the landscape essay.

All essays, to be sure, embody cognitive acts, and the best essays provoke them in the reader as well. In the view of philosopher Eduardo Nicol, the chief cognitive function of the essay form is to illuminate a particular phenomenon by relating it to the general -- to ideas and concepts. Nicol characterizes the essay as a mixed genre that moves between image and concept, thereby condemned to remain "almost literature and almost philosophy."(3) If the essay thus falls short of systematic philosophy, which deals in universals, the landscape essay is doubtly stigmatized, for it is a minor form of an already marginal genre. Whereas systematic philosophy bans particularity in discourse, the landscape essay thematizes its context of discourse, thereby making contingency -- its "here and now" quality -- into a rule of the genre. By respecting the specific contours of its objects, as well as the contexts in which they appear, the landscape essay is truer to lived experience than are systems, which purge all traces of spontaneity.(4) We shall return to this opposition at the end of the present essay.

Genres do not arise in a vacuum; they emerge from the attempt to fashion formal solutions to ideological problems. The Spanish landscape essay, first appearing as a recognizable form in the writings of the "Generation of '98," was an aesthetic response to the problems confronting Spain around the turn of the century. Ortega's most important precursors in this genre were Azorín and Unamuno. For them, as for most of their contemporaries, the Spanish landscape held conflicting associations. On the one hand, primarily in their early essays, they saw in the Spanish landscape -- particularly in the barren Castilian countryside -- a reminder of Spain's agricultural and industrial backwardness vis-a-vis northern Europe since the seventeenth century. This essentially positivistic attitude toward the land owed much to the reformist programs of Francisco Giner de los Ríos and other members of the "Institución Libre de Enseñanza."(5)   It was reinforced by determinist ideas then in vogue, notably those of Hyppolite Taine, whose popular formula, "race, moment, milieu," stressed the impact of ethnic and environmental forces on culture.(6)   On the other hand, as Azorín and Unamuno retreated from their early positivism -- the former into quietist aestheticism, the latter into increasing subjectivism -- they adopted a more nostalgic and contemplative attitude toward nature. Now they saw the Castilian landscape as a positive symbol of Spain's national and cultural identity -- in short, of her legitimate differences from the rest of Europe. Although the positivistic and the contemplative attitudes overlap to some extent in the transitional writings of Azorín and Unamuno -- most notably in the latter's pivotal work, En torno al casticismo (On Spanish Traditionalism; 1895) -- the contemplative stance prevails in the writings of both authors after 1900.(7)   Roughly sketched, this was the ideological setting for Ortega's landscape essays.

Between 1906 and 1929, Ortega produced a dozen-and-a-half essays either devoted entirely to, or containing significant passages on, landscape. Properly speaking, only six of these writings make a genuine contribution to the landscape essay as a literary form, for in them the landscape figures at once as occasion, theme, and structural device: "Pedagogía del paisaje" ("Pegagogy of the Landscape;" 1906), Meditaciones del Quijote (Meditations on Quixote; 1914), "De Madrid a Asturias o los dos paisajes" ("From Madrid to Asturias, or Contrasting Landscapes;" 1915), "Azorín: primores de lo vulgar" (The Delights of the Commonplace;" 1917), "Temas de viaje" ("Travel Themes;" 1922), and "Notas del vago estío" ("Notes from a Vagabond Summer;" 1925).(8)   All six essays employ the device of a first-person narrator who relates his experiences and impressions while traversing a particular Spanish region.   It is significant that ten out of eighteen of Ortega's writings on landscape, and all but one of the most important six, fall within the period 1914-1925.   Referred to by José Gaos as Ortega's "early mature period," it was the height of his digressive, essayistic style of thought.(9)   This period also saw the development of his crucial concept of perspective, the implications of which were explored in his landscape essays.

Behind those essays were both patriotic and philosophical motives. From Francisco Giner de los Ríos and Joaquín Costa, Ortega had inherited the desire to "regenerate" Spain by reappropriating her most authentic values, beginning with a revalorization of the land itself, as both the material and symbolic ground of national life.   Ortega's version of this project is expressed most clearly in his Meditaciones del Quijote, specifically in the long prologue and the "Meditación preliminar" ("Preliminary Meditation"). There, he urged Spaniards to cultivate a reverence for the particulars of their surroundings. "Man achieves his full potential only when he becomes fully conscious of his circumstances. Through them he communes with the universe. . . . I am myself and my circumstances, and unless I redeem them, I cannot redeem myself" (I, pp. 318-22).

But this redemption of Spanish circumstances entailed a reform of perception. The Spaniard's approach to reality was visceral, relying on immediate sensation alone, Ortega argued. One needed to temper the chaos of sensory experience by the discipline of intellect, to integrate, as he put it, "Mediterranean sensualism" and "Germanic conceptualism" (I, pp. 356-57). Ortega thus offered his readers "new ways of looking at things," and invited them to essay these new perspectives for themselves. This reliance on vision as a metaphor of cognition was hardly accidental. Ortega thought naturally in images, and this eidetic bent doubtless predisposed him to make the landscape a leitmotif in his essays. Even in his serious philosophical works, he turned instinctively to landscape analogies to illustrate an epistemological point or a mode of cognition.(10) And is not the entire "Meditación preliminar" an ars speculandi, a disquisition on the art of visual thinking? Elsewhere in that work, Ortega's changing metaphors, described his project as one of "extracting the logos from things which are prelogical, and do not yet have meaning" (I, p. 321) -- producing, in other words, cultural interpretations of natural phenomena. What better laboratory for this operation than the Spanish landscape itself, replete, as we know, with latent ideological associations, waiting to be "extracted"? And if the landscape was the privileged testing-ground for Ortega's "experiments toward a new Spain" (I, p. 328), the landscape essay was the form in which the experiments would be conducted.

The great ideological question raised in those essays -- and the terms of the question were inevitably those of Taine -- was the nature of the influence of Spain's geography upon the Spanish history and character. Could the problems of modern Spain be traced to its arid land and climate, as they fatefully molded the Spanish character? In Ortega's first landscape essay, "Pedagogía del paisaje" (1906), the narrator looks out over the Guadarrama mountain range and muses: "Tell me which landscape you live in, and I will tell you who you are. . . . Consider this wretched countryside. . . . Thus, we of Madrid are among the most sullen and hostile beings on earth" (I, pp. 55-56).

One finds many echoes of this geographical determinism in Ortega's subsequent work. But his later essays reveal the writer's growing conviction that the people of a country or region in a sense choose or interact with their surroundings, rather than being strictly determined by them. In his 1922 essay, "Temas de viaje," Ortega rejects the geographical theory of Spanish history as an intellectual bromide. Geography is not the cause of national character, he argues paradoxically, but the symptom and symbol of that character. "Each people (raza) carries in its primordial soul an ideal landscape which it strives to recreate within the geographical framework of its surroundings. Castile is so terribly arid because Castilian man is arid. We have accepted the barren environment because of its affinity with the inner steppe of our soul" (II, pp. 373).(11) Here, Ortega exchanges geographical for ethnic determinism, thus shifting his emphasis from one term of Taine's formula to another (from milieu to race).

But Ortega's dialectical instincts told him that neither kind of determinism was strictly tenable; there had to be a middle way between the two extremes. The concept of perspective would furnish the necessary mediation. Central to his philosophical work of the period, it embodied the conflict between an objective or "rationalist" epistemology and a subjective or "relativist" one. How can truth be permanent and objective, he asked, when it can only be experienced from the ephemeral standpoint of particular human subjects (III, p. 157)? In a 1914 essay on aesthetics, moreover, he doubted whether it was possible to comprehend a point of view other than one's own.(12) This raised the question of perceptual determinism: Is each human subject a prisoner of his point of view, as it is conditioned by the accidents of time and place?

In what is arguably his finest landscape essay, "De Madrid a Asturias o los dos paisajes," Ortega offers at once a dramatic illustration and a metaphorical answer to this question. He begins by showing that the topography of one's native region strongly conditions the way one perceives reality.(13) A journey from Castile to Asturias occasions a comparison of the two regions and of the distinct worldviews to which they give rise. The eye trained by the stark Castilian mesa, where "to live is to hurl oneself forward," finds it difficult to adjust to the topography of Asturias, "where both the landscape and the hearts of its inhabitants are embroidered with subtle hues and transitions." So it is all the more remarkable when the traveler learns, in the course of his journey, to suspend his rude Castilian perspective, allowing it to be transformed by the gentler Asturian landscape. "Our eyes have learned to observe tactfully. . . .   They have stopped being Castilian, which is to say, ascetic and bellicose, . . . hostile, or indifferent to things." Ortega calls the capacity to transcend one's narrow perspective "the most delicate human faculty," and exhorts Castilians to respect the other regions and viewpoints of Spain (II, pp. 253-60). His own essay is a cogent example of such pluralism, for it provides an object lesson in comparative culture while demonstrating a way of overcoming the limits of one's regional perspective.

Nor is it the sole example. "Temas de viaje" and "Notas del vago estío" are similar in strategy and structure to the essay just described. In each of these travel essays, the visual contrast between two regions engenders in the traveler a deeper reflection upon the antithetical cultures which they represent -- France and Spain in the first case, urban and rural Spain in the second. While all three essays successfully carry out the "new ways of looking at things" proposed in Meditaciones del Quijote, it is well to recall that this ostensibly visual enterprise is primarily a rhetorical accomplishment. The first-person narration gives a sense of immediacy to these travel essays. Self-references convey the pleasure and enthusiasm of the essayist as he sets about exploring the landscape.(14) The constant interplay between sensuous detail and abstract argument effects the integration of sensation and intellect recommended in Ortega's "Meditación preliminar." The image of the traveler journeying through the countryside lends plastic dimension to the appropriation of circumstances called for in Ortega's earlier program. Such devices -- the first-person narration, the playful digressions, the juxtaposition of abstract and concrete -- combine to produce the dynamic mode of cognition apparent in these writings. The journey becomes in them a metaphor for a way of discovering reality. To admit that these essays are rhetorical tours de force rather than rigorous philosophical argument, that they offer aesthetic solutions to ideological problems, does not diminish them. Metaphorical resolutions can have practical consequences. Ortega's best landscape essays suggest a cognitive model for transcending geographically induced ethnocentrism. As for their place in Ortega's work, they are fertile experiments in perspectivism, leading up to the philosophical position of "ratiovitalism," which he would define in his 1923 work El tema de nuestro tiempo (The Modern Theme; III, pp.197-203).

Yet the quality of spontaneous subjectivity one finds in Ortega's essays has caused some critics to dispute the philosophical merits of his essayism. Eduardo Nicol claims that the personalism of Ortega's style betrayed his philosophical intentions, and led to a "confusion of genres" between philosophy and the essay. In Nicol's view, both Unamuno and Ortega were guilty of making the self, instead of truth, the protagonist of their philosophies. By constantly highlighting the self and its surroundings, Ortega left the impression, reinforced by his doctrine of perspectivism, that truth was always relative to the individual perceiving subject, and that philosophy was equivalent to self-expression. "The alternative is clear: either one serves the self, or one serves philosophy." Calling personalism the main problem of Hispanic philosophy, Nicol argues that the rightful mission of that philosophy is "to raise itself to the level of universality proper to science."(15)

While Nicol's critique of personalism is a powerful one, it disregards how consciously Ortega employed the rhetoric of subjectivity in his writings. It would be instructive to compare the landscape essays of Azorín, Unamuno, and Ortega in this regard. One would find in each a distinct cognitive style based on a discrete ratio of subject to object. Whereas Azorín depicts the landscape as a static scene received passively by the viewer, Unamuno makes it a pretext for introspection and self-affirmation. Both Unamuno and Ortega call attention to the cognitive process through frequent allusions to the self and the circumstances of discourse. But in Ortega, the perceiving subject neither dominates the scene, as in Unamuno, nor disappears from it, as in Azorín. Rather, it interacts with the scene, as we have observed in the essay, "De Madrid a Asturias o los dos paisajes."

For Ortega, the device of self-reference is motivated both by methodological and by rhetorical considerations. Methodologically, self-reference serves to ground perspective, situating the essayist in relation to the scene. Just as, in Ortega's epistemology, each individual point of view is "an irreplaceable instrument for the conquest of truth" (III, p. 200), so, in his landscape essays, the perspective of the essayist is an essential aspect of the cognitive venture. By keeping the viewer in the picture, as it were, Ortega draws our attention not only to the object seen but also to his way of seeing it. Rhetorically, deictic expressions -- especially first-person pronouns -- are used by Ortega to solicit the reader's empathy and participation, as when he invites the reader of Meditaciones del Quijote to essay his "new ways of looking at things." This accounts for the "rallying tone" that Juan Marichal accurately perceives throughout Ortega's writings.(16) Similar motives led him to decry Unamuno's strident egocentrism, while extolling Azorín's self-effacing style.(17) It should be recalled, finally, that Ortega's landscape essays stem from his attempt to inculcate in his countrymen a heightened respect for the empirical qualities of the world around them. If personalism was as common in Spanish readers as many claim it was in Spanish writers of the time, then it is small wonder that Ortega chose to communicate through the essay rather than through the impersonal system. Given a public inveterately personalistic, it would have been bad rhetorical strategy to adopt a discursive form that precluded subjectivity.

To say this is to defend Ortega's occasional essays not only against Nicol and other critics, but also against the opinion that Ortega himself later came to hold. From the late 1920s on, his work reveals an increasing will-to-system, and a concomitant dissatisfaction with the essay as a vehicle for his philosophical ideas.(18) The reproach that systems make implicitly to the essay is best expressed by Nicol's remark that "philosophy, at its highest, lacks local color."(19) Aiming at universality, systematic philosophers try to eliminate what Hegel once termed "the stain of the particular." Accordingly, they shun all reference to the writing subject and the circumstances of discourse. If by philosophy one means the formulation of propositions whose truth is independent of the philosopher and his milieu, then Ortega's landscape essays are admittedly not philosophy. Whether or not this be the proper criterion for systematic philosophy, it is decidedly not the right one for evaluating the landscape essay, in which, by definition, the context of discourse and the "local color" of experience are of the essence. As Ortega suggested in Meditaciones del Quijote, the project of his essays was to redeem precisely those aspects of sensuous reality that are ignored by systems in their rush to generalization.

Ultimately, the landscape essays themselves are the most compelling justification of that project. Their legacy is not a set of theses on the Spanish land or people; it is rather the model of cognitive praxis which they embody. As we have noted, albeit elliptically, these essays display an empathetic mode of cognition that proceeds by comparing and integrating perspectives. Insofar as they instill in the reader a desire and a method for the interpretation of external reality, it may be said that they redeem both the essayist and his circumstances.

NOTES

1.   Juan Marichal, "Persona y sociedad en la España moderna (1837–1936)," in El nuevo pensamiento político español (México: Finisterre, 1966), p. 103. Throughout this chapter, translations from the Spanish are mine.

2.   Theodor W. Adorno, "Der Essay als Form," in Noten zur Literatur (Frankfurt am Main: Suhrkamp, 1958), p. 41.

3.   Eduardo Nicol, "Ensayo sobre el ensayo," in his El problema de la filosofía hispánica (Madrid: Tecnos, 1961), p. 207.

4.   The notion that the essay is inherently opposed to systems is from Adorno. His view of the essay as a distinct mode of cognitive experience is discussed in R. L. Kauffmann, The Theory of the Essay: Lukács, Adorno, and Benjamin, University of Wisconsin Press (forthcoming).

5.   María del Carmen Pena, Pintura de paisaje e ideología: la generación del 98 (Madrid: Taurus, 1982), pp. 9–10.

6.   Pedro Laín Entralgo, La generación del 98, 8th ed. (Madrid: Espasa–Calpe, 1975), p. 195.

7.   This view of the evolution of Azorín and Unamuno relies upon Carlos Blanco Aguinaga La juventud del 98 (Madrid: Siglo XXI, 1970), pp. 293–322.

8.   All references to Ortega's works in this paper are from his Obras completas (Complete Works), 4th ed., 6 vols. (Madrid: Revista de Occidente, 1957). Hereafter, unless otherwise indicated, volume and page numbers from these works will be cited parenthetically in the text.

9.   José Gaos, "Los dos Ortegas," in his Sobre Ortega y Gasset (México: Imprenta Universitaria, 1957), p. 89. For my purposes, I have extended the period proposed by Gaos by one year to include "Notas del vago estío" (1925), an essay that otherwise fits his criteria for the period.

10.   For example, see "La doctrina del punto de vista" ("Doctrine of the Point of View") in Ortega's El tema de nuestro tiempo (III, p. 199).

11.   This passage has overtones of krausismo, the philosophy which guided Francisco Giner de los Ríos and his followers at the "Institución Libre de Enseñanza." From German idealism, Spanish krausismo had borrowed, among other things, the idea that landscape reflected the soul of a people. (María del Carmen Pena, p. 55). But the passage also echoes the ethnic determinism found at the end of Ortega's España invertebrada (III, p. 128; Invertebrate Spain), the interpretation of Spanish history which he had published a few months earlier, and to which he alludes in the essay under discussion (II, p. 369).

12.   Ortega, "Ensayo de estética a manera de prólogo" (VI, pp. 247–64; "An Essay on Aesthetics by Way of a Prologue"). Ortega's essay raises complex epistemological issues that go beyond the scope of this essay. He questions, for instance, whether it is possible for a thinking subject to have an immediate comprehension of itself. For further commentary on

Ortega's essay, see Nelson R. Orringer, Ortega y sus fuentes germánicas (Madrid: Gredos, 1979), pp. 119-26.

13.   Ortega holds that only in the guise of the región natural or "geographical region," which can be visually apprehended by a subject, does geography influence us in any vital way: "The very thing we call Spain is a political and historical abstraction.   One can't get an adequate image of it. . . .   In contrast to such abstract entities, the geographical region proves its reality in a very simple way: by penetrating us through our eyes (II, p. 261).

14.   Consider the ludic aspect of this passage from "Notas del vago estío:" "In this hunting for landscapes which the sightseeing trip represents, castles and cathedrals are the main trophies we bring back." (II, p. 419).

15.   Nicol, El problema de la filosofía hispánica, pp. 125-50,239. Gonzalo Fernández de la Mora, in Ortega y el 98, 3rd ed. (Madrid: Rialp, 1979), claims that Ortega inherited egotism (yoísmo) from the "Generation of '98." He maintains, however, that Ortega's work represents a considerable advance in rigor and objectivity over the writers of that generation.

16.   Marichal, "La singularidad estilística de Ortega," in La voluntad de estilo (Barcelona: Seix Barral, 1962), p. 212.

17.   In "Azorín: primores de lo vulgar," Ortega conducts a lengthy if indirect polemic against Unamuno (II, pp. 186-89). See also Marichal, "La singularidad estilística de Ortega," p. 213.

18.   Gaos, "La salvación de Ortega," in Sobre Ortega y Gasset, pp. 73-86. Gaos defends the "authentic reactive spontaneity" of Ortega's early essays against the "adventitious will-to-system" (p. 79) evident in his later writings.

19.   Nicol, El problema de la filosofía hispánica, p. 69.

18.
Ortega's Philosophy of Art

ROBERTO J. VICHOT

The history of philosophy of art in the West can be summarized under the history of esthetics. Esthetics is that branch of philosophy of art concerned with the standards and critical principles by which questions about judgement of taste can be answered upon premises of rational character. Ever since Kant, when esthetics first came into being as a branch of theoretical knowledge isolated from the "main stem of philosophy," the task of estheticians, according to the Earl of Listowell, has been to provide a critique of esthetic judgement by harmonizing the empirical dimension of artistry in artistic production and the causal artistry of nature with speculative esthetic principles and the qualities of the esthetic experience.(1) Not until the twentieth century, when philosophers like José Ortega y Gasset and Martin Heidegger began their criticism of idealist transcendental consciousness coupled with their elucidation of the vital and existential grounds of human reality, did esthetics appear as one aspect of the broader philosophical concern with understanding the roots and presence of art in human life. In this sense, Ortega's esthetics becomes part of a broader analysis and study of art in terms of its fundamental existence in human reality, both as a historical fact and as a part of the vital activity of being.

For Ortega, esthetic contemplation is an effort of "transposition," of imposing an imaginative reality upon a thing and the transposing of the thing into an (material) esthetic object. Art, like science, assumes the fact of its vital reality and functions by supplanting the clear and tranquil world of theoria, of meditations, with the meaningful and solicitous world of art, of the spectator. While philosophy tries to be absolutely "transparent" to life by the practice of aletheia, art tries to affect an experience, to solicit a perspective. Art, like philosophy, is contemplative and transparent, but unlike philosophy it is not theoretical but rather suggestive of meaning and thereby transferable. Art is transferability by excellence, symbolization. Ortega calls it idiom.(2) He captures this and the "inclusive" meaning of philosophy, stating that while the philosophic phrase is hermetic and systematic, literary expression spills its meaning as it overflows with excess life.(3) Michael Weinstein, recapturing the distinction, states that while the primary feature of philosophy is to strive to eliminate mystery and present its conclusions at the beginning, showing how it reached them, literature supresses the fullness of its meaning until the last word has been written, thus flourishing through mystery.(4)

In art, contemplation does not function in the pure theoretical sense that it does in philosophy, where it is an effort of "transmigration," an exercise that life makes to unveil itself from things and make life transparent.(5) The role of the poet is premised on the ability to create the language that presents the intimate reality of human life.(6) However, lan-

guage, says Ortega, is already doctrine, thought.(7)   The tongue is a symbol, a custom of reference to a thing.(8)   The authentic name is also a
cloak, a mask, a word that conceals. In this sense, the product of philosophic activity, like all thought or contemplative expression, includes a
secondary form of reality superimposed by the individual and not spontaneously sustained by the immediate reality of vital life.   Primary, vital
reality is only manifested as modus nascendis: any attempt at thingifying
it or substantiating it is already a secondary activity of doctrinaire
thought or intellect.

Philosophy, which is the most radical kind of interest, the interest in
the universe, in all there is, is a part of culture and is not exempted from
the primacy or radicalness of life. Philosophic contemplation, like artistic and scientific activity, finds the activity of being, as the fundamental
datum of reality. For Ortega, the most radical problem of philosophy is to
define our life, and Ortega does so through the concept of intransferability: "To live is what no one else can do for me . . . it is my utmost
individual being."(9)   Intransferability makes my life "the radical mode of
living; every other thing or mode of living I find in my life.   In it,
everything is what it is to life, as it is being lived."(10)   Life is what
one does not doubt and, hence, what can never become an ideal object.(11)
Once one accepts that life is the radical reality, "anyone who tries to
speak of a more indubitable or primary reality will find that not even
thinking" with its order of principles is prior to it.(12)   Although life
may be theorized, to live is not theory.

In ¿Qué es filosofía? (What is Philosophy?), Ortega claims that whatever does not define philosophy as the activity of philosophizing is not a
radical definition.   A philosophical doctrine, he tells us, that which can
be in a book, is only an abstraction of the authentic reality philosophy --
it is only its precipitated and semidead body.(13)   In an earlier work, he
criticized Aristotle for having made beatitude or perfect life depend on
theoretical activity; he writes that he does not asseverate that the theoretical attitude is supreme nor that one should philosophize first and then
live.(14)   Rather, what he wants is to accentuate the difference between
culture and spontaneity, contemplation and life, in order to comply with the
mission of his time, which was to bring culture to trial before the infallible judge Dionysus and show that reason, ethics, and art should serve
life.(15)

However, the fact that life is the object of philosophy means that the
attitude of "being in oneself," of ensimismamiento, that defines life, is
the object and essence of philosophic activity.   Indeed, the elements of
contemplation and transparency suggested by the attitude of "being in oneself" and ensimismamiento are shown by the primogenial name of philosophy,
aletheia, and by the etymological meaning of the word theoria, which is the
primary characteristic of philosophic thinking since its inception in
Greece, especially since Aristotle.(16)   According to Ortega, in "Greece
philosophy began by calling itself aletheia, which means disocultation,
revelation, or unveiling; in sum, manifestation. And to manifest is but to
speak, logos. If mysticism is silent, philosophy is to say, to discover, in
the great nakedness and transparency of the word the being of things, to say
the being; ontology."(17)   Aletheia is truth in the sense of stating what is
already there; what is absolutely present.(18)

The philosopher, to perceive the primary reality of living, must disregard the particular manifestation of life and retrieve her or his gaze on
life as such as if it were a crystal. My primary intimacy with life, as
earlier stated, makes my life transparent to me. This transparency of life
means that like a crystal my life is a means by which other objects, things,
become apparent to me and that in order to perceive it, as a crystal, one
must disengage one's attention from the thing represented in the transparency.(19)

The work of art, like philosophic work, is transparent but it effects
itself; it transpires the metaphorical meaning in its own object.(20)

Artistic contemplation interposes into its own transparent element a delusion, suffusing the theoretical world of philosophy with an inspiring or illusory artistic "inner world." What occurs is that through a process of metaphorical thinking, art, unlike philosophy, limits or "brackets" one's "beliefs," which essentially are the immediate pre-theoretical meaning that things bear in one's life and are usually expressed with everyday language in an ordinary situation. The metaphor originates with a belief.(21)   The metaphor limits, brackets, or "dehumanizes" a belief, creating a secondary language of signs and symbols whose meaning is only made patent by the imagination's intimate reality. It is the imagination's intimate reality that creates a meaning, not present in the effective, everyday meaning of things, which gives the object its esthetic quality and the appearance of existing as an absolute moment within a vital present.(22)   The esthetic object and the metaphorical object are the same thing, states Ortega.(23) However, the metaphor, though the most radical instrument of dehumanization, is not the only one.(24) All power of imagination has a dehumanizing force. The illusionary and inspirational inner world created through metaphorical thinking, gives art its "expansive" secondary meaning, which distinguishes it from philosophy and gives it its "dehuman" character.

By affirming the primordiality of life, Ortega was able to avoid the reduction of life to philosophy and affirm the independence of philosophy and art. This also allowed him to avoid the tendency of abstracting art from life by maintaining a theoretical or philosophical perspective on art. Ortega's willingness to apply this theoretical perspective allowed him to carry his vital critique of art and the contemporary state of culture in Spain, Europe, and the Occident further than previous philosophy of art ever did. The result was a philosophy of art with greater insights about art and civilization than any of its predecessors.

One of these insights is the critique of the humanization or politicization of art. According to Ortega, nineteenth-century artists, "perhaps perceiving (presintiendo) a twilight in their history, became ungrateful and threatening like distanced prophets. All the difficulties of the struggle for existence assaulted the author's fantasies and gained the right to citizenship in literary creation."(25)   For Ortega, it seemed that "with the downfall of religion and the inevitable relativism of science, art was expected to take upon itself nothing less than the salvation of mankind."(26) This was done according to Ortega by claiming importance for art on either of two counts -- either on account of subjects that deal with the most profound problems of humanity or on account of art's significance as a human pursuit from which the species derives justification and dignity.(27)

Nineteenth-century art seems to have been caught up in an estheticism in two senses -- in an ideological sense, in that it projected the quest for vital security and immortality onto art, turning esthetics into religious compensatory dogma; and in a metaphysical sense in that it still grounded art upon some principle of esthetic consciousness and not in human life. The culmination of the second metaphysical sense occurs in twentieth-century philosophy in the works of such great philosophers as Alfred North Whitehead, José Vasconcelos, and George Santayana, all of whom reduced not only philosophy of art but philosophy in general to basic principles of esthetics.

The humanism and estheticism remaining faithful to life also surpasses, goes beyond, or "constructs," life. The poet "aggrandizes the world by adding to reality, which is there by itself, the contents of his imagination,"(28) writes Ortega. This illusory quality of art permits artists to project or identify their lives with the experience solicited by the art object, and, reflectively, to treat and interpret themselves not in terms of their own lives but in terms of the art object. This process of "thingifying" the ego, circumstances, and the art object is partially responsible for what Ortega calls the humanization of art.(29) As a consequence of this, an artist can lead a life which is "effectively mundanized" in the sense that the illusory meaning that forms and sustains the esthetic object blocks the life of the artist out of the art object. What occurs is that the primary attitude or the radical reality Ortega calls "my life," which is "to inform oneself," "to be transparent," "to communicate" and to ensimismarse,(30) is flashed out be the meaning, in this case, of the esthetic experience. Consequently, the whole life of the artist becomes effectively overwhelmed by a particular structure of meaning, or mundanized. In this situation, the product of the work of the artist is a mass-object, in the sense of its being defined and getting its meaning like all mass from a source "outside," alien to it, in this case alien to the vital aspect of the life of the artist, the primary attitude of which is ensimismamiento.

Insofar as art expresses a nonvital reality, Ortega believes that art has contributed to the devitalizing tendency, a culturalist trend, that has prevailed throughout the modern period and of which the humanism and estheticism of nineteenth-and twentieth-century philosophy of art are but particular manifestations. Ortega believed that in the Renaissance began a social trend that stressed the growth of the cultural aspects of human life over its vital dimension. This culturalist trend in history has been the common denominator of what has come to be known as a modern epoch in which the fascination with science becomes dominant. What this culturalist trend meant for Ortega was the contraction of the vital elements of art, leading to the mundanization of artistic experience and precipitating the existence of modern mass society.

The historical trend of culturalism is continuous for Ortega with the development of the cultural (as opposed to class) phenomenon of the bourgeoisie. Indeed, Ortega considers modern mass-society to be essentially an outgrowth of bourgeois society. The fact of the modern masses comes into being when the bourgeoisie, loosening tensions between living and culture, takes control of the available "level" of "vital gravitation" that belongs to others and unsuccessfully endeavors to expand the vital horizons of bourgeois life. What the culturalist trend, along with the "effective mundanization" of life, had accomplished by 1929, when Ortega wrote La rebelión de las masas (The Revolt of the Masses), was a reduction of the vital aspects of life and philosophy to a minimum and the contraction of human action to the quest for security and manipulation characteristic of bourgeois life values. La rebelión de las masas can be interpreted as a thoroughgoing indictment of any culturalist theory, which claims that history can be ruled through transvital laws. For Ortega, art, philosophy, science, and all other cultural phenomena originate in the vital aspects and needs of the individual. All culture must perform a vital function, which may be subjected to intravital values and regimentation, but which, when separated from its vital function, "effectively mundanizes" life and experience, and with them, art, philosophy, science, and many other forms of cultural objectification. In El tema de nuestro tiempo (The Modern Theme),Ortega argues for a new philosophic synthesis of culture and vitality, ideas and beliefs, that can be used as an indictment against the culturalism prevalent in the history of modern pilosophy.

The basic thesis of La rebelión de las masas, written in 1929, is that the modification of the cultural infrastructure of society caused by the industrial revolution has had as one of its major consequences the "effective mundanization" of our life. According to Ortega, our life has become radically routinized or "mundanized." For him, we live a life so full of order that "novelty," such as that of heroism, has become an impossibility, while "vulgarity" has become one of the fundamental virtues of life giving it basic impetus that "technicism" produces toward "mediocrity."

The consequences of this "mundanization" for art had been presented by Ortega in a work written four years before La rebelión de las masas, La deshumanización del arte (The Dehumanization of Art). In the latter, Ortega announced the thesis that the arts have transcended their supposed semantic quality and have effectively invaded every sphere of human life. In La

deshumanización del arte, Ortega argues for a halt to the effective mundanization of our life by the arts and endorses what he considers to be the
qualities and elements of a new style of art.(31) In the later La rebelión
de las masas, extending the arguments he makes in La deshumanización del
arte, Ortega argues that the effective mundanization of life has produced at
the social level a mass-society that is characterized by a culture where the
places and utensils created by civilization are stripped of all esthetic
quality, turning them into mere things, the collection of which comes to
form the frames of experiences for a world empty of vital possibilities and
actions.(32) At the psychological level, the mass consequences of the effective mundanization of life are identified by Ortega as the presence of a
lack of self-appreciation and self-esteem, as a "thingification" of the
self. Mass individuals are "ones who do not value themselves";(33) ultimately, they are those who completely treat themselves as objects, suffering
intense self-alienation.

The ultimate political implication of La rebelión de las masas is that
what has been known as Western civilization is on the verge of collapse and
that it had its support founded upon what is thought to be the most free,
unnecessary, insignificant, and sprightly kind of human activity: art. La
rebelión de las masas contends that it is possible for Western civilization,
the product of human activity, suddenly and effectively to be separated from
the artistic quality of living that constitutes it. The result of this is a
civilization without art where life is thrown into a magnificent culture but
is not adequately able to appreciate it. It is for this reason that our
civilization is under the constant absolute threat of collapsing.(34) Since
mass-individuals have little appreciation for themselves, there is little
reason to hope or expect that they will develop appreciation for the effects
of human action and the consequent ability to be socially responsible.

Faced with the extirpation of the primary attribute of human reality --
ensimismamiento -- from the life of the artist, the "effective mundanization" of the artist's world into a mass-society and the decadence of art and
European civilization to a mass level become simply a matter of time for
Ortega. The task of the philosopher under these circumstances would be to
remind the artist of the radicality of her or his life, of the fact that to
live is to live for oneself, which is what no one else can do for anyone
else. Philosophers need to discover and redefine life for the times, not
only in a theoretical sense but in an artistic sense, on those frontiers
where art and life meet and the art of living begins. Art is as proper to
philosophy as theorizing about the universe.

It was previously stated that Ortega defines life as intransferability,
and the primary attribute of this intransferability is that of "being-in-
oneselfness" or ensimismamiento. What this primary category constitutive of
life, of finding oneself, of being for oneself, means for Ortega is that
life is a kind of affair, a living for, which gives life a horizon of vital
possibilities, and like all horizons, is defined by a margin of liberty and
fatality: of mission and destiny. These aspects of liberty and fatality
that are suggested by the preposition for, and which constitute life's circumstances, the horizon of vital possibilities, also give life its dramatic
attribute, its element of "theoretical heroism" which the safe, tranquil,
and bourgeois step of science never has.(35) Dramatism, Ortega tells us, is
the abnormal tension of our soul, "produced by something which announces itself for the future, to which we become more proximate in each instance."(36) According to Ortega:

> Because life is constructed by fatality on one side, but
> by the necessary liberty of deciding ourselves in front
> of it on the other, there is in its very roots material
> for an art, and nothing symbolizes it better than the
> situation of the poet who rests upon the fatality of the
> rhyme and the rhythm the elastic liberty of his

> lyricism. All art implies acceptance of a shackle, of a
> destiny, and as Nietzsche said: "The artist is the one
> that dances enchained." The fatality which is the pre-
> sent is not a disdain but a delight, the delight that
> the chisel feels when it encounters the resistance of
> the marble.(37)

The beauty of life lies precisely not in that destiny be favorable or unfa-
vorable, since it is always destiny, but in the gentleness with which one
meets it and carves of its material a fatal and noble figure.(38) The fact
that in the very roots of life there is material for an art means that there
is such a thing as an art of living, which consists of a dramatic melody
that always keeps consciousness awakened to the problem of life. This art
of life is not a reduction of life to art; it sets the enjoyment of artistic
experience at the very marrow of human life or, as Ortega would say: "The
destiny of each one is, at the same time, one's greatest delight."(39)

NOTES

1.   The Earl of Listowell, "The Present State of Aesthetics in this
Country," Proceedings of the Aristotelian Society NS 35 (1934–1935): 195.

2.   José Ortega y Gasset, "Ensayo de estética a manera de prólogo,"
Prologue to El pasajero by J. Moreno Villa (1914); reprinted in Obras completas, 5th ed., (Madrid: Revista de Occidente, 1961), vol. VI, p. 256.

3.   José Ortega y Gasset, "Guillermo Dilthey y la idea de la vida,"
Revista de Occidente, No. 125, 126, 127 (Nov., Dec., 1933 and Jan. 1934);
reprinted in Obras VI, pp. 169–170.

4.   Michael A. Weinstein, Structure of Human Life: A Vitalist Ontology (New York: New York University Press, 1979), p. 1.

5.   José Ortega y Gasset, ¿Qué es filosofía?, Colección Austral (1957;
reprint Madrid: Espasa-Calpe S.A., 1973), p. 207.

6.   José Ortega y Gasset, Origen y epílogo de la filosofía, Colección
El Arquero, 3rd ed. (1960; reprint Madrid: Revista de Occidente, S.A.,
1972), p. 102.

7.   José Ortega y Gasset, "Ideas y creencias," Obras V, p. 393.

8.   Ortega y Gasset, Origen y epílogo, pp. 91, 98.

9.   Ortega y Gasset, ¿Qué es filosofía?, p. 177.

10.   Ibid., pp. 177, 183.

11.   Ortega y Gasset, "Ideas y creencias," Obras V, p. 393.

12.   Ortega y Gasset, ¿Qué es filosofía?, pp. 199, 200.

13.   Ibid., p. 208.

14.   José Ortega y Gasset, "Verdad y perspectiva," El Espectador (Feb.
– March, 1916); reprinted in Obras completas, 7th ed., (Madrid: Revista de
Occidente, 1966), vol. II, p. 18.

15.   José Ortega y Gasset, "El tema de nuestro tiempo," (1923); reprinted in Obras III, p. 178.

16.   Ortega y Gasset, ¿Qué es filosofía?, p. 74; Origen y epílogo, pp. 201-203.

17.   Ortega y Gasset, ¿Qué es filosofía?, p. 98.   Translation made by the author.

18.   Ortega y Gasset, Origen y epílogo, p. 101.

19.   Ortega y Gasset, "El tema de nuestro tiempo," Obras III, p. 188.

20.   Ortega y Gasset, "Ensayo de estética," Obras VI, p. 257.

21.   Ortega y Gasset, "Ideas y creencias," Obras V, p. 392.

22.   Ortega y Gasset, "Ensayo de estética," Obras VI, pp. 254, 262.

23.   Ibid., p. 257.

24.   José Ortega y Gasset, La deshumanización del arte (Madrid: Revista de Occidente, 1925); reprinted in The Dehumanization of Art and Other Essays on Art, Culture, and Literature, trans. Helene Weyl, 2nd ed. (Princeton, N.J.:   Princeton University Press, 1972), p. 35.

25.   José Ortega y Gasset, "La Sonata de estío de Don Ramón del Valle-Inclán," La lectura (Feb. 1904); reprinted in Obras I, p. 21.   Translation made by this author.

26.   Ortega y Gasset, Dehumanization of Art, pp. 49-50.

27.   Ibid., p. 50.

28.   Ibid., p. 31.

29.   For a discussion of the manipulative "thingification" of the self and its relation to the art object, see Ortega, "Ensayo de estética," Obras VI, pp. 250-254.

30.   Ortega y Gasset, ¿Qué es filosofía?, p. 202.

31.   Ortega y Gasset, Dehumanization of Art, p. 14.

32.   José Ortega y Gasset, La rebelión de las masas, (1929); reprinted in Colección Austral, 20th ed., (1937; México, Espasa Calpe Mexicana, S. A., 1976), p. 39.

33.   Ibid., p. 40.

34.   In his Prologue to La rebelión de las masas, Ortega wrote: "Anyone would say that those two things -- civilization and culture -- are not an issue to me.   The truth is that they are precisely what concerns me since my first writings," p. 35.

35.   Ortega y Gasset, ¿Qué es filosofía?, p. 55.

36.   Ibid., p. 94.

37.   Ibid., pp. 215-216.   Translation made by this author.

38.   Ibid., p. 216.

39.   Ibid., p. 17.

Part III

Ortega y Gasset:
Ambivalence and Echoes

19.
Spanish Son and German Father: Ortega y Gasset and Goethe

ELIZABETH BOHNING AND JUDY B. McINNIS

Udo Rukser, in Goethe in der hispanischen Welt, (Goethe in the Hispanic World) summarizes Ortega y Gasset's explicit statements about Goethe, especially those in "Pidiendo un Goethe desde dentro" and "Goethe, el libertador" (1932), essays commemorating the one hundredth anniversary of Goethe's death. Although he does not analyze Ortega's philosophy in depth, Rukser does observe that Ortega frequently cited Goethe's dicta with cavalier disregard of their contexts to support his own conclusions.(1) Yet, we might point out that even in this, Ortega was following Goethe's advice to use reading as a spur to one's own creativity: "In short, everything is odious that merely instructs me without increasing my activity or giving it new life immediately."(2) In an earlier work Joaquín Iriarte, emphasizing Goethe's pervasive influence upon Ortega, concluded that it is difficult to separate the ideas of the two men.(3) In essays published in 1961, Julián Marías isolated two moments in Ortega's relationship to Goethe: friendship in which Ortega viewed Goethe as his godfather and the harshly critical reassessment of the centennial essays, in which Ortega distanced himself to pose the question "Who is Goethe?" as the preliminary to "Who am I?"(4) Here again Ortega does not escape Goethe's influence, for he follows the advice expressed in Faust: "What thou hast inherited from thy forbears, thou must earn thyself to make it thine own"(I, p. 135; VI, p. 405).

Egon Schwartz observed that both Georg Simmel, Ortega's teacher at Marburg in 1906, and Ortega himself looked for reflections of their own culture in Goethe. In his analysis of the centennial essays, Schwartz suggests that Ortega projected the dichotomy in his own personality onto Goethe. Nevertheless, he points out, subsequent Goethe scholarship has centered on the questions Ortega posed.(5) In his invaluable study of Ortega's German sources, Nelson Orringer demonstrates the similarities and differences between Ortega's and Simmel's conceptions of Goethe: while Ortega consistently stressed the individualistic movement towards the center of the soul, Simmel stressed the universal movement from the soul to the outer world.(6) Although he offers convincing proof of Ortega's dialogue with Simmel, Orringer fails to explain the impassioned tone of Ortega's defense and subsequent attack on Goethe. José Sánchez Villaseñor, despite the bias that prevented him from crediting Ortega with the slightest degree of originality, had already suggested in 1949 an explanation worth examining: "Goethe, says Ortega, came to feel a mixture of terror and hatred before everything which demanded an irrevocable decision. Is not this the case with Ortega himself? . . . Ortega feared the truth; like Goethe he felt a horror for all irrevocable decisions."(7)

Villaseñor, Marías and Schwartz implicitly rely on Freud's Oedipus complex to explain the fluctuations in Ortega's attitude to Goethe. Throughout The Anxiety of Influence Harold Bloom applies this theory to the writer's

relationship with the giants of his cultural tradition.(8)   In this essay,
we hope to shed additional light upon Ortega's ambivalent view of his acknowledged mentor by explicitly demonstrating its Oedipal aspects within the
context of Bloom's adaptation of Freud's theory.

In Ortega's hands, Goethe's biography assumed as much importance as his
literary and scientific works.   It was precisely the relation of Goethe to
his works, to his society, and to his German and European heritage that most
fascinated the Spanish formulator of the perspectivist philosophy.

Investigation of Ortega's allusions to Goethe throughout his works reveals the startling degree to which the son–father pattern is repeated.   For
Ortega, Goethe was the first Romantic, the inventor of lyricism, and the
first man to perceive clearly the value of life in itself.   In "Musicalia"
Ortega declared that in Goethe's work the world became an expression of the
soul as the distinction between the author and his persona was lost.   Goethe
and Chateaubriand "heroically opened their veins and let the vital flow of
their blood run through the stream of verse and estuarine curve of the time.
More or less faithful, all of us who write today are grandchildren of these
two demigods" (II, p. 242; see also IV, p. 389).   Ortega admired Goethe's
passion for taking possession of his own life through reflective meditation
on the significance of his heritage and his activities (II, p. 161).   He
appreciated Goethe's idea of the fateful coincidence emerging from all past
times of the feeling, modulus, style and circumstances of a person (II, p.
167) –– and the protophenomenon –– the discovery of Nature's secrets through
study of the most humble things (I, p. 322).   Goethe's proverb that "things
are differences which we impose" (II, pp. 106 and 391; V, p. 442) generated
Ortega's perspectivist philosophy.   He cited Goethe's perception that the
song is the singer's best reward to support his theory that all vital processes begin in the superfluous and free energy of play or sport (II, p.
611).   He also cited Goethe to prove that a religious, that is, respectful,
rather than a frivolous attitude towards life is the logical consequence of
this theory (I, p. 435).   Finally, he recalled Goethe's emphasis on energy:
"In the beginning was the deed" (VI, p. 417n), to support his own concept of
vital reason.   Goethe's heroes, Ortega declared, confronted "gray theory
with life, with the palpitating rainbow of existence" (II, p. 17).   Goethe
transformed the medieval germ of Faust into "a gigantic philosophical poem,
a universal song, in which every cardinal reality is granted a voice, a
smile and a lament" (VI, p. 122).

Despite such repeated tributes to Goethe and acknowledgement of his own
debt to him, we find a critical stance at other points, especially in the
centennial essays.   His hostility here cannot wholly be explained by his
avowed intention to shock his German readers out of their complacent, almost
institutional, reverence for Goethe.   In "Pidiendo un Goethe desde dentro,"
he interprets what he calls the "failure" of Werther, Faust, and Wilhelm
Meister to discover their destiny as a reflection of Goethe's betrayal of
his own vocation in the retreat to Weimar and in the substitution of a spectral symbolic life.   Holding himself in reserve because he wished to keep
all possibilities open in an eternal youthfulness (eudaemonia), Ortega says,
Goethe developed a philosophy of cosmic optimism that contradicted real insecurity over his personal destiny.   In his earlier essays, Ortega adopted
the more generally held view that through the court life at Weimar and his
relationship with Charlotte von Stein, Goethe learned self–discipline and
restraint.   Frau von Stein corrected his "atrocious youthful Teutonism"
(III, p. 321).   In the 1932 essay, Ortega cites the relationship as an
illustration of Goethe's flight from reality into a symbolic life midway
between "poetry and reality":

> Accustomed to that, Goethe ends up not needing reality,
> and, just as for Midas everything turned into gold, so
> for him everything changes, evanesces into a symbol.
> Hence his strange, post–juvenile almost love affairs.

Indeed his affair with Charlotte von Stein is equivocal: we would not understand if the almost adventure with Marianne von Willemer did not make definitely clear the capacity for unreality which this man had achieved. Once it is acknowledged that life is a symbol, one thing is the same as another: it is all the same to sleep with Christelchen as to marry in an ideal Pygmalion-sense a sculpture of the Palazzo Caraffa Colobrano. But destiny is strictly the opposite of the "it's all the same" of symbolism! (IV, p. 414)

Goethe's error was not in going to what Ortega calls "a ridiculous Lilliputian court;" a season there to correct his "furor teutonicus" with a dose of restraint would have allowed him to make German literature the foremost in the world: "That German literature which only Goethe could have restored is characterized by the union of intensity and restraint. The intensity of feeling and fantasy, two things other European literatures do not possess: the restraint which, in a different way, France and Italy possess to a great degree" (IV, p. 412). Ortega laments that Goethe, who had the unique fortune to have been able to unite the two qualities, cut himself off from his "roots in the German soil," from the "furor teutonicus," by remaining at that isolated court to become a petrified statue. He takes little account of Goethe's friendship with Schiller, which blossomed at Weimar and which is generally regarded as highly fruitful for German literature. Indeed, he cites Schiller's first impression of Goethe's cool aloofness to contrast the two writers: Schiller, "infinitely less gifted than Goethe," nonetheless discovered and embraced his destiny while Goethe never fully committed himself to anything (IV, p. 415). In fairness to Goethe, we must point out that at Weimar he was inspired to resume writing many long neglected works, among others, Faust.

Ortega is critical of the emphasis that during his classical period Goethe placed upon the universal and cosmic rather than the individual and particular. He concludes the essay with an implied comparison of Goethe to an orchid: "There was a time when it was believed that orchids were born in the air, without roots. There was a time when it was believed that culture needed no roots . . . not long ago, and still so long ago. . . ." (IV, p. 419) The comparison gains significance from the fact that Ortega also criticized Goethe for his reliance on botanical images of life. Earlier in the essay, he praised Goethe for being the first to realize that man's major task in life is to discover and fulfill his individual destiny. Goethe's concept of the entelechy remained "the best expression to designate that vital purpose, that inexorable calling of which our real ego consists. Each one is 'the one he must become,' although perhaps he will never succeed." (IV, p. 405) Ortega bases what he perceived as the contradiction between Goethe's life and his ideas upon the inadequacy of Goethe's botanical images to trace man's development:

For the plant, the animal or the star, to live is to have no doubt in regard to one's own being. None of them has to decide what it is to be the next moment. Consequently their life is not drama, but . . . evolution. But a man's life is quite the opposite: it is having to decide at every moment what he is to be in the next, and, for this reason, having to discover the exact plan, the exact purpose of his being. (IV, p. 407)

Ortega's uncharacteristically sarcastic tone in this essay reveals the extent to which the son-father rivalry dominates his assessment of Goethe. He seems intent upon establishing his own uniqueness by belittling that of his mentor. In both centennial essays he points out that Goethe was no

philosopher, thus fencing off a terrain in which he felt he could be superi-
or to the more versatile father figure. The first instance occurs at the
beginning of the more critical essay, "Pidiendo un Goethe desde dentro,"
discussed above: "It is surprising that the constant contradiction in the
thinker Goethe's ideas about the world has not been stressed -- the least
valuable part of Goethe. . . ." (IV, p. 407) The second ends the otherwise
laudatory "Goethe, el libertador" where Ortega nearly announces his succes-
sion, hiding his "I" only behind an editorial "we": "It is a pity that
Goethe was not naturally endowed as a philosopher. His ideas usually under-
mine his intuition. Let us take renewed life from his promise; let us press
upon the broad outline the secret and programmatic profile of our own ego"
(IV, p. 427).

In addition, Ortega in a two-page footnote directly reveals his antago-
nism to the German intellectual tradition of which Goethe was the exemplar.
Justifiably piqued at being regarded as an apostle of his contemporary,
Heidegger, Ortega abjures any debt to him and suggests that the relationship
might be the obverse: "There are scarcely one or two important concepts of
Heidegger that do not pre-exist in my books, sometimes by thirteen years"
(IV, p. 403). Ortega then generalizes his defense by declaring that he may
have obscured his own originality by over emphasizing his debt to German
philosophy in adopting as one of the missions of his work "that of improving
the Spanish mind with the torrent of German intellectual treasure" (IV, p.
404n).   Thus it becomes apparent that Ortega hoped to accomplish for
philosophy what he judged Goethe had failed to accomplish for literature.

Ignoring the vast changes that Goethe's thinking underwent in the
course of a long life, Ortega accused Goethe of having formulated all his
major works by the age of thirty and of having spent all his remaining years
simply elaborating and completing them. Goethe himself maintained, for example, that when he resumed work on Faust after a long hiatus the figures he
had created in his youth were almost total strangers to him. Nevertheless,
Ortega repeated the pattern he perceived in Goethe in his own life, as we
shall see through analysis of his earliest works that already contain in em-
bryo his perspectivist philosophy. In these works Ortega, who would judge
Goethe not to have been German enough in 1932, perceives Goethe as having
been perhaps too German.

In the Meditaciones del Quijote (Meditations on Quixote, 1914) Ortega
endeavors to convert his countrymen to an ideal exemplified in his own philosophy -- the union of Spanish corporality and German spirituality. He assumes a more reverent attitude towards Goethe than in the 1932 essays, while
at the same time holding himself above his mentor as one in whom the two
qualities are more thoroughly fused.

In Chapter 7, Ortega introduces Goethe's famous account of the Italian
captain who reprimanded him for silently meditating on the scene: "Man
should no longer think, by thinking he grows old. Man should not limit himself to one thing alone, because then he becomes dull and one-sided; it is
necessary to have a thousand things, a confusion of things, in one's head"
(I, p. 346). Ortega uses this episode to illustrate the distinction between
the Mediterranean man who sees clearly and the German who thinks clearly.
In an earlier essay, he had developed the idea that in German cultural history Greek idealism had been imposed on Gothic transcendentalism with its
denial of material existence (I, p. 188; see also IV, p. 475).   Hence,
Ortega maintains in the Meditaciones, Germans are doubly removed from Mediterranean sensuality: theirs is a culture of "profound realities," while
the Latin is a culture of the surface (I, p. 341).

He admits that Goethe possessed more visual imagination than most of
his compatriots and elsewhere praises Goethe's painterly style (II, p. 337).
However, in comparison to Mediterranean writers, and especially Cervantes,
"for Goethe seeing is rather thinking with his eyes" (I, p. 348).   For
Ortega, Goethe's images lack immediacy: "Things and people float at a

welldefined distance. They are like a memory or dream of themselves" (I, p. 347); this "remembered" realism idealizes life, giving the form or concept but not the sensuous impression. Nevertheless, Ortega continues, it supplies the physical and moral sense of things that the simple impression can never supply. Ortega uses Goya as the cardinal example of Spain's frontier culture: "Savage culture, culture without a yesterday, without continuity, without certainty; culture in continuous struggle with the fundamental, disputing every day the possession of the territory it holds" (I, p. 355). Ruled by the impression, the Spaniard, in Ortega's view, cannot build upon the past as do cultures based on the concept. Each artist, like Goya, has to create his style from the beginning.

In essay 12, Ortega makes an impassioned plea to Spaniards for the integration of sensual imagination and thought: "Why does a Spaniard insist on living anachronistically in his own time? Why does he forget his germanic heritage" (I, p. 356)? Once more he returns to Goethe to cry: "I declare myself to be descended from those who out of the darkness aspire toward light" (I, p. 357). Ortega thus reveals a profound conviction that his personal destiny is to turn Spain's face to Europe through the lucid exegesis of modern philosophical, historical, and aesthetic currents.

Ten years later in "Vitalidad, alma, espíritu," Ortega abstracted the psychological system implicitly contained in the Meditaciones. Here he describes the psyche as consisting of three overlapping parts: vital corporality, spirit (intelligence and will), and emotion. He holds that in the German psyche emotion dominates the spirit, and vital corporality scarcely exists, while in the Spanish psyche corporality dominates the emotions, and spirit remains embryonic (II, p. 480). Kant's "Viking" philosophy represents the inevitable development of German subjectivity and the will to power (II, p. 467), an idea he expanded in "Kant (1929)": "For Kant thought is a controller of nature. To know is not to see, but to command. A quiet truth becomes an imperative" (IV, p. 46). Ortega often returned to Goethe's poetic expression of this idea:

> Nothing is inside, nothing is outside.
> What there is inside, is outside too. (II, pp. 585 and
> 85)

However dimly he regarded Goethe's philosophy, as he understood it, Ortega always gave him credit, even in the centennial essays, for liberating humanity by demonstrating that man creates his own world and finally himself. Spaniards, ever prone to relapse into the pattern of nonreflective Mediterranean sensuality, could learn to think vitally by following Ortega's philosophy.

Just as a son's feelings toward his father are ambivalent and often self-contradictory, so Ortega often vacillates in his attitude toward the father figure Goethe. He tends to overlook the changes that the experience of life brought about in Goethe. Perhaps his occasional failure to see Goethe in perspective is due to his preoccupation with his own philosophy of life; as his own ideas evolved, his view of Goethe changed. He relied upon Goethe as an authority far less in his later works as is evident in the sharp decline in the frequency of allusions to the mentor. In the Obras completas he alluded to Goethe twenty times in volume I; twenty-four times in volume II, ten times in volume III, six times in addition to the centennial essays in volume IV, twice in volume V, and thrice in volume VI.(9)

The Spanish philosopher tended to take Goethe to task when the German poet's philosophy at a certain stage in his life no longer harmonized with Ortega's current ideas. On the other hand, he used many opportunities, particularly the 1932 anniversary, to drape his own ideas with homage to the genius whom he truly revered(10) despite fleeting outbursts, perhaps of jealousy. The relationship is perhaps best expressed by Iriarte who says Ortega was so close to Goethe that it is often impossible to see where one begins and the other ends.(11)   Ortega had Goethe constantly before his eyes.

NOTES

1.   Udo Rukser, Goethe in der hispanischen Welt (Stuttgart: J. B. Metzler, 1958), p. 192.

2.   José Ortega y Gasset Obras completas, 2nd ed. (Madrid: Revista de Occidente, 1950), vol. II, p. 168.   Subsequent references shall appear in the text.

3.   Joaquín Iriarte, Ortega y Gasset (Madrid: 1942), p. 204.

4.   Julián Marías, Ortega ante Goethe (Madrid: Taurus, 1961), p. 20.

5.   Egon Schwartz, "José Ortega y Gasset's Verhaltnis zu Goethe," Studies in Germanic Languages and Literatures, ed. Erich Hofacker Liselotte Dieckmann (St. Louis: Washington University Press, 1963), p. 74.

6.   Nelson Orringer, Ortega y sus fuentes germánicas (Madrid: Gredos, 1979), p. 303.

7.   José Sánchez Villaseñor, Ortega y Gasset: Existentialist (Chicago: Henry Regnery Company, 1949), p. 150.

8.   Harold Bloom, The Anxiety of Influence, (New York: Oxford University Press, 1973); in Yeats (New York: Oxford University Press, 1970), p. 5, Bloom observes: "Freud thought all men unconsciously wished to beget themselves, to be their own fathers in place of their phallic fathers, and so 'rescue' their mothers from erotic degradation.   It may not be true of all men, but it seems to be definitive of poets as poets.   The poet, if he could, would be his own precursor, and so rescue the Muse from her degradation."

9.   Ortega cites Goethe's Viaje de Italia (Roma: abril, 1788) as his source for this biographical note.   It is extremely rare for Ortega to give exact references for his allusions to Goethe.

10.   Rukser, Goethe, p. 190.

11.   Iriarte, Ortega y Gasset, p. 204.

20.
"Consciousness of Shipwreck": Ortega y Gasset and Malcolm Lowry's Concept of the Artist

SHERRILL E. GRACE

"Consciousness of shipwreck, being the truth of life, constitutes salvation."(1)   Malcolm Lowry first read these words from Ortega's essay "In Search of Goethe from Within" shortly after it appeared in Partisan Review (Dec., 1949), and thus began his considerable interest in the philosopher. We know from a long letter dated 23 June 1950 that Lowry was deeply impressed by the Goethe essay and that he had been reading, with even greater interest, Toward a Philosophy of History.(2)   Whether or not Lowry read more than the Partisan Review articles of 1949 and 1952 and Toward a Philosophy of History is difficult to say because only scraps of precise information about Lowry's reading have survived. But whatever he read, it is important to remember that he was a writer, not a philosopher, and with the ruthless eclecticism of the artist he appropriated and transformed the ideas of others. What I am primarily concerned with here is when Lowry discovered Ortega, why Lowry admired him, and what he chose to use from Ortega's work.

My first two questions are, in part, answered. If ever there was a man who believed that the "consciousness of shipwreck . . . constitutes salvation," it was Lowry. Both his works and his life were founded (and foundered) on that belief. One can only begin to imagine what Lowry must have felt, early in 1950, when he read Ortega's description of Goethe as a shipwrecked man and of the individual as a "poor human being (who), feeling himself sinking into the abyss, moves his arms to keep afloat."(3)   Three years previous to this, Lowry had published his masterpiece, Under the Volcano, a novel with important allusions to Goethe, a dramatic portrayal of a man who chooses not to move his arms and ends up in the abyss. Moreover, Lowry, who was a powerful swimmer, tried more than once to drown himself, and after the publication of Under the Volcano, claimed that success was "like some horrible disaster" and that he wished he "had been left in darkness forever to founder and fail."(4)   Certainly Lowry knew first hand what Ortega meant by shipwreck.

But apart from biographical anecdotes, there are several important aspects of Ortega's philosophy which were of value to Lowry and these can be determined by examining Lowry's comments in letters and manuscripts in conjunction with the developments in his art, both before and after 1950, and by comparing these with what we know Lowry read of Ortega. For example, in the 1950 letter referred to above, Lowry heartily approves Ortega's emphasis on history, his philological bent, his brand of optimistic existentialism and his affinity with Heidegger and, as Lowry thought, Kierkegaard. He even goes on to comment, at some length, on Ortega's discussion of liberalism and Communism (issues Lowry had grappled with throughout Under the Volcano) in Toward a Philosophy of History.(5)   But while there are several points on which Ortega may have influenced Lowry's thinking -- or at least corroborated what Lowry was groping towards -- there is one area in which Lowry's

reading of Ortega was crucial, and that is the influence of Ortega's theory
of self-fabrication upon Lowry's concept of the artist, or what Lowry came
to speak of as "Ortega's fellow."(6)

In order to assess the role played by Ortega in Lowry's thinking, it is
necessary to go back at least to 1929 when Lowry met the American writer
Conrad Aiken, who was the first distinct and major influence upon the young
writer.   Under Aiken's tutelage, Lowry learned how to portray the inner
world of human consciousness which he had already chosen as his special concern. But Aiken's writing also reveals an obsession with time, in particular the mythical, historical, and personal past, and it is the combination
of these two interests -- in consciousness and time -- that would be most
fruitful for Lowry.

Sometime during the early thirties, when Lowry spent his vacations from
Cambridge with Aiken, he must have been introduced to the ideas of Freud and
Henri Bergson, both of whom were influential for the older man, but while
Lowry never acquired Aiken's enthusiasm for Freud (in later life he specifically praises Jung over Freud), he developed a lasting interest in Bergson
whom he continued to allude to in his later work. During the period from
1930-1950, Lowry was absorbing Aiken's lessons and moving beyond him into
some rather unusual mystical and quasi-philosophical areas.(7) But Bergson
continued to fascinate Lowry, and it is Bergson who provides the link with
Ortega.

The Bergsonian principles of value to Lowry, who was gradually coming
to see life, art, and the development of consciousness as endless voyage,
are not difficult to discover. In Creative Evolution (1911; trans. 1931),
Bergson argued that existence consists of continual change and that maturity
only comes from endless self-creation. In addition, the individual's past
persists, accumulates, and follows him, thereby providing him with a personal duration. A danger in Bergson's theory arises from the fact that the
passive individual may become psychically trapped in his past and hence
cease to become, and it is a danger that plagued Lowry and each of his protagonists. At the same time that he was grappling with these ideas on continual change, time and consciousness, Lowry was beginning to formulate
plans for a trilogy of novels modeled on Dante, and by 1940 he was calling
this opus The Voyage That Never Ends. This plan, however, was never final,
and he rapidly outgrew the Dantean structure.

Although there are several reasons for the radical changes Lowry was
soon to make in his Voyage plans, three stand out: first, he was almost
incapable of bringing his major works to a conclusion because he was psycho-
logically and aesthetically committed to the need to continue writing; second, he suffered a serious back injury in a 1949 fall and while in the hospital experienced unusual psychic phenomena that he then wanted to use in
his work; third, after approximately twenty years of avid, if eclectic reading and constant self-doubt about his "philosophical equipment," Lowry discovered Ortega. The result was his 1951 "Work in Progress" statement, a
thirty-four page discussion of a revised Voyage that was then to consist of
seven novels in which a man in hospital, and on the threshold of death, is
called upon to give an account of his existence. Simply put, this account
takes the shape of six complex interrelated novels as the dying man presents
the manuscript of his life. In Lowry's words this man, whom he called Sigbjørn Wilderness, is not only the "editor . . . cutter, and . . . shaper
(but) as Ortega observes, a sort of novelist, God help him: the idea of
death as the accepted manuscript of one's life . . . strikes me as a profound one."(8)

Fully aware that in Toward a Philosophy of History Ortega was stressing
the importance of history not fiction, Lowry nevertheless seized upon the
idea of man as "a sort of novelist of himself" who invents his life and then
becomes an engineer in order to convert it into reality. This view of man,
which is also the basis of Ortega's argument in the essay on Goethe, appealed to Lowry so strongly because he was, in fact, ready for such a

formulation. That life was "essentially a drama . . . a desperate struggle. . . to succeed in being in fact that which we are in design"(9) was not
only Lowry's view, but the theory upon which he was trying to base his
Voyage with its constituent novels. But before examining Lowry's development of this concept in his chief character-cum-novelist, Sigbjørn Wilderness, something more should be said about those aspects of Ortega's theory
of man and history that appealed to Lowry and contributed to his conception
of the Wilderness figure.

In the important seventh section of "History as a System" from Toward a
Philosophy of History, Ortega sets forth three interrelated principles:
one, that life is a drama actively imagined and carried out by the individual; two, that the individual ego is the "vital program" of being, the drama
that a man chooses to create (indeed, must choose as a consequence of his
"constitutive instability"); and, three, that being must be understood as
Heraclitean or non-Eleatic. Concerning the first of these principles,
Ortega draws a most useful distinction between his view and Bergson's. By
isolating the phrase "l'être en se faisant" and the verbal "se faisant,"
Ortega points to a certain passivity inherent in Bergson's idea of merely
"becoming" (devenir), in contrast to his own emphasis upon the activity of
"making" or "fabricating oneself." With Bergson, despite his emphatically
Heraclitean position, man is acted upon; with Ortega, man is the actant.

For Lowry's protagonists the problem is always whether or not they will
act or merely be acted upon, and to the degree that they can act they will
succeed in making themselves. As we are reminded by the writing on the wall
in Volcano: "No se puede vivir sin amar," -- "one cannot live without loving." And Lowry insisted (as does Ortega) upon the activity instead of the
state. The second of these principles takes clearer shape in Lowry's post-
Volcano work where, with Ortega's help, he consciously begins to dramatize
the struggles and more hopeful, creative efforts of the master "ego" (in
Ortega's sense) and writer of the Voyage, Sigbjørn Wilderness, who is making
up his life as he goes along in the effort to realize his "vital program"
and in the full terrifying awareness that he is "able to be other than what
(he) was."(10)

But before turning to a closer examination of the Wilderness character,
the consequences of the third principle mentioned above, Ortega's non-
Eleatic concept of being, should be considered. According to Ortega,

> human life is thus not an entity that changes acciden-
> tally, rather the reverse: in it the "substance" is
> precisely change, which means that it cannot be thought
> of Eleatically as substance. Life being a "drama" that
> happens, and the "subject" to whom it happens being, not
> a thing apart from and previous to his drama, but a
> function of it, it follows that the "substance" of the
> drama would be its argument.(11)

From this essentially phenomenological position, Lowry could draw valuable
support for his belief that life and art are perpetually protean and must
constantly change, and that the best art is a type of mimetic art that mir-
rors the flux of reality at the same time as it stands (in the Voyage novels) in metonymic relation to Sigbjørn Wilderness' drama of self-fabrication.

Two brief examples from Lowry's work should clarify these points. In
the posthumously published novel, October Ferry to Gabriola, Lowry's protagonist, who is "beginning, beginning, beginning again" on his outward bound
voyage of life, must realize that he has become a "misoneist," a hater of
change, who will only survive if he can overcome this problem. Faced with
eviction from his beloved cabin home beside the sea, he learns that, "imper-
manence, indeed, the ramshackle tenuity of the life, were part of its beauty, . . . why then be afraid of change?"(12)

Tackling this same problem of non-Eleatic being and its consequences for art in a late metafictional story called "Ghostkeeper," Lowry's artist-protagonist ruminates over the fact that the "minute an artist begins to try and shape his material -- the more especially if that material is his own life," he realizes that his "shaping . . . is absurd, that nothing is static . . . that everything is evolving or developing into other meanings."(13) This leads the man in the story to Ortega, whom he paraphrases to the effect that man becomes an engineer in order to give form to the fiction of his life. The man then concludes that the story which he is writing (in fact, the story the reader is reading) must "give the illusion of things . . . in a state of perpetual metamorphosis."

It is hard to say with certainty just when Lowry began to create Sigbjørn Wilderness as a self-fabricating artist figure. Manuscript and biographical evidence suggest sometime between 1949, when he broke his back, and 1951, when he wrote his "Work in Progress" statement -- in other words, at or around the time he was reading Ortega. It was also at this time that he began the two-part "Ordeal of Sigbjørn Wilderness," which was intended as a frame for the Voyage novels. Lying close to death in hospital, Sigbjørn would recall his entire life in the form of the novels he had written in the process of self-fabrication, which, in turn, comprise the life-text that the Voyage reader reads. But instead of dying, Wilderness struggles back to life; in a sense he refuses to drown and is able to continue his never-ending voyage. Wilderness is, in fact, the author of Volcano and the other Voyage novels, and through the writing of these texts he has created, imagined, or fabricated his life.

In a 1953 letter to his editor, Albert Erskine, Lowry described and defended his theory of the artist in some detail. He maintained that Wilderness, although a novelist, was not typical of the self-conscious, articulate writers usually found in novels. To the contrary, he is unsure of himself -- "he is Ortega's fellow, making up his life as he goes along, and trying to find his vocation."(14) Lowry agreed with Ortega that the novelist was an excellent image of man and, therefore, he liked to think of his Wilderness character in this way. Lowry's defense was intended to allay Erskine's doubts about the role of Wilderness in the fourth Voyage novel, Dark as the Grave, where Wilderness, as author of Under the Volcano, revisits Mexico and the scenes of his novel only to find alarming parallels between events in the fiction he has written and in the fiction he is presently living. This realization leads him to the suspicion that, contrary to being free to choose his own drama, he is no more than a character in someone else's fiction. Furthermore, since arriving in Mexico he has been unable to write, to act, indeed to live at all; he is drinking heavily, has attempted suicide, and refuses to leave his apartment.

Dark as the Grave is by no means as complex or profound a work as Volcano; nevertheless, it is not possible to summarize briefly all the issues Lowry was tackling. If he had lived to finish it and others of its Voyage companions, the philosophical burden carried by the Wilderness character would have been more convincingly dramatized. Even in its present form, however, it is obvious that Lowry was exploring the ontological and aesthetic problems faced by an artist who must continuously create his life story in a world that is perpetually protean.

He achieved some success in Dark as the Grave in several senses. First, the very structure of the text duplicates in its opening narrative stasis the paralysis of the man who can neither write nor live. Second, Sigbjørn Wilderness does eventually move his arms in order to swim free of the psychological and fictional pasts which threaten to drown him. He comes face to face with shipwreck, and he saves his life, his marriage, his vocation -- at least for the time being. Third, in Dark as the Grave, Lowry provided his only major portrayal of the Voyage Wilderness character, and through a close and informed study of the text we are able to watch him struggling with some of the most philosophically challenging concepts of our time. Unfortunately, <u>Dark as the Grave</u> has been dismissed and disparaged, but when it is viewed in the light of the revised <u>Voyage</u> and the consistent development of Lowry's thinking on questions of consciousness, time, change and being, which culminate in his discovery of Ortega, then the novel can be seen to contain some fascinating material and much genuine merit.(15)

Outside the entire <u>Voyage</u> cycle stands Malcolm Lowry who drew deeply on his own experience for the shape and subject matter of his fiction. In his writer/protagonist, Sigbjørn Wilderness, Lowry created an alter ego (a <u>Doppelgänger</u> as he called him) who represents what he understood as the central human endeavor of self-fabrication, and Lowry's image for that activity was the manuscript of his life — <u>The Voyage That Never Ends</u>. The concept was not simple nor the task easy. Because he believed in a non-Eleatic concept of being, a perpetually protean reality that is nonetheless a unity in multiplicity, and an art that must mirror these truths, Lowry (or Wilderness) also believed that the elements and form of his art must be in constant flux. As Sigbjørn complains in <u>Dark as the Grave</u>, artistic despair arises, in part, from the fact that "the universe itself . . . is in the process of creation," and that, therefore, an "organic work of art, having been conceived, must grow in the creator's mind, or proceed to perish."(16)

Several dangers spring from this philosophical position, and these too are part of Sigbjørn's drama, and thereby scenes in each of the novels; he is frequently tempted to withdraw from action due to various guilts, minor defeats, or temporary setbacks, and allow himself to drown; he is increasingly plagued by the fear that instead of writing his life, he is being written; and, finally, he is overwhelmed by the emotional, psychological and artistic burden he must carry, for the minute he stops creating — in Lowry's own and in his character's case — he has ceased to live. What is so often mistaken for autobiography masquerading as fiction in Lowry's post-<u>Volcano</u> work is the beginning of a fascinating metafictional mimetic enterprise that, if completed, would have forced us to redefine autobiography.(17) Without his discovery of Ortega y Gasset in 1950, Lowry would not have pushed as far along in his project as he did.

But it seems to me that something further be said by way of conclusion to this discussion; otherwise I will simply have charted a few points on the intersecting trajectories of two important twentieth-century writers. Beyond the questions of influence and adaptation lies the larger question of what our writers tell us about the time in which they and we live. Both Lowry and Ortega strike me as very much early-to-mid-twentieth-century men. They speak to and of their time, no more so than when they recognize, whether through philosophical or literary systems, the centrality of individual consciousness in a world stripped of absolutes, where man must create his identity within an ever-changing historical process and his art within the ineluctable constraints of his medium.

Ortega touches upon precisely this point in his conclusion to "On Point of View in the Arts" when he speaks of the modernists' "progressive de-realization of the world" that has resulted in intrasubjectivity and the "virtual objects"(18) of a phenomenological system. Lowry's fiction shows that he was attempting to understand and portray just such a world in an art that was often (as Ortega notes of contemporary art in general) expressionistic. That Lowry destroyed himself before he could finish this task by writing those novels that embody a positive vision of <u>living with</u> the world,(19) or indeed that he had undertaken a task which by definition could not be finished, may be personally tragic, but it is scarcely surprising. He was a man who accepted the "consciousness of shipwreck," and what salvation can be derived from that truth lies in his art.

NOTES

1. José Ortega y Gasset, "In Search of Goethe from Within," in <u>The Dehumanization of Art and Other Essays on Art, Culture, and Literature</u>

(Princeton, N.J.: Princeton University Press, 1968), p. 137. Lowry probably read the essays included here when they appeared in Partisan Review for
1949 and 1952.

2.   Selected Letters of Malcolm Lowry, eds. Harvey Breit and Margerie
Bonner Lowry (Philadelphia & New York: J. B. Lippincott 1965), pp. 208-13.

3.   Ortega y Gasset, Dehumanization, p. 136.

4.   Selected Poems of Malcolm Lowry, ed. Earle Birney (San Francisco:
City Lights Books, 1962), p. 78.

5.   José Ortega y Gasset, Toward a Philosophy of History (New York:
W. W. Norton, 1941).

6.   Lowry, Selected Letters, p. 331.

7.   These influences (including William James, J. W. Dunne, P. D.
Ouspensky, Annie Besant and Charles Stansfeld-Jones), together with Aiken,
are discussed in my book The Voyage That Never Ends: Malcolm Lowry's Fiction (Vancouver, B.C.: The University of British Columbia Press, 1982), and
in several articles cited in its bibliography.

8.   From the unpublished MS entitled "Work in Progress" in the Lowry
Collection at The University of British Columbia Library, Box 37:9, pp. 2-3.
At the time of his death, the Voyage was to consist of "The Ordeal of Sigbjørn Wilderness, I", Ultramarine, Lunar Caustic, Under the Volcano, Dark as
the Grave Wherein My Friend Is Laid, "La Mordida," "Eridanus" (published
posthumously as October Ferry to Gabriola), and "The Ordeal of Sigbjørn
Wilderness, II."

9.   Ortega y Gasset, Dehumanization, p. 141.

10.   Ortega y Gasset, Toward a Philosophy, p. 203.

11.   Ibid., p. 205 (Emphasis is mine).

12.   Malcolm Lowry, October Ferry to Gabriola (New York: World Publishing, 1970), p. 171.

13.   "Ghostkeeper," Malcolm Lowry: Psalms and Songs, ed. Margerie
Lowry (New York: Meridian, 1975), p. 223.

14.   Lowry, Selected Letters, p. 331.

15.   Dark as the Grave Wherein My Friend Is Laid, eds. Douglas Day and
Margerie Lowry (New York: World Publishing, 1969).

16.   Lowry, Dark as the Grave, p. 154.

17.   For a discussion of the relationship between metafiction and mimesis, notably the process mimesis of much contemporary metafiction, see Linda
Hutcheon's Narcissistic Narrative: The Metafictional Paradox (Waterloo, On-
tario: Wilfrid Laurier University Press, 1980), pp. 39-47.

18.   Ortega y Gasset, Dehumanization, p. 129.

19.   The novella, "Forest Path to the Spring," from Hear us O Lord from
Heaven Thy Dwelling Place (London: Jonathan Cape, 1961), was the closest
Lowry came to portraying what Ortega seems to mean by living with the world,
and it is a work of unique, meditative beauty.

21.
José Ortega y Gasset and Federico García Lorca

JUDY B. MCINNIS

José Ortega y Gasset exerted a profound influence on Federico García Lorca in the late twenties when Lorca was most engaged in defining his aesthetics. The great Spanish intellectual shaped the young poet's mind both through his published works and through his lectures at the Residencia de Estudiantes, where Lorca lived while in Madrid. Lorca published some of his poems and prose works in the Revista de Occidente, which Ortega founded and edited. In "The Psychological Map of García Lorca's Aesthetics: Granada as Universal Image," I traced Lorca's borrowings from Ortega's psychological system for the personifications of three kinds of poetic inspiration: the angel, the muse, and the daemon.(1) Ortega had fleshed out the skeleton of the psychological system informing the Meditaciones del Quijote (Meditations on Quixote), 1914, in his article "Vitalidad, alma, espíritu" ("Vitality, Soul, Spirit"), 1924. In this essay I shall endeavor to elucidate the surprising degree of Lorca's reliance upon Ortega not only for the content but especially for the form -- the structure and metaphors -- of his lectures and surreal prose poems.

Ortega prefaced his article "Vitalidad, alma, espíritu" with a discussion of what a lecture is and how it should be reviewed. Comparing a summary to "bird scraps" because it "extirpates the wing and leaves the gizzard and the claw behind,"(2) he urged journalists to remember that a lecture is "a small drama which happens" (Ortega, OC II, p. 451) in a particular salon to a particular audience and with a particular speaker. He described the lecture's title as a net that reaches down into the depths of society to capture a marine booty, sometimes even a few sirens. Each lecture is an organism, an animal, with its own particular history, Ortega asserted. Thus, he held that it should not be summarized but rather recounted like an automobile accident or a football game; the journalist should take account of the coughs, the tension, the boredom, and the excitement of orator and public.

Ortega's emphasis on the particular circumstance of each lecture illustrates the extent to which his philosophy of vital reason permeated all his utterances. Through the development of vital reason Ortega sought to overcome the isolation of the spirit within which he included intelligence and will both from the outer world whose images constantly stimulate the imagination and from the inner world where all impressions are shaped by the psyche's emotional responses. Similarly in the Meditaciones del Quijote, Ortega devoted the first meditation to setting the ideal scene for the work. He believed that his hillside perspective of the Escorial put him in the right frame of mind for achieving man's primary task in life: the reabsorption of his circumstance. In another continuation of ideas implicit in the Meditaciones, Ortega in "Vitalidad, alma, espíritu" identified corporeal vitality, spirit, and emotive soul as the three components of the human psyche. He then outlined a cultural anthropology, a theory of psychological development, and a national typology based upon the prevalence of one of the components in the individual or in the composite national character. Thus, the child "scarcely possesses spirit, has a small volume of soul and a great periphery of vitality" (Ortega, OC II, p. 473). Ortega believed that the ancient Greeks based their worldview in corporeal vitality from which they passed directly to spirit without experiencing the emotive state. Looking at modern nations, Ortega declared that the northern peoples have less corporeal vitality but more spirit than the southern ones.

Lorca kept his mentor clearly in mind when he began his own lecturing career in the United States and South America in 1930. Both the content and the form of "Las nanas infantiles" ("Children's Cradlesongs"), where he presents nursery rhymes as the culture's and the individual's most important artifacts of literary awareness, reveal Ortega's influence. At the beginning of the lecture, Lorca followed the method Ortega had used in the Meditaciones and described in "Vitalidad, alma, espíritu." Lorca too asserted that his purpose was to suggest and incite rather than to define and he insisted upon studying the object within its circumstance. To understand cradlesongs one must study them from within; one must enter into the world of the child, a world where analysis is conducted within a frame of vital, immediate experience unlike the world of the erudite scholar whose analysis consists in removing and isolating the object from its circumstance. Lorca, like Ortega, insisted on the need to study living things, the small things that truly define the character of a people. Ortega cited Goethe in his letter to Jacobi on one of his botanical-geological excursions as example and authority for this attitude: "I am here climbing up and down hills and searching for the divine in herbis et lapidibus" (Ortega, OC I, p. 322). Ortega also adopted as his own Goethe's statement of the heroic nature of intellectual investigation: "A fighter I have been, and this means that I have been a man" (Ortega, OC I, p. 319). Lorca unself-consciously presented himself within this tradition in his self-portrait of his normal poetic activities which he left behind to study the cradlesongs: "I am in this moment far from the poet who watches the clock, far from the poet who struggles with the statue, who struggles with dreams, who struggles with anatomy."(3) Ortega's metaphor comparing the lecture to a fishing expedition also recurs in Lorca's lecture: "I have wished to go down to the bank of bulrushes" (Lorca, OC, p. 48), he declared.

Lorca also developed the motif of the dead bird, which Ortega used repeatedly in the Meditaciones del Quijote and once again in "Vitalidad, alma, esp{ritu." Lorca's association of this motif with the child had already appeared in the Surreal prose poem "Degollación de los inocentes" ("Massacre of the Innocents"): "Do you remember the nightingale with the two little broken legs: It was among the insects, creators of shivers and mouth waterings" (Lorca, OC, p. 21). In the lecture Lorca presented the child in harmony with Ortega's psychology as a being who lives primarily from his center of corporeal vitality and who is slowly discovering the world of spirit and soul. Again projecting the image through Surreal lenses, Lorca depicted the child coolly, almost scientifically, studying the ants devouring a bird smashed by an automobile.

In Ortega's Meditaciones del Quijote, the image of birds falling dead in flight over the swamp became a symbol of the memories or thoughts of the past disintegrating in the Spanish soul. Ortega believed that it was only by giving life to the past, "opening our veins and injecting their blood into the empty veins of the dead" (Ortega, OC I, p. 324), that the Spaniard could dominate the past and achieve a vital culture. Spain's error was not that it was a country dedicated to its ancestors but that it removed life from them without gaining any vitality for those still living; it merely let the dead dominate the living: "The death of the dead is life" (Ortega, OC I, p. 324), Ortega maintained. In his lecture on cradlesongs, Lorca also emphasized Spain's death culture. Falling asleep is a rehearsal for death in Spain: "A deadman is more dead in Spain than in any other part of the world.   And he who wishes to fall asleep wounds his feet on the blade of a barbarous knife" (Lorca, OC, p. 51).   Lorca reiterated his belief that the most vital element of Spanish culture arises from its preoccupation with death in his "Teoría y juego del duende" ("Theory and Play of the Daemon"), delivered in New York in 1930.   This lecture simultaneously reveals Lorca's dependence and independence of Ortega.   His angel, muse, daemon trinity translates Ortega's corporeal vitality, spirit, and emotive soul from the psychological to the aesthetic realm, but while Ortega deplores the pre-dominance of the emotional or the irrational in the Spaniard, Lorca exalts it as source of the highest art and claims that the daemonic constitutes Spain's unique contribution to the world.

Lorca's sense of the circumstance of the lecture reveals the extent to which he had absorbed Ortega's philosophy of vital reason.   He was acutely aware of the irony of subjecting the irrational daemon to spiritual analysis or, in terms of his own aesthetic theory, to muse-inspired intellectualiza-tion.   He and his audience occupied the very salon that he so disparagingly associated with the muse both in this essay(4) and in the prose poem "Nada-dora Sumergida" ("Submerged Swimmer").   In the former, Lorca attempted to dispel the tedium of this ambiance through a virtual exorcism -- naming and abjuring its presence -- so that he might speak to his audience as a poet giving "a simple lesson on the dark spirit of aching Spain" (Lorca, OC, p. 36).   The subtitle of the latter, "Pequeño homenaje a un cronista de salones" ("A Small Homage to the Chronicler of Salons"), establishes the ironic tone used throughout the poem.

In both poem and lecture, the muse is associated with snow, northern countries, the salon, marble, mollusks, and decapitated sirens.   In the poem Lorca's narrator seduces his listener, the Countess, with a vivid monologue describing his love affair with a frigid, ethereal woman who always eluded his grasp.   The narrator confides that he only possessed that woman when the devil drove him to approach her at three in the morning.   He had a scalpel bisecting his throat, she a large silk scarf, or rather the tail of the horse about to carry him away.   Only when each mutilated themselves -- he by slashing his forehead, she by cutting her cheek -- were they able to em-brace.   The narrator describes the three fold development of this embrace with images alluding to the author's works: the gypsy poetry, the drama Mariana Pineda, and the odes.   Allowing the allegorical level of this ac-count of his relationship to the muse to surface on the literal level, the narrator declares: "Since then I left the old literature which I had culti-vated with great success.   It is necessary to break it completely for dogmas to be purified and for norms to have a new tremor" (Lorca, OC, p. 32).   The poem ends with the murder of the new muse, Countess X.   Although her death is attributed to her love of swimming, a reference recalling Ortega's de-scriptions of fishing and sirens in the article "Vitalidad, alma, espíritu," the murder is actually the handiwork of the narrator who has left a note tied to a wormwood fork stuck in the Countess' throat with the message, "Since you couldn't turn into a dove, you are better off dead" (Lorca, OC, p. 32).

In this poem Lorca allegorized his flirtation with Surrealism and sup-plied a paradigm of his own process of creation in which the muse is first courted by the angel (imagination), then annihilated by the daemon as the poet seeks to create his unique variation on the literary tradition.   Lorca deliberately undercuts the marine and aviary motifs on which the poem is based with the cold, clinical irony typical of the Surrealists.   The muse as the agent who enables the poet to go on a fishing expedition in the sea of his unconscious here herself becomes the prize: a siren who fails to reach the sea and one who is immediately cast aside since she can neither fly nor swim.   The Countess with the wormwood fork in her neck ironically recalls Garcilaso de la Vega's portrait of the dead Elisa in the Third Eclogue.   Un-like Elisa whose sacrificial beheading allowed the flow of blood and song, the stabbing of the Countess' throat stifles song. Lorca's perception of Surrealism as an overintellectualized movement that kills the spirit of poetry is revealed in his metaphorical description of his own poetry (including the present poem): "On the French coast the assassins of the sailors and those who rob fishermen of salt were beginning to sing" (Lorca, OC, p. 31).

A "spiritual" ideal in the Orteguian sense had inspired Lorca's Surreal prose poems as well as his most classical poems, the didactic "Oda a Salvador Dalí" ("Ode to Salvador Dalí"), 1926, and the unfinished "La sirena y el carabinero" ("The Siren and the Rifleman"), 1927, both written in alexandrines. In the latter Lorca was striving for luminescence and serenity of form in the creation of the "myth of the useless beauty of the sea" (Lorca, OC, p. 1564). In an amorous, tranquil meditation, the poet was to extract and give disinterested expression to the pure concept beneath the sensual image. In his lecture on Góngora (1926), Lorca presented the poet as a nocturnal hunter in a distant forest, a poetic elaboration of a motif Ortega developed in the Meditaciones (Ortega, OC I, p. 327). Góngora tied down his imagination like a sculptor, Lorca declared in an echo of Ortega: "Plato says that impressions escape us if we do not bind them with reason, as, according to legend, Demetrius' statues used to flee from the gardens nightly if he did not tie them down" (Ortega, OC I, p. 353). Góngora, Lorca declared, did not create from the immediate sensuous impressions of Nature but from the meditation upon these impressions that come out of "the dark room of the brain and from there leave transformed in order to make the big jump upon the other world with which they are fused" (Lorca, OC, p. 76).

Through the "equestrian leap" of the metaphor, he joined the external world of impressions and the interior visionary world. The result was an autonomous poetic reality distinct from Nature: "A world of essential features of things and characteristic differences" (Lorca, OC, p. 77). The dark side of poetic inspiration and its alliance to the subconscious combine with the desire for the terra firma of logic in Lorca's portrait of Góngora as a lover of islands who gazes out to sea in meditative reverie. In his discussion of the conflict between the culture of the abstract intellect and spontaneous life, Ortega in El tema de nuestro tiempo (The Theme of Our Time), 1923, declared that pure reason "is only a brief island floating on the sea of primary vitality" (Ortega, OC III, p. 177). Lorca suggested that Góngora, like himself an Andalusian poet, achieved the vital reason that Ortega proposed as the new ideal. He accomplished the union of the impression and the concept. In the Meditaciones, Ortega, in oblivious disregard of the Baroque art of the conceit in Góngora, Quevedo, Calderón, Gracián, etc., had affirmed: "We represent in the moral map of Europe the extreme predominance of the impression. The concept has never been our element" (Ortega, OC, I, p. 359).

Of course, Góngora exercised the "spirit" to exalt the images of everyday reality with little concern for poetry's moral dimension. For this the poets of his time had labeled him an atheist.(5) In Ortega's theory the concept gives the essence of a thing -- its moral and physical dimensions. In his own essay on Góngora in 1927, Ortega stressed the diabolic nature of Góngora's alchemy with a comparison to Faust. Góngora's euphemistic, recreative art forced the reader to perceive simultaneously the new world of mythical beauty and the old one of everyday objects: "Bedeviled operation. Rejuvenation. Young Faust who carries within the decrepit Faust" (Ortega, OC III, p. 581). Ortega accommodated Góngora within his theory of Mediterranean sensuality by emphasizing the overabundance of his images, which approached the vegetative exuberance of Indian sculpture: Góngora's art represented "the unformed and the chaotic within the very zeal that wants to create forms. It has been said that exuberance of all Hindustani life gives it a vegetal sense. It is the forest that suffocates in its own fecundity" (Ortega, OC III, p. 584). Ortega agreed that the poet had reduced art to its purest element: pure jest, agreeable fable" (Ortega, OC III, p. 586).

Recognizing the validity of this artistic purpose, he nevertheless warned young poets to temper their enthusiasm for Góngora: "Without limits, there is no outline or physiognomy.   It is necesary to define Góngora's grace, but, at the same time, his horror" (Ortega, OC III, p. 587).

As a poet and an Andalusian, Lorca had a deeper appreciation of Góngora than did Ortega.   However, as Laffranque points out, the seeds of Lorca's disenchantment were already present in his description of Góngora's "objective beauty, pure and useless," but also "exempt from communicable anguish."(6)   Lorca produced his most Surreal poetry under the influence of the Gongorine muse: poetry characterized by an obsession with aesthetics so extreme that the creative process itself becomes the primary theme of each work.(7) The "horror" of beauty -- bloody sacrifice, suicide, mutilation -- became the poet's métier in precisely organized short narrations.   Contrary to Ortega's prophecy that such poetry would become formless, Lorca imposed concept over image in works with the clarity of vision of the allegorical parable.   The price of this clarity was the literal assassination of the living image.   In the "Degollación del Bautista" ("Beheading of the Baptist"), Lorca identified equally with victim and assassin:(8) "It is necessary to go against the flesh.   It is necessary to raise factories of knives. So that horror moves its intravenous forest.   The specialist in beheading is the enemy of emeralds" (Lorca, OC, p. 19).   In the "Degollación de los inocentes" the conflict between image and concept was given its most pathetic expression as Lorca particularized the victims by giving them diminutive names: "Jorgito. Alvarito. Guillermito. Leopoldito. Julito. Joseíto. Luisito. Innocents. Steel needs heat to create nebulas and -- let's go to the indefatigable leaf! It is better to be a medusa and to float than to be a child" (Lorca, OC, p. 21).

In Ensayos filosóficos: biología y pedagogía (Philosophical Essays: Biology and Pedagogy), 1921, Ortega had described the reduced world of the mollusk, sensitive only to pressure and without the senses of sight, hearing, smell, or taste to illustrate the necessity of understanding a creature's "landscape" to understand its life. Very much in the Romantic current, he developed the idea that the best part of the adult is the child that remains imprisoned in his soul. The ability to expend effort in activities that have no immediately useful application stems from the survival of the child's values in the poet, the wiseman, the politician, the general, and the inventor.

In the "Degollación de los inocentes," Lorca allegorized the strange conjunction of the spirit and the subconscious in the Surrealist credo. A creation of the spirit (the conscious mind) however much it glorifies the subconscious, Surrealist dogma serves the intellect as an instrument for the assassination of the child's vision. The reward is entrance into the world of the medusa where all things simply exist without evoking emotional response.   In the elemental world of the prehuman, things are at last seen in utmost simplicity: life and death; blood seeking to flow into the sea at the planetary bloodletting of the sunset. The inhumanity of this soulless aesthetic is apparent in the poet's brutal statement: "It is necessary to have two hundred sons and to hand them over to the massacre. Only in this way will the autonomy of the wood lily be possible" (Lorca, OC, p. 21).   The objective art of the "spirit" requires the sacrifice of the poet's childlike vision of an integrated cosmos, the world of things as they ought to be, for it is a world created by his own desire.   In Orteguian terminology, the spirit kills the emotive soul that is exemplified in Lorca's icy, detached narration of the events; the spirit also kills the vital (corporeal) soul as the parents eagerly turn their children over to the butcher. Art and life are absolutely divorced.

This reader, like Ortega and eventually like Lorca himself, comes away from these poems with serious questions about the validity of an aesthetic that requires such violent symbols for its expression. Should emotional and moral responses to such atrocities be converted into an utterly dehumanized aesthetic response? Lorca's goal was to sympathize equally with assassin and victim, both doomed to play out the drama. The only motive given the faceless assassins is completion of an instinctual pattern.

As Lorca explained in his lecture "Imaginación, inspiración, evasión" ("Imagination, Inspiration, Evasion"), 1929, the Surrealists wanted to reduce poetry to the creation of the poetic deed. By liberating poetry from the anecdotal element, they evaded reality and created a distinct world of "virgin emotions, staining poems with a planetary feeling. Evasion of reality by way of dreams, by way of the subconscious, by the way that dictates an unheard of deed that inspiration presents" (Lorca, OC p. 1546). In, his revision of this lecture, Lorca added that this poetry was "very pure, scarcely diaphanous" and admitted the Latins' preference for "profiles and visible mystery. Form and sensualities" (Lorca, OC, p. 1548).

In 1927 Lorca had lamented that he and his contemporaries were following two false roads: "one which goes to Romanticism and another that goes to the snake's skin and the empty locust;" he could not escape condemnation of this "empty poetry or decorative scabbard" (Lorca, OC, p. 1590). By 1935 he was deploring the fact that Zorrilla's Romantic dramas were no longer staged; they had been superseded by the dramas of Naturalism and Modernism: "Because of that the verses that are recited today are fang-toothed. People say: 'How well they rhyme, how well they sound . . .,' but nobody weeps, nobody feels tears in his eyes, as they do feel when Zorrilla speaks" (Lorca, OC, p. 1729). The same could not be said of Lorca's own dramas, for he had ultimately heeded his mentor's warning against the excesses of Gongorism. In his great rural tragedies, Lorca turned away from Gongorism's modern resurgence in the Surrealist movement to forge a new compromise between modern technique and tradition.

NOTES

1. Judy B. McInnis, The Comparatist, 8 (1984), 33–42.

2. José Ortega y Gasset, Obras completas, 2nd ed., 6 vol. (Madrid: Revista de Occidente, 1950), vol. II, p. 451. Subsequent references to this edition will appear in the text. All English translations from Spanish are my own.

3. Federico García Lorca, Obras completas, 4th ed., ed. Arturo del Hoyo (Madrid: Aguilar, 1960), p. 48. Subsequent references to this edition will appear in the text.

4. Ibid., p. 38. Lorca declares: "The muse awakens the intelligence, she brings a landscape of columns and the false flavor of laurels, and the intelligence is often poetry's enemy, because it imitates too much, because it elevates the poet on a throne of cliffs and makes him forget that suddenly the ants can devour him or a great arsenic locust can fall on his head against which the muses in monocles or in the tepid lacquered rose of the small salon are powerless."

5. Francisco Cascales, in Cartas filológicas, ed. Justo García Soriano (Madrid: Espasa-Calpe, S.A., 1930), vol. I, p. 221. Cascales declares that Góngora aspired to be "prince of light" but became "prince of darkness." Dámaso Alonso has pointed out the similarity of culteranismo and luteranismo in Góngora y el "Polifemo" (Madrid: Editorial Gredos, 1961), vol. I, pp. 69–70. Andrée Collard develops this argument in Nueva poesía: conceptismo, culteranismo en la crítica española (Waltham, Mass. and Madrid: Brandeis University and Editorial Castalia, 1967).

6. Marie Laffranque, Les idées esthétiques de Federico García Lorca (Paris: Centre de Recherches Hispaniques, 1967), p. 120.

7.   Although he does not link Lorca and Góngora, Paul Ilie suggests a
connection between Gongorism and Surrealism in the poetry of Rafael Alberti
who moved from an initial period of "obscure Gongorism" to "cryptic personal
baroque" that was expressed in the collection Sobre los ángeles in The Surrealist Mode in Spanish Literature (Ann Arbor: The University of Michigan
Press, 1968), p. 122.   Ilie observes the divorce between feeling and metaphor in this collection, a divorce which I also see in Lorca's narraciones.
In his concluding chapter Ilie does relate Surrealism to Gongorism: "Many
of its antecedents can be found in the tradition of the Spanish grotesque,
and perhaps even in the dehumanizing techniques of Gongorism" (p. 193).   The
general influence of Góngora on the Generation of 1927 has been treated by
Dámaso Alonso, Estudios y ensayos gongorinos (Madrid: Editorial Gredos,
1960), pp. 532–79.

8.   In a letter to Jorge Guillén, Lorca (OC, p. 1564) declared that he
wished to communicate equal sympathy for the rifleman and the siren he kills
in his new poem "La sirena y el carabinero."

22.
José Ortega y Gasset and Arthur Koestler: Meditations on the Two-faced Forest
RONALD G. JONES

1983 — the centenary year of Ortega y Gasset's birth. 1983 — the year that Arthur Koestler took his own life, at age seventy-seven. Perhaps not much of a coincidence, yet this essay is meant to celebrate the centenary of Ortega's birth and to be a tribute to Koestler's work.

It is questionable whether this centenary celebration of Ortega's birth would please him. Let me play a little game: in preparation for this centenary, I began by looking through the serried volumes of his works. But I immediately felt that my goodwill would soon be exhausted. I am not in favor of centenaries. It is a sad and depressing business to go over a treasure of depreciated coins. Will the contributions at this centenary merely work on Ortega, work underneath Ortega, and simply be concerned with going around Ortega? Will our work be sterile Orteguian bigotry?

Do you recognize this? The above paragraph, with obvious changes, is taken directly from Ortega's remarks when he participated in the centenary of Goethe's death. This appears in "In Search of Goethe from Within."

I am sure that Festschrifts and centenaries will be organized for Koestler at the appropriate times. Koestler showed some displeasure with such goings-on in his novel The Call Girls. This novel is a satire on those professors that travel from conference to conference, repeating their never-changing ideas.

This year my students were required to read both La rebelión de las masas (The Revolt of the Masses) and Darkness at Noon. One of the exciting discoveries of this is the fact that modern, thoughtful, and critical students find both Ortega and Koestler relevant. The former book was first published in 1930, the latter in 1940. One in the midst of Spain's turmoil, the other at the beginning of World War II. Both have become modern classics. Why? My theme is that both deal, on the socio-political level, with the most fundamental problem — the individual in society — which, expressed on the philosophical level, is the problem of the One and the Many.

The history of this problem is easily traced from the ancient Chinese I Ching, through the ancient Greek problem of the One and the Many as clearly seen in Plato's Parmenides, through the fifteenth-century Nicolas of Cusa, the sixteenth-century Shakespeare, the eighteenth-century Goethe, to great moderns such as Teilhard de Chardin and Alfred North Whitehead. Beyond the problem of the One and the Many, both authors deal directly with the issue of whether there is a reality greater than the individual — Ortega in terms of "limits," and Koestler in terms of the "tragic" plane in his autobiographical writing, and the "greater" in Darkness at Noon.

Whether Ortega and Koestler like it or not, their work enjoys and will continue to enjoy a certain timelessness and timeliness. It is this that will make both men "contemporary" at any time. Ortega and Koestler deal with this classic problem in different ways, of course. But to focus on the differences is to miss their greatness and the importance of their diagnoses of man's eternal predicament, along with their prescriptions.

The title of this essay includes reference to the Roman god Janus, the god able to look in two directions at once -- having a kind of "double vision" -- and refers to forest, or I could have referred to the Roman god Sylvanus, the god of forests. Koestler's second-to-the-last book was entitled Janus: A Summing Up (1978). I also rely on Ortega's beautiful essays "The Forest" and "Streams and Orioles" in Meditaciones del Quijote (Meditations on Quixote). In the works I have mentioned, one readily finds the bases for my claim that Ortega y Gasset and Arthur Koestler enjoy a certain timelessness and timeliness. And further, they can claim to have made significant contributions to problems psychological, socio-political and philosophical in nature.

While La rebelión de las masas is a socio-political treatise, Darkness at Noon is a socio-political novel. In interpreting each, it is well to recall Ortega's advice. He tells us that we need not adhere strictly to the text, that all articulate language leaves something unsaid, that there are "tacit suppositions." He tells us that a thinker's ideas always possess a "subsoil." In his Origen de la filosofía (Origin of Philosophy) he writes that "Every text is a fragment of an unexpressed context."

In addressing problems in the field of the professional preparation of teachers, I work in terms of a hierarchy of three levels, from most inclusive to least -- that is, on the philosophical, sociological, and educational levels. It could be said that I think and work in terms of a Philosophical Sociology of Education. The principle of subsumption provides the basis for the relationships among the levels. These levels are isomorphic with the hierarchy of Meta-theory, Theory, and Practice. Or as Lancelot Law Whyte put it so nicely, Mystical Love, Intellectual Clarity, and Appropriate Action.

Using these levels, Ortega and Koestler contribute differently. Both obviously contribute to the middle level of science, theory, or, in this case, socio-political clarity. Ortega intended to contribute in a major way to education. Koestler seldom concerned himself with what I would identify as the concerns of education. Indeed, there is a sense in which he could be seen as anti-education. In recent years he raised the controversial question of whether a drug is possible that could reconcile our self-assertiveness with our ability to transcend ourselves. He gave up on sweet reason.

Ortega never gave up being interested in political questions. Koestler did. In 1955 Koestler wrote what he called his "farewell to arms." He said the "bitter passion" chad burnt itself out. His work from that time shows the different "vocation," and over a decade later, in personal correspondence, he reasserted that he was "now grazing in different fields."

Beginning, then, with the middle level, the socio-political level, both men raise the essential issue of the individual in society. This is a special case of the problem of the One and the Many. If Ortega is to be known for one thing, it will surely be his great emphasis on the individual and his circumstances, his famous "I am I and my circumstance." Central to Koestler's work is his emphasis not only on "hierarchy," but on the concept of "holon." I argue that of all the modest differences and of all the major similarities, this one is of the greatest importance. It explains at once their easy affinity and their lasting relevance to contemporary issues.

So much has been written about Ortega's central notions of "I" and "circumstance" it hardly seems necessary to say much. On the middle level of the hierarchy, this has to do with the individual in society, the individual and his environment -- social-cultural, political, and psychological. On the highest level, it has to do with the problems of transcendence and immanence, or as Alfred North Whitehead put it, the problem of "personal autonomy and cosmic dependence."

In La rebelión de las masas, Ortega writes about individuals who are "hermetically closed," an obvious denial of a "Greater." In one of the most succinct passages, Ortega criticizes "mass-man" as having failed to learn the basic idea that "here I end and here begins another more powerful than I am." The "vulgar" fail to understand the concept of organization, that is, the concepts of parts, wholes, and systems. It is in the understanding of these ideas that we distinguish between the vulgar and the noble. The former are unwilling to engage in disciplined effort, the latter are understood precisely in terms of sustained, disciplined effort to comprehend, to see the trees and the forest, surface and depth, patent and latent, trivial and tragic planes, and to love.

In Darkness at Noon the main character Rubashov wrestles throughout with the problem of "I" and "we." Indeed, one section of the novel is entitled "the grammatical fiction," and is directly concerned with the status of the first-person singular. And in his last thoughts, Rubashov asks pathetically, "Could there be a greater?"

Koestler uses, sometimes skillfully, other times almost with triteness, images of seeing. One prisoner wears a monocle, Rubashov wears his pince-nez, always hard to see through, always being cleansed on his sleeve so he can see more clearly. Everytime Rubashov thinks about "I" his tooth aches -- his eyetooth. This speculative bent finally costs Rubashov his life, which is reminiscent, of course, of the Stalin purges.

Both writers are concerned, then, with the problem of the individual and his surroundings -- social, psychological, and political. Each develops these ideas in his political writings, and each considers the same question in other contexts and on different levels of the hierarchy. As Ortega develops extensively his concept of "I" and "circumstance," Koestler, in later work, goes on to develop the "Janus principle" so central to his work.

The main concept in Koestler's work after he gave up his political involvements is that of "holon." "Hol-" is from the Greek "whole," and the suffix "-on" suggests "part" or "particle," as in neutron. Whatever level of a hierarchy, the holon is Janus-faced. As a position (or status) in a hierarchy, the holon looks within to see itself as a whole, and looks out to see itself as a part of a larger whole. Insight and outlook. The concept of holon is meant to bridge the gap between oneness and manyness, between holism (monism) and atomism. All of this was too much for Rubashov.

"I" and "my circumstance," "I" and "we," the existence of a "Greater" -- in barest outline these ideas bring Ortega and Koestler together. Still on the middle level, there is another important similarity. It has to do with the individual as he transcends himself. This is a very delicate business. Some transcendence is obviously necessary. For the individual to fail to recognize the importance of his circumstances, his larger surroundings, to fail to look outward, is to court disaster. Such a failure is the most natural breeding ground for pride.

Ortega and Koestler point out so beautifully the necessity of transcending the self, but each warn of the problem of "too much" self-transcendence. Each becomes almost scathing in this context. Koestler reveals the "chronic indignation" he likes to mention. Ortega writes in El tema de nuestro tiempo (The Modern Theme) that the glory and perhaps the gory European heritage is built on the highly developed transcending dimension. Koestler makes the identical point in writing that the greatest creative accomplishments and the gory annals of war result from our ability to transcend our selves. It is for this reason that Koestler inquired about a drug to limit one's patriotism, identification with causes, not his aggressiveness and mature integration.

Ortega expressed concern about those that thoughtlessly love this or that person, cause, or flag. Ortega was powerful in his insistence that such self-transcendence must be accompanied by the effort to understand these loyalties. Both expressed great misgivings about public opinion, direct action, oversimplification, and violence. Both were concerned with the disproportion between the complexity of problems and the minds that study them.

With respect to this disastrous over self-transcendence, I employ the expression "sympathy for the whole." It refers to the important idea of recognizing and identifying with our circumstances, larger whole, and so on. It is equated with mutuality, reciprocity, and love. The vision is of unity and diversity, where opposition serves integration. It includes what Ortega means by synoikismos -- the resolution to live together. But "sympathy" is a complex matter. There is sympathy that is antipathetic -- too little sympathy, the begrudging of other's good fortune. I call this the "Antipathetic Fallacy."

There is too much sympathy -- as with those that "vibrate in unison" with any cause. Of course I am talking about a balanced, healthy sympathy -- as Aristotle understood it. When sympathy begins to result in excessive identification with cause or flag, I call this the "Sympathetic Fallacy," and if Ortega and Koestler are right, what I have dubbed "Sympathetic Fallacy" and the "Antipathetic Fallacy" may isolate and identify the great problem of our time.

The ideas of Sympathy for the Whole, the Sympathetic Fallacy, and the Antipathetic Fallacy, intimately related as they are to the ideas of Ortega and Koestler, show the way to an exciting definition of education goals. While to my knowledge neither author developed his thinking about education in this way to any great extent, it is completely consistent with the spirit of their thinking to do so. Ortega writes extensively about vision, uses expressions like "active vision" and "sensitive to environment." Koestler emphasizes repeatedly the importance of "hierarchic awareness," "holarchic awareness," and places major emphasis on the notion of "the discovery of hidden analogy." Koestler uses Aha!, Ha Ha, and Ah to refer to the discovery of hidden likeness in science, art, and humor. In my view, these ideas suggest a very fruitful direction for further use of Ortega's and Koestler's insights.

Paralleling the levels mentioned earlier, when it comes to education and curriculum I refer to levels, from top to bottom, as the Spiritual-Mystical, Abstract-Rational, and Concrete-Sensuous. Using these levels, Ortega and Koestler have striking similarities. It is here that Ortega's use of the forest image is relevant. Koestler's The Invisible Writing is particularly relevant.

These levels I call "Commodular Levels." The idea of Commodulation entails the notion of growth from within and according to a principle (logos). Ortega's levels of "Latent and Patent," Koestler's "Tragic" and "Trivial Planes" fit the upper and lower levels. Both agree the middle level is characterized by form, relational structure, and that the way to the highest level from the lowest is through the middle. For Ortega the notions of surface and depth are relevant. This terse treatment scarcely does justice to the beauty of Ortega's essays and the excitement they evoke.

It is in the context of the "Tragic Plane," the "Latent Dimension," and the idea of depth that the important matter of mysticism emerges. I would argue that both men ultimately share views on the mystical, though one must be very careful, as they are, to avoid the many problems by distinguishing among various kinds of mysticism. They are, at minimum, concerned with only that mysticism that always has an articulate carry-over.

Ortega and Koestler seem to be using Spinoza's vision sub specie aeternitatis differently, but this is not troublesome. In terms of subsoil they concur. To me, this aspect of their work, the concern with something greater than ourselves, is the most exciting and most related to the everyday problems confronting us as human, loving beings. The idea of "Commodulation" and "Commodular Levels," and these levels as exemplified by Ortega and Koestler, form an exciting basis for curriculum design -- given their diagnosis, prognosis, and prescription.

But as space is running out, it will have to suffice to mention only in passing other areas of agreement. They would agree on the importance of hierarchy, the importance of "elite" -- properly understood, and rarely understood properly. Ortega has his concept of <u>alteración</u>, and Koestler writes about "The Swing" between extremes. Both recognize the importance of awe and wonder. Both use the "shipwreck" metaphor the same way. Koestler also speaks of sailing without ballast. Koestler adopts over and over again the notion of <u>reculer pour mieux sauter</u>, and while not using the exact expression, Ortega uses the same argument. Both talk about "leveling" as seen in Ortega's "The Height of Our Times" and Koestler's (Rubashov's) "Theory of Relative Maturity." Ortega refers to the Dead Sea, Koestler refers to "sea level." Both pay careful attention to the concepts of analogy and metaphor. And so the similarities come into focus as one studies their work.

This short essay does not do justice to the wealth, to the beauty of the metaphors employed by each. This essay suggests several areas of agreement, fails to mention others, but for an exciting discussion of mankind's critical issues, José Ortega y Gasset and Arthur Koestler serve contemporary times well.

Part IV

Postscript

23.
The Centenary of José Ortega y Gasset and William Carter
JOHN R. HÉBERT

On August 14, 1983, Dr. William E. Carter, Chief of the Hispanic Division of the Library of Congress, died after a year long struggle with cancer. There is no doubt that he would have wanted to be here today. Through my presentation, "The centenary of José Ortega y Gasset and William Carter," I will attempt to weave both the event and the individual into a single story. It is obvious that neither began in that fashion.

To those who are not aware, Bill Carter had become the chief of the Hispanic Division in January 1979, following a prestigious career as director of the Center for Latin American Studies at the University of Florida. While there, he had established himself as an authority on Andean indigenous culture, and he continued anthropological research on the area while at the Library of Congress. A former Methodist minister, Bill Carter throughout his life had pursued programs of assistance to the under-represented in society in an attempt to give them a voice or to help them to preserve their culture and their way of life.

In was with the love for the indigenous culture of Bolivia that he came directly to the Hispanic Division, where he immediately sought to foster greater understanding of Hispanic culture. The division has since 1939 served as a center for the study of the cultures of Latin America, Spain, and Portugal, and it was with this study in mind that he immersed himself into the work of the division. Among the qualities that he possessed was a great desire to complete what he had started; in fact, this important trait was evident in practically every project in which he became involved. Once a promise to produce publishable results or to convene a symposium had been made, every effort was exerted to complete the promise, on time and, even more importantly, with high standards for content and for participation.

His contact with the ideas for programs to honor the great Spanish twentieth-century philosopher José Ortega y Gasset came early in his tenure as chief of the Hispanic Division. In the first part of 1979, Don Jaime Benítez, the Puerto Rican educator and statesman who was also a very close friend of Ortega and Ortega's daughter, visited the Library of Congress to discuss the development of several events tied to the celebration of the centenary of the birth of Ortega y Gasset. It was at that time that the fiftieth anniversary of Ortega y Gasset's The Revolt of the Masses had just been observed and Don Jaime envisioned even bigger and better programs. It is noteworthy that Daniel Boorstin, Librarian of Congress, also held great respect for the writings of Ortega y Gasset, having been favorably impressed by The Revolt of the Masses when it first appeared, and he was profoundly interested in the convening of a conference in the Library of Congress on the theme of Ortega y Gasset.

Under Bill Carter's direction, two courses of action were pursued. First, the microfilming of the personal papers and notes of Ortega y Gasset

was considered; secondly, the convening of a major conference on the theme
of Ortega y Gasset at the Library of Congress was discussed. Both proposals, as we know now, were successfully completed. Both proposals were successful because of the continuing effort and dedication of Bill Carter to
see them through to completion.

In June 1980, Bill Carter journeyed to Madrid to visit Soledad Ortega
and the Fundación Ortega y Gasset to investigate the possibility of microfilming the Ortega papers. From the beginning we had been interested in the
possibility, given the fact that Ortega y Gasset was Spain's foremost philosopher and essayist during the twentieth century and since writings and
teachings had an important influence on the development of United States'
thought. As Bill said in his report, "Our problem in proceeding with the
matter (of microfilming) was that we had only vague notions as to the organization of the collection and even vaguer ones as to the eventual cost of
microfilming. Without a clearer idea of both, we had no way of judging the
feasibility of a microfilming project." At that time, the Fundación Ortega
y Gasset had received a three-year grant from the Ministry of Culture to
create a center for the study of Ortega y Gasset, but by no means sufficient
money to microfilm the collection. Bill discovered in Madrid that the
Ortega y Gasset Archive was in excellent order; Soledad Ortega had worked
with assistants for nearly fifteen years retrieving and ordering the material, and the state of the material reflected that fact. Other than final
collation of the correspondence file and the preparation of targets for the
filming process, the collection seemed to be in good order for a microfilming project.

Bill's careful survey of the collection turned up nearly 50,000 items
for microfilming. These included 10,000 research notes; 4,300 letters to
and from varions personages, 700 family letters; 12,500 miscellaneous letters; 20,000 pages of manuscript; and 2,500 class and lecture notes. This
is surely a treasure trove for the study of Ortega y Gasset and twentieth-
century Spanish thought. The research notes, found in 27 file boxes, contain Ortega y Gasset's personal definitions and interpretations of basic social and human issues; as such, these are keys to his thought and personality. These notes are arranged by subject blocks, for example, problems of
philosophy, notes on philosophers, sociology and politics, sundry thoughts,
bibliography.

The collection of letters in the archive provides the researcher a
unique understanding of Spanish intellectual life preceding the Civil War,
how it was affected by that war, and the problems of adjustment faced by intellectuals during the diaspora following the war. In them, one can trace
the development of Ortega y Gasset as a thinker, from the times he was in
Germany for schooling to the period when he had gained worldwide respect and
regularly traveled throughout Europe and the New World. These letters were
familial, and from and to various personages, such as Azorín, Gómez de la
Serna, Ramiro and María de Maeztu, Julián Marías, Victoria Ocampo, Helene
Weyl, and Miguel de Unamuno.

The manuscripts in the Ortega y Gasset collection consist basically of
original drafts of his works, set in order by year. Most of these materials
are available in print. Finally, his class and lecture notes are also
available.

In Bill Carter's summation of his report on the collection he said:

> The archive is of great relevance for American scholar-
> ship. First of all, it represents the development and
> thought of the most influential Spanish contributor to
> Western philosophy in the twentieth century. Second, it
> documents the involvement by Spanish intellectuals in
> events leading up to, during, and following the Spanish
> Civil War -- a war in which many Americans fought and
> which set the stage for the World War that followed.

> Third, it contains valuable insights into the Spanish
> perception of United States culture through the personal
> observations of both Ortega himself and of his friends
> and colleagues as they toured and/or took up residence
> in this country. We are fortunate that the Ortega fam-
> ily has given us the opportunity to microfilm this
> unique collection. . . . It would . . . serve as elo-
> quent testimony to the Library's commitment adequately
> to document the Hispanic heritage. . . . I therefore
> strongly recommend that we proceed with the matter
> forthwith.

And proceed we did; within the year, i.e., 1980-81, the collection had
been microfilmed by the Centro Nacional de Microfilmación and in the winter
of 1982 Señora Soledad Ortega formally presented to the Library a copy of
the microfilm. The Library of Congress became the sole depository of the
microfilm of the Ortega y Gasset Archive in the Western hemisphere, and one
of only two locations in the world to have the microfilm of the collection,
the other copy remaining with the Fundación Ortega y Gasset in Madrid. That
microfilmed collection, at least those items available to the researcher,
have been identified in Everette Larson's Microfilmed Papers of José Ortega
y Gasset Open for Research in the Library of Congress.(1) That guide is a
publication distributed without charge by the Hispanic Division of the
Library of Congress. Of 82 reels of microfilm of the entire collection, 39
have been opened for research.

It is appropriate that the José Ortega y Gasset Archive is accessible
to scholars through one of the world's major research libraries. Ortega y
Gasset would have been proud, since he was a strong believer in libraries,
librarians, and their importance to the development of civilization.   In
1908 he had urged Spain to establish a modern and international scientific
library without which the country would be disgraced. In 1935 he was invited to give the inaugural speech to the Second International Congress of
Librarians and Bibliography held in Madrid. He chose as the title of his
address "The Mission of the Librarian,"(2) and based his lecture on the fact
that books, defined by Plato twenty-six centuries earlier as written say-
ings, allowed civilization to advance, building the present upon the past.

Simultaneous to the Library of Congress' efforts to have microfilmed
the José Ortega y Gasset papers, planning under Bill Carter's direction had
begun for the convening of a major conference on the Spanish philosopher.
The date of the event, the fall of 1982, was to provide for maximum international academic participation and the timing of the event was to allow the
symposium to serve as the inaugural event in the plans for the centennial of
the birth of Ortega y Gasset. Again, assistance in the planning was provided by Jaime Benítez and Soledad Ortega, as well as by an advisory committee formed in the spring of 1982 to plan other events in honor of the Spanish philosopher; among those on that committee were Professors Nora de
Marval-McNair, Roberto Esquenazi-Mayo, Manuel Durán, Juan Marichal, Antonio
Ramos, Nicolás Sánchez Albornoz, Philip Silver, Luis Arocena, Alberto
Campillo, and Ricardo Gullón, and Dr. Javier Malagón of the Spanish Embassy.
In fact Dr. Malagón had become a vital individual on the committee and con-
tinued to work tirelessly throughout the duration of the symposium.

The September 30-October 1, 1982 program at the Library received finan-
cial support from the Consejo Conjunto Hispano-Norteamericano para Asuntos
Educativos y Culturales, the Tinker Foundation, and the Embassy of Spain
directed to the Fundación Ortega y Gasset; the Organization of American
States and the Hispanic Division of the Library of Congress also expended
resources for the success of the program. A two-day program was planned in
which the writings of Ortega y Gasset would be explored through four major
themes -- the visionary, man as actor, self-awareness, and education. The

symposium featured presentations and commentary by a wide range of scholars and was well attended.

Since that event, many more programs have been planned and successfully concluded in honor of this centennial year. And from a perusal of this symposium's program, it is evident that José Ortega y Gasset will receive the discussion and debate that his works have inspired.

The program at the Library of Congress was not the final task in which Bill Carter participated, as he sought the preparation of the papers and commentaries of the symposium for publication. Today, thanks to Bill Carter's initiative, the publication of those proceedings is closer to reality, as Professor Pucciarelli in Buenos Aires is preparing the papers for publication in Sur, and the Library of Congress, after having all of the papers and commentary translated into English, is preparing the papers for publication in the United States.

As you can tell, this long accounting of Bill Carter's relationship to the centenary of José Ortega y Gasset has not been easy to prepare. To compare the result of the activities surrounding the centenary and the contributions of Bill Carter and to weave both of them into a succinct statement seems impossible. But Bill's participation in the remarkable Ortega y Gasset events of the past four years, the microfilming of the papers, and the planning and conducting of the inaugural symposium on the theme of the Spanish philosopher, are testimony to his drive and vision. Bill had learned shortly before the convening of the fall 1982 symposium at the Library that the metastasis of a previous cancer had reappeared. Obviously shattered by this discovery, he still pushed on to the successful completion of the symposium, without notice to the participants, and then endured, within a week following the program, an operation to halt the spread of the cancer. After returning to the office several weeks later, he fought on for nearly a year before the disease grew out of control and at last conquered him. During that year he spent practically the entire time hard at work at his post in the Library. In honor of his contributions to the diffusion of Hispanic culture, Bill Carter was awarded the Order of Isabel la Católica, in the knight's rank, by King Juan Carlos of Spain on June 14, 1983. He was cited not only for his work on the José Ortega y Gasset program at the Library of Congress, but also for the other symposia (e.g., 1001 years of the Spanish language), the concerts, and the scholarly activities that he advanced in the Library and at the University of Florida.

As Julián Marías said in an eloquent eulogy to Bill Carter:

> Not only Spain, but the entire Hispanic world has lost one of its most loyal and brilliant friends. . . . Not a bit ostentatious, rather modest and of a profound religiosity . . . his studies on Hispanic America . . . were not confined to research and knowledge but reflected a heartfelt affection, a deep sincerity and love.(3)

He brought with him "the conviction that what one does is for eternity — and because of this, one has to do it well." No better summary of Bill's career can be uttered; no better summary of his deep interest with the celebration of the centennial of José Ortega y Gasset can be found.

And as our rich Hispanic collection of the Library of Congress — a necessary source of knowledge of Hispanic reality at all times — was passed into Bill Carter's hands, he propagated it, made it alive, tried to enrich it with new stimuli up until his last day, because he wanted it, more than for himself, to continue being the great tool of study of Hispanic literature, philosophy, art, and history.

NOTES

1. <u>Hispanic Focus</u> 2. (Washington, Library of Congress, Hispanic Division, 1982).

2. José Ortega y Gasset, <u>Obras completas</u> (Madrid: Revista de Occidente, 1974), vol. V, pp. 207–32.

3. Julián Marías, <u>ABC</u>. Madrid, October 25, 1983.

ESPECTADOR UNIVERSAL

International Conference
in Celebration of the
100th Anniversary
of the Birth of

JOSÉ ORTEGA Y GASSET

HOFSTRA UNIVERSITY
HEMPSTEAD, NEW YORK 11550

**Thursday, Friday, Saturday,
November 10, 11, 12, 1983**

HOFSTRA CULTURAL CENTER

Director:	Joseph G. Astman
Associate Director:	Peter D'Albert
Music Coordinator:	Paul Hefner

GALLERIES:

David Filderman Gallery

Marguerite M. Regan
Assistant to the Dean of Library Services

Nancy E. Herb

Emily Lowe Gallery

Gail Gelburd
Director

Mary Wakeford
Directorial Assistant

MUSICAL ORGANIZATIONS:

American Chamber Ensemble

Blanche Abram
Naomi Drucker
Directors

Hofstra String Quartet

Seymour Benstock
Artistic Coordinator

HOFSTRA CULTURAL CENTER

UNIVERSITY CENTER FOR CULTURAL & INTERCULTURAL STUDIES

Assistant Directors and Conference Coordinators:	Natalie Datlof Alexej Ugrinsky
Secretary:	Marilyn Seidman
Assistants:	Karin Barnaby Jo-Ann Graziano Michael E. Hurley Doris Keane Nel Panzeca Sinaida U. Weber

An Acknowledgement from the Director

I would like to express my gratitude to those who have contributed so notably to making this a truly international conference. I am especially indebted to His Excellency Lucio García del Solar, Ambassador of the Argentine Republic, to His Excellency Gabriel Mañueco, Ambassador of Spain, to The Honorable Dr. Javier Malagón, Cultural Attaché of the Embassy of Spain, to The Honorable Dr. Adolfo Saracho, Counsellor for Cultural and Academic Affairs of the Embassy of the Argentine Republic, to The Honorable Mr. Tomás R.-Pantoja, Cultural Counsellor of the Spanish Consulate General in New York, to Dr. Diodoro Urquía Latorre and to Doña Soledad Ortega, President of the Fundación José Ortega y Gasset in Madrid.

I would like to render special tribute to the memory of Dr. William E. Carter, Chief of the Hispanic Division of The Library of Congress, whose guidance, assistance and dedication to Spanish culture and to José Ortega y Gasset studies aided us greatly in making this conference a reality.

This symposium would not have been possible without the strong leadership of Dr. James M. Shuart, President of Hofstra University, the counsel and steady encouragement of Dr. Joseph G. Astman, Director of the Hofstra Cultural Center, and the professionalism and outstanding enterprise of the Assistant Directors, Ms. Natalie Datlof and Dr. Alexej Ugrinsky, who have so generously given me their unflagging support since the inception of this project.

I am also deeply indebted to the distinguished scholars who have graciously agreed to participate, as well as Dr. Zenia Sacks Da Silva, Professor of Spanish at Hofstra University, the faculty of the Department of Spanish, Mrs. Hada Rivera, the departmental secretary and to all those others of the Hofstra University community who helped us bring about the Espectador universal Conference.

Dr. Nora de Marval McNair
Chair, Department of Spanish
Conference Director

JOSÉ   ORTEGA   Y   GASSET

LA REBELIÓN
DE LAS MASAS

Revista de Occidente
Madrid
1929

Thursday, November 10, 1983

Conference Opening:	Registration: David Filderman Gallery
	Department of Special Collections
9:00 - 11:00 A.M.	Hofstra University Library - 9th floor

11:00 A.M.

Greetings from the Hofstra University Community

James M. Shuart
President

Joseph G. Astman
Director
Hofstra Cultural Center
Professor of Comparative Literature & Languages

Nora de Marval McNair
Chair, Department of Spanish
Conference Director

The Honorable Mr. Tomás R.-Pantoja
Cultural Counsellor of Spain in New York
New York, NY

Special Address: John Hébert
Acting Chief
Hispanic Division of
The Library of Congress
Washington, D.C.

"The Centenary of Ortega y Gasset and William Carter"

Opening Address: Ignacio Götz
Teaching Fellow in the Humanities
New College, Hofstra University

"Ortega y Gasset: A Tribute"

Opening of Conference Exhibit:

José Ortega y Gasset: The Man and His Circumstance

Reception

12:00 Noon   Lunch: Student Center Cafeteria/The Netherlands

1:30 - 3:30 P.M.   PANEL I: PHILOSOPHY AND HISTORY - Dining Rooms ABC
                                                Student Center

Moderator: John T. Marcus
Department of History
Hofstra University

"Historiology and Interdisciplinarity: Ortega's
'Basic Discipline' for the 'Human Sciences'"
John T. Graham
University of Missouri at Kansas City

Thursday, November 10, 1983 (cont'd.)   Dining Rooms ABC, Student Center

1:30 P.M. (Continued)   PANEL I: PHILOSOPHY AND HISTORY

                             "Ortega y Gasset and the Limits of Conservatism"
                             Victor Ouimette
                             McGill University, Montreal, Canada

                             "The Real and the Ideal: Two Europes in the
                             Thought of Ortega"
                             Harold Raley
                             University of Houston, Houston, TX

                             "Ortega, Hegel y América"
                             Leopoldo Zea
                             Universidad Nacional Autónoma de Mexico
                             Mexico City, Mexico

3:45 - 5:45 P.M.   PANEL II: ART, AESTHETICS AND LANGUAGE

                             Moderator: Ignacio Götz
                                          Teaching Fellow in the Humanities
                                          New College, Hofstra University

                             "Ortega y la metáfora"
                             Antonio F. Cao
                             Hofstra University, Hempstead, NY

                             "The Ludic Element in Orteguian Aesthetics"
                             Rafael E. Hernández
                             College of Wooster, Wooster, OH

                             "Ortega's Phenomenology of Language versus
                             Linguistic Philosophy"
                             William F. Lawhead
                             University of Mississippi, University, MS

                             "Ortega's Philosophy of Art"
                             Roberto J. Vichot
                             Purdue University, West Lafayette, IN

6:00 P.M.   Dinner: Student Center Cafeteria/The Netherlands

7:00 P.M.   Evening Program

                             Ortega y Gasset: Images of a Life

                             Slide Presentation

                             Commentary: Nora de Marval McNair, Chair
                                           Department of Spanish
                                           Director, Jose Ortega y Gasset Conference

Friday, November 11, 1983   Dining Rooms ABC, Student Center

9:00 - 10:30 A.M.   PANEL III: ORTEGA AND SPAIN

                            Moderator: Roberto Esquenazi-Mayo
                                         Department of Modern Languages
                                         Director, Institute for International Studies
                                         University of Nebraska at Lincoln

                            "The Problemacity of Life: Towards the Orteguian
                            Notion of Universal Spectator"
                            Jorge García Gómez
                            Southampton College/LIU, Southampton, NY

                            "Between Antitheses: Subject and Object in the
                            Landscape Essays of Ortega y Gasset"
                            Robert Lane Kauffman
                            Rice University, Houston, TX

                            "Ortega y Gasset and Federico García Lorca"
                            Judy B. McInnis
                            University of Delaware, Newark, DE

10:45 - 12:00 Noon   PANEL IV: DON QUIXOTE

                            Moderator: Zenia Sacks Da Silva
                                         Department of Spanish
                                         Hofstra University

                            "Between Philosophy and Literature: Ortega's
                            Meditations on Quixote"
                            Anthony J. Cascardi
                            University of California, Berkeley, CA

                            "Ortega in Quest of Don Quixote"
                            Warren Hampton
                            University of South Florida, Tampa, FL

12:00 Noon   Lunch: Student Center Cafeteria/The Netherlands

2:00 P.M.   DAVID FILDERMAN GALLERY - Hofstra University Library
                                                      9th floor

                            Special Address: Csejtei Dezső
                                               Attila József University
                                               Szeged, Hungary

                            "Bridges Between Western and Eastern Europe:
                            The Influence of José Ortega y Gasset's Thought on
                            Hungarian Spiritual Life - 1928--1945"

Friday, November 11, 1983 (cont'd.) - <u>David Filderman Gallery - Hofstra University Library</u>
<u>9th floor</u>

3:00 - 4:30 P.M.   <u>PANEL V: ORTEGA AND EUROPEAN THOUGHT</u>

                                    Moderator: Frank S. Lambasa
                                                   Department of Comparative Literature & Languages
                                                   Hofstra University

"Ortega and Johann Wolfgang von Goethe"
Elizabeth Bohning & Judy B. McInnis
University of Delaware, Newark, DE

"Ortega y Gasset and Malcolm Lowry's Concept of the Artist"
Sherrill E. Grace
University of British Columbia, Vancouver, Canada

"José Ortega y Gasset and Arthur Koestler:
Meditations on the Two-Faced Forest"
Ronald G. Jones
University of British Columbia, Vancouver, Canada

4:45 P.M.   <u>Special Address</u>:   Ezequiel de Olaso
                                                   Universidad Nacional de La Plata
                                                   Buenos Aires, Argentina

"Seeing, Thinking, Understanding:
Reflections on the <u>espectador universal</u>"

5:30 P.M.   <u>Presidential Reception</u>

Guests of Honor:

His Excellency Lucio García del Solar
Ambassador of the Argentine Republic
Washington, D.C.

The Honorable Dr. Adolfo Saracho
Counsellor, Academic and Cultural Affairs
Embassy of the Argentine Republic
Washington, D.C.

The Honorable Mr. Tomás R.-Pantoja
Cultural Counsellor of Spain in New York
New York, NY

6:30 P.M.   Cash Bar   <u>Dining Rooms ABC, Student Center</u>

<u>JOSÉ ORTEGA Y GASSET CONFERENCE BANQUET</u>

<u>Introductions</u>: Nora de Marval McNair, Director

<u>Greetings</u>:   James M. Shuart
                   President

                   His Excellency Lucio García del Solar
                   Ambassador of the Argentine Republic
                   Washington, D.C.

MUSIC FOR GUITAR BY SPANISH COMPOSERS

William Zito, Classical Guitarist

November 11, 1983   Dining Rooms ABC

Pavanas   Gaspar Sanz
Passacalle de la Cavalleria de Napoles
Canarios

Omaggio - Scritto per le Tonbeau de Debussy   Manuel de Falla
Cancion del Fuego Saturo

Elogio de la Danza   Leo Brouwer

Asturias   Isaac Albéniz

Saturday, November 12, 1983   Dining Rooms ABC, Student Center

8:00 - 9:00 A.M.   Continental Breakfast

9:00 - 10:00 A.M.   PANEL VI: ORTEGA AND LATIN AMERICA

                           Moderator: Elio Alba-Bufill
                                        Department of Foreign Languages
                                        Kingsborough Community College/CUNY
                                        Brooklyn, NY

                           "José Ortega y Gasset and His Three Visits to Argentina"
                           Jesús Méndez
                           Barry University, Miami Shores, FL

                           "Presencia de Ortega y Gasset en Hispanoamérica"
                           Humberto Piñera, Professor Emeritus
                           New York University, New York, NY

10:00 - 11:30 A.M.   PANEL VII: CONTEMPORARIES AND ANTI-ORTEGANS

                           Moderator: Philip Silver
                                        Department of Spanish and Portuguese
                                        Columbia University
                                        New York, NY

                           "From Ortega y Gasset to Robert S. Hartman:
                           Thoughts on Value Theory"
                           Gary Acquaviva
                           Walters State Community College, Morristown, TN

                           "Philosophy as Performance: The Anti-Ortegans"
                           Paul Ilie
                           University of Southern California, Los Angeles, CA

                           "From Ortega y Gasset to Karl Jaspers:
                           Thoughts on Situating Vital Reason"
                           Erling Skorpen
                           University of Maine at Orono

12:00 Noon   Complimentary Brunch

GREETINGS

" . . . felicitándoles por el trabajo de organización que han realizado . . .

les envía un cordial saludo."

> Soledad Ortega
> Presidente
> Fundación José Ortega y Gasset
> Madrid, Spain

"Deseándoles toda clase de éxitos, . . ."

> Gabriel Mañueco
> El Embajador de España
> Washington, D.C.

" . . . en mi calidad de Secretario de la Comisión de Homenaje a Ortega y Gasset en los

Estados Unidos, le agradezco lo que Vd. está haciendo para difundir la obra de Don

José y por tanto la de España."

> Javier Malagón
> Agregado Cultural
> Embajada de España
> Washington, D.C.

Cooperating Institutions:

Aerolíneas Argentinas

Cultural Office of the Embassy of Spain
Washington, D.C.

Embassy of the Argentine Republic
Washington, D.C.

Hempstead Plaza Hotel
Hempstead, NY

Lectorum Publications, Inc.
New York, NY

Library of Congress
Washington, D.C.

Nassau County Office of Cultural Development
Roslyn, NY

Nassau Library System
Uniondale, NY

New York Public Library
New York, NY

Suffolk Cooperative Library System
Bellport, NY

HOFSTRA CULTURAL CENTER

CONFERENCES AT HOFSTRA UNIVERSITY

George Sand Centennial - November 1976

Heinrich von Kleist Bicentennial - November 1977

The Chinese Woman - December 1977

George Sand: Her Life, Her Works, Her Influence - April 1978

William Cullen Bryant and His America - October 1978

The Trotsky-Stalin Conflict in the 1920's - March 1979

Albert Einstein Centennial - November 1979

Renaissance Venice Symposium - March 1980

Sean O'Casey - March 1980

Walt Whitman - April 1980

Nineteenth-Century Women Writers - November 1980

Fedor Dostoevski - April 1981

Gotthold Ephraim Lessing - November 1981

Franklin Delano Roosevelt - March 1982

Johann Wolfgang von Goethe - April 1982

James Joyce - October 1982

Twentieth-Century Women Writers - November 1982

Harry S. Truman: The Man from Independence - April 14-16, 1983

John Maynard Keynes - September 22-24, 1983

Romanticism in the Old and the New World - Washington Irving,
    Stendhal, and Zhukovskii - October 13-15, 1983

HOFSTRA CULTURAL CENTER

CONFERENCES AT HOFSTRA UNIVERSITY

Espectador Universal: José Ortega y Gasset - November 10-12, 1983

Dwight D. Eisenhower - March 29-31, 1984

George Orwell - October 11-13, 1984

Friedrich von Schiller - November 8-10, 1984

Harlem Renaissance - February 28-March 2, 1985

John F. Kennedy - March 28-30, 1985

Conference on Higher Education - April 1985

Eighteenth-Century Women Writers - October 10-12, 1985

Avant Garde Art and Literature - November 14-16, 1985

Lyndon B. Johnson - April 1986

Carl Gustav Jung - October 1986

George Sand: Her Life, Her Works, Her Influence - November 1986

Richard M. Nixon - Spring 1987

Bicentennial of the United States Constitution - Fall 1987

Gerald R. Ford - Spring 1988

Jimmy Carter - Spring 1989

Bicentennial of the French Revolution - Fall 1989

Ronald Reagan - Spring 1990

"Calls for Papers" available

CREDIT for the success of this Conference goes to more people than can be named in
    the program, but those below deserve a special vote of thanks:

HOFSTRA UNIVERSITY OFFICERS: James M. Shuart, President
                               Sanford S. Hammer, Provost & Dean of Faculties
                               Robert C. Vogt, Special Advisor to the Provost
                               Robert A. Davison, Acting Dean, Hofstra College of
                                           Liberal Arts & Sciences

ARA SLATER: Tony Internicola, Director, Dining Services

DAVID FILDERMAN GALLERY: Marguerite M. Regan, Assistant to the Dean of Library Services
                           Nancy E. Herb
                           Anne Rubino

DEPARTMENT OF ART HISTORY: Robert Myron, Chair

DEPARTMENT OF MUSIC: Edgar Dittemore, Chair
                       Eleanor Geddes, Secretary
                       Joan Stadler, Supervisor, Music Library

DEPARTMENT OF SPANISH: Hada Rivera, Secretary

HOFSTRA UNIVERSITY LIBRARY: Charles R. Andrews, Dean

OFFICE OF THE SECRETARY: Robert D. Noble, Secretary
                           Margaret Mirabella
                           Stella Sinicki, Supervisor, Special Secretarial Services
                           Jack Ruegamer, Director, Art & Printing Production
                           Vicki Anderson
                           Veronica Fitzwilliam
                           Doris Brown & Staff

OPERATIONAL SERVICES: James Fellman, Director

PUBLIC SAFETY AND TELECOMMUNICATIONS: Robert Crowley, Director

SCHEDULING OFFICE: Charles L. Churchill, Assistant Facilities Manager
                     Dorothy Fetherston, Director

TECHNICAL AND MEDIA SERVICES: Elizabeth Weston, Media Services Librarian
                                Robert J. Kleinhans, Director, Technical Services
                                Albert Nowicki
                                William Gray

UNIVERSITY RELATIONS: Harold A. Klein, Director
                        James Merritt, Assistant Director
                        M.F. Klerk, Editor/Writer
                        Frances B. Jacobsen, Administrative Assistant

The continuous assistance by the following student organization is greatly
appreciated:
                        The Spanish Club

                   President: Ruth A. Beckles
                   Vice President: Diana C. Octave
                   Secretary: Linda Olivo
                   Treasurer: Susan Ward

Forthcoming:

INTERNATIONAL CONFERENCE

NATIONAL UNION OF JOURNALISTS

7 John Street, Bedford Row, London, W.C 1

Phone
HOLborn 2258

Telegrams
Natujay Holb. London

This is to certify that

Mr. GEORGE URWELL

of The Tribune

is a member of the   F . + P .
Branch of the National Union of Journalists

Leslie R. Aldous   Branch Sec

(Address) 66, Priory Gans., N.6.

Member's No.

By permission of University College London Library.

Deadline for papers, which may deal with any aspect of the conference theme: April 1, 1984

Papers are not to exceed 20 minutes presentation time.

Papers must be submitted in duplicate.
Selected papers will be published.

FOR FURTHER INFORMATION:
Courtney T. Wemyss, Conference Director
Natalie Datlof & Alexej Ugrinsky, Conference Coordinators

University Center for Cultural &
Intercultural Studies (UCCIS)
(516) 560-5669, 5670

*An intercultural
and interdisciplinary
inquiry into his works,
his world and the
validity of his views*

**Thursday, Friday, Saturday
October 11, 12, 13, 1984**

**HOFSTRA
UNIVERSITY**
HEMPSTEAD, NEW YORK 11550

NOTES

Index

DARLA KOWALSKI

About the Editor and Contributors

GARY J. ACQUAVIVA is Associate Professor of Philosophy at Walters State Community College. His research involves applying R. S. Hartman's formal value theory and he is currently doing extensive testing within the Tennessee prison system to revalidate a pilot study which distinguished felons from nonfelons.

ELIZABETH BOHNING is Professor Emeritus and former Chairman (1971-78) of the Department of Languages and Literature at the University of Delaware. Her principal research interests are in eighteenth- and nineteenth-century German literature. With Judy McInnis she has co-authored a number of articles on Goethe's influence on García Lorca and Ortega y Gasset.

ANTONIO F. CAO is Assistant Professor of Spanish at Hofstra University and previously held positions at Vassar College and Harvard University. He has published extensively on modern Hispanic drama, the theory of the metaphor, and Golden Age theater. He is the author of *Federico García Lorca y las vanguardias: Hacia el teatro* (1984).

ANTHONY J. CASCARDI is Associate Professor of Comparative Literature and Spanish at the University of California, Berkeley, where his principal area of research is the relationship between philosophy and literature. He is the author, most recently, of *The Bounds of Reason: Cervantes, Dostoevsky, Flaubert*, and editor of *Literature and the Question of Philosophy*.

DEZSØ CSEJTEI is Professor of Philosophy at Attila József University in Szeged, Hungary. He has been concerned primarily with the history of life-philosophies and existentialism. He has written extensively for scientific journals in Hungary and in Yugoslavia. He is the author of *José Ortega y Gasset* and *History of Spanish Existentialism* (in Hungarian).

JORGE GARCÍA-GÓMEZ is Professor of Philosophy at Long Island University. He has taught for over twenty years in various universities, both American and foreign. He has published extensively, including books and research articles. A recent book is his translation and edition of José Ortega y Gasset's *Psychological Investigations*, with his introductory essay to the work.

IGNACIO L. GÖTZ is Professor and Coordinator of the Humanities at New College, Hofstra University. His principal research interests center around the relationship between individuals and institutions, especially communes, schools, religion, and art. His contributions include *No Schools*, *The Psychedelic Teacher*, and *Creativity*, as well as numerous monographs for scholarly journals.

SHERRILL E. GRACE is Associate Professor of English at the University of British Columbia, Canada, and was formerly at McGill University. She has lectured at universities across Canada and in the United States and Europe. She has published numerous articles on modern and contemporary literature, two books on Margaret Atwood, and is the author of *The Voyage That Never Ends: Malcolm Lowry's Fiction*.

JOHN T. GRAHAM is a historian (Modern European Intellectual) at the University of Missouri, Kansas City. His current research is on the philosophy and philosophy of history of Ortega y Gasset, and the history of crisis thinking. He is the author of *Donoso Cortés, Utopian Romanticist and Political Realist*.

WARREN HAMPTON is Associate Professor of Spanish at the University of South Florida. He has been a Gulbenkian Foundation fellow and has done extensive translation work in Latin American history. He has written a number of articles and papers on José Ortega y Gasset.

JOHN R. HÉBERT is Acting Chief of the Hispanic Division of the Library of Congress. He is a Latin American historian with research in Argentine and U.S. Borderlands history and has been a regular contributor to the *Handbook of Latin American Studies*. His interest in Ortega y Gasset stems from his institutional work in the collecting of the Ortega papers at the Library of Congress.

RAFAEL E. HERNÁNDEZ is Assistant Professor of Spanish at Converse College in South Carolina. His professional interests include Spanish and Latin American literature, cultural philosophy, international education and the curriculum, and the problem of cultural identity in the Hispanic World. He is co-author of *Le cultura hispana: Dentro y fuera de los Estados Unidos*.

PAUL ILIE is Professor of Spanish and Comparative Literature at the University of Southern California and held the same title previously at the University of Michigan. His research includes the history of ideas in the eighteenth and twentieth centuries, and French-Spanish cultural relations. Among his books is *Unamuno: An Existential View of Self and Society*, and more recently *Literature and Inner Exile*.

RONALD G. JONES is Professor of Social and Educational Studies at the University of British Columbia, Canada. He has held appointments at other universities including the State University of New York at Buffalo and Pennsylvania State University. His main work deals with the relationships between types of society and modes of thought, especially how the latter influence the former. He has published extensively in national and international journals.

R. LANE KAUFFMANN is Assistant Professor of Spanish and Semiotics at Rice University in Houston, Texas. His main research interest is comparative literature, and he has published articles on literary theory and criticism. He is the author of a forthcoming study, *The Theory of the Essay: Lukács, Adorno, and Benjamin*.

WILLIAM T. LAWHEAD is Associate Professor of Philosophy and Religions at the University of Mississippi at Oxford. His research and published articles have been in the areas of phenomenology, philosophy of language, and the philosophy of religion.

JUDY B. McINNIS is Associate Professor of Spanish and Comparative Literature at the University of Delaware. She devotes her literary research to the aesthetics of Lorca and the major Golden Age poets. As director of the AATSP National Spanish Examinations, she conducts pedagogical research on error analysis and language transfer.

NORA DE MARVAL-McNAIR is Associate Professor and Chairperson of the Department of Spanish at Hofstra University.

JESÚS MÉNDEZ is Assistant Professor and Coordinator of the Department of History at Barry University in Miami, Florida, and was previously a member of the faculty at the State University of New York at Binghamton. His areas of special interest include Argentine intellectual history and Spanish–Latin American relations in the twentieth century. His articles have appeared in *Inter-American Review of Bibliography*, *Journal of Church and State*, and *SECOLAS Annals*.

VICTOR OUIMETTE is Professor of Spanish at McGill University in Montreal, Canada. His principal research interest is modern Spanish intellectual history. He is the author of *Reason Aflame: Unamuno and the Heroic Will*, *José Ortega y Gasset*, and the editor of Miguel de Unamuno, *Ensueño de una patria: periodismo republicano, 1931-1936*.

HAROLD C. RALEY is Professor of the Department of Hispanic and Classical Languages at the University of Houston. His research interests involve modern Spanish philosophy and literature. He is the author of *José Ortega y Gasset: Philosopher of European Unity*, *Responsible Vision: The Philosophy of Julián Marías*, and several other books and articles.

ERLING SKORPEN is Professor and Chair of Philosophy at the University of Maine, and has previously taught at Yale University and the University of Nevada. His journal articles and conference papers exhibit strong interest in the role of human self-knowledge in perennial philosophy, theory of the person in philosophy and psychology, and in pure and applied ethics.

ROBERTO J. VICHOT is Assistant Professor of Political Science at Texas A&M University and was formerly on the faculty of Texas A&I University. His principal fields of research are political theory, American government, international relations, and philosophy. He is the author of a number of articles on philosophy of law, sociology of art, and American political thought, as well as Iberian and Latin American thought.

Hofstra University's
Cultural and Intercultural Studies
Coordinating Editor, Alexej Ugrinsky

Walt Whitman: Here and Now
(*Editor: Joann P. Krieg*)

Harry S. Truman: The Man from Independence
(*Editor: William F. Levantrosser*)

Nineteenth-Century Women Writers of the English-Speaking World
(*Editor: Rhoda B. Nathan*)

Lessing and the Enlightenment
(*Editor: Alexej Ugrinsky*)

Dostoevski and the Human Condition After a Century
(*Editors: Alexej Ugrinsky, Frank S. Lambasa, and Valija K. Ozolins*)

The Old and New World Romanticism of Washington Irving
(*Editor: Stanley Brodwin*)

Woman as Mediatrix
(*Editor: Avriel Goldberger*)

Einstein and the Humanities
(*Editor: Dennis P. Ryan*)

Dwight D. Eisenhower: Soldier, President, Statesman
(*Editor: Joann P. Krieg*)

Goethe in the Twentieth Century
(*Alexej Ugrinsky*)

Franklin D. Roosevelt: The Man, the Myth, the Era, 1882-1945
(*Editors: Herbert D. Rosenbaum and Elizabeth Bartelme*)

The Stendhal Bicentennial Papers
(*Editor: Avriel Goldberger*)

Faith of a (Woman) Writer
(*Editors: Alice Kessler-Harris and William McBrien*)

George Orwell
(*Editors: Courtney T. Wemyss and Alexej Ugrinsky*)